Media Technologies and Posthuman Intimacy

Media Technologies and Posthuman Intimacy

Jan Stasieńko

BLOOMSBURY ACADEMIC
NEW YORK • LONDON • OXFORD • NEW DELHI • SYDNEY

BLOOMSBURY ACADEMIC
Bloomsbury Publishing Inc
1385 Broadway, New York, NY 10018, USA
50 Bedford Square, London, WC1B 3DP, UK
29 Earlsfort Terrace, Dublin 2, Ireland

BLOOMSBURY, BLOOMSBURY ACADEMIC and the Diana logo
are trademarks of Bloomsbury Publishing Plc

First published in the United States of America 2022
This paperback edition first published in 2023

Library of Congress Cataloging-in-Publication Data
Names: Stasieńko, Jan, author.
Title: Media technologies and posthuman intimacy / Jan Stasieńko.
Other titles: Niematerialne Galatee w wehikułach rozkoszy i bólu. English
Description: New York : Bloomsbury Academic, 2021. |
Includes bibliographical references and index.
Identifiers: LCCN 2021023811 (print) | LCCN 2021023812 (ebook) |
ISBN 9781501380518 (hardback) | ISBN 9781501380525 (epub) |
ISBN 9781501380532 (pdf) | ISBN 9781501380549
Subjects: LCSH: Social media–Psychological aspects. | Intimacy (Psychology) |
Mass media–Social aspects. | Communication and technology.
Classification: LCC HM742 .S82713 2021 (print) |
LCC HM742 (ebook) | DDC 302.23/1–dc23
LC record available at https://lccn.loc.gov/2021023811
LC ebook record available at https://lccn.loc.gov/2021023812

ISBN: HB: 978-1-5013-8051-8
         PB: 978-1-5013-8055-6
       ePDF: 978-1-5013-8053-2
      eBook: 978-1-5013-8052-5

Typeset by Integra Software Services Pvt. Ltd.

To find out more about our authors and books visit www.bloomsbury.com
and sign up for our newsletters.

To Agnieszka, Szymon, Łukasz and Pola for being super(b)humans

Contents

Figures

Acknowledgements

One could hardly mention everybody who has contributed to the creation of this book. I would like to thank the former president of the University of Lower Silesia, Professor Robert Kwaśnica, for his support for the first study trip on this project. Without the hospitality of Donna Kowal of SUNY College at Brockport that trip could not have happened. I extend a big thank you to Richard Smith, the former director of the Centre for Digital Media in Vancouver, and the Centre's other staff who gave me a warm welcome on my second trip to North America. It is thanks to them that I was able to finish the book. My gratitude goes also to all those who have left their direct or indirect imprint on this tome: Beata Sierocka, Ireneusz Sierocki, Stefan Bednarek, Sonia Fizek, Maciej Sedlaczek, Maciej Czerniakowski, Carmel Vaisman, Francesca Ferrando and Stefan Lorenz Sorgner. I received a wealth of precious feedback from Krystina Madej, Bert Olivier, Evi Sampanikou and Curtis D. Carbonell.

I thank especially my publisher, Katie Gallof of Bloomsbury Academic, for her propitious support for me and my project ever since I first approached the publisher with it.

As is often the case when working on academic projects, the help received from others also has other dimensions than the purely academic aspects of the work. For this reason I would like to thank Agnieszka Chodorowska, Tom Kowal, Wojciech Wojciechowski and Małgorzata Wojciechowska, Kathy and Henry Herdzik, Stanisław Figaj, Danuta Adzińska and Alek Bester, Katarzyna and Tomasz Żemojtel.

Last but not least, my greatest thanks go to my wife, children, parents and parents in-law, without whom this posthuman adventure could not have been a success.

Introduction

Is it possible to show affection for immaterial objects? Is it possible to place our feelings in algorithms, digital representations, images and sounds? Can media content become a lover or friend, or a conscious or unconscious oppressor? What of our lust, hate, fear and other emotions when they are filtered and mediatized by modern digital vehicles such as the internet, virtual reality or video games? What of our humanity when its limits are constantly undermined by material and immaterial transfers of stimuli, affects and cravings? Who controls the transfers and who benefits from them? Who or what is the non-human other situated in the media apparatus?

All of these questions surface more and more frequently in the public space in a time of increasingly sophisticated AI scripts, developing companion bots or sex-bots, fictional characters and avatars taking the place of physical human subjects. These trends contribute to the emergence of highly complex posthuman intimacy and emotionality. Their biological, technological and informational elements together construct complicated and vivid assemblages, and have for a long time formed hybrid subjects of either material or immaterial structure, often called human, or otherwise.

It turns out, however, that this melting away and reconfiguration of intimacy and the associated subject idea of a diversity of 'apparatus of pain and pleasure' is not just a characteristic feature of our own post-digital age but appears to have been presented in many historical media orders. The greater, therefore, the perceived importance of their analysis, for we then understand the evolution of media technologies as an unending, perennial game of formation of nomadic subjecthood constituting the product of autonomy and subordination, algorithmic action patterns and spontaneous entropy, as well as the dynamic relationship between subjectivation and objectification.

Posthuman intimacy thus seems to be an incredibly important category capable of showing, in an interesting light, the deep time of media, as Siegfried

Zielinski writes, from an archaeological perspective (or anarchaeological, rather). Such a close look on both media pasts and the media present through the lens of posthuman affects and assemblages is what I would like to make the subject matter of this book.

The posthuman reflection that is gaining increasing popularity is currently practised in a great many fields within humanities. The foundational works to this area of thinking by Donna Haraway, Katherine Hayles, Rosi Braidotti, Cary Wolfe or Karen Barad, along with other scholars associated with this current of thought or contributing valuable inspiration to it even before it received its name, delimit various territories of reflection, from technological contexts, wherein the cyborg figure and artificial intelligence have pride of place, through social aspects associated, for example, with the actor-network category, to interspecies relations and bio-art. The various diverse perspectives of employing the posthuman idea in humanities have in many cases a common denominator in the pursuit of demystification of the category of the liberal humanist subject with its own autonomous substantiality (essentiality) and the capacity for self-governance and as a rational and integral being with clearly defined boundaries. The construability and impermanence of that which is human and that which is non-human, the problem of autonomy and ethics, and attempts to redefine the category of the 'other' are subjects of singular importance in the wake of the change brought by the advances in information technologies, digital media, genetic engineering, as well as other problems, e.g. in the area of Foucaltist bio-politics.

Posthuman reflection in its current shape builds on two strong provenances of the 'other'. One of its enduring 'legs' is the category of the animal, the other of the machine. Haraway, in publishing her two manifestos – of the cyborg[1] and of the companion species[2] – laid out the route for these two paths of thinking, channelling the considerations that had until then featured separately in different places. When deliberating on the scope of reflection within these positions it is not difficult to note that in both cases there are both similarities in the perspective adopted, the observations and the theoretical toolset constructed, and differences, for example, in the philosophical, historical and social background relied on. One can also look for attempts at integrated thinking about the relations that happen on the human–machine–animal axis.[3]

The purpose of my study in this book will be an attempt to demonstrate that it is possible within posthuman reflection to determine and describe a third 'instance' associated with the information category. While information is, in posthuman thought, indeed present from nearly the beginning, it is rarely established as a separate 'entity' or 'quality' beside the animal and the machine.[4] Until present, primarily due to cybernetic expressions and informational concepts of life, information has often been characterized as the 'spirit' of communication systems – data that, in cybernetic systems, have been exchanged, transmitted and confirmed. Information is, in this perspective, the fruit of the operations of autopoietic systems. Transmissible consciousness, artificial intelligence, artificial life and virtual corporeality are select figures of this reflection, whereof the informative aspect is its immanent property. The information contexts of this reflection have on the one hand often entailed negating the idea of subjectivity altogether (or giving it an aleatory constitution), and on the other hand it has usually been a reflection emerging from technological thinking from the onset of information technology embodied in the computer machine. Information was, therefore, in this case, a category from a different plane, from outside the above triad. As Joanna Żylińska writes, 'the human is positioned much more ostensibly as an element in the information system, a nodal point for the flow of data, rather than a skin-bound, self-contained rational moral agent'.[5] Hayles, in turn, notes that information 'is a pattern rather than a presence, defined by the probability distribution of the coding elements composing the message'.[6]

The purpose of my study is not so much to discuss the possibility of combined analysis of information systems through a cybernetic perspective enabling structures with each a different ontological status (human subjects, computer systems, ecosystems) to be discussed on a uniform plane, as to show how, in the anthropological sense, such dilution of the boundaries of the human subject may take place under the influence of information. Theses challenging the integrity of this subject are based, *inter alia*, on pointing towards other species, technologies or other inanimate objects as equiponderant instances. It appears equally important to show to what extent we can so speak of information creations, even though as until now they have not fully been linked with subjectivity, or at least only in select cases, being at that ones in which the analysis is clearly marked with the technological perspective. Here, Hayles cites examples of artificial life, which in itself is defined by technological discourse, but also introduces the interesting category of data humanization.[7]

By contrast, the bilateral process of giving subjecthood the status of immaterial information and on the other hand uplifting informational creations to the status of subjects took shape over a long time. An explanation for these transformations is provided, for example, in the early works of Allucquere Rosanne Stone, who, correspondingly to the technologico-biological foundation of Haraway's cyborgicity, puts more emphasis on the informational background of the cyborg's status. In *Will the Real Body Please Stand Up. Boundary Stories about Virtual Cultures*,[8] on the basis of the previous concept by Frances Barker,[9] she demonstrates how the development of the internet and of the cyberspace has contributed to the gradual separation of the body from the subject and the bestowal of a textual status on subjecthood.[10] This, too, is one of the reasons why in my book I will strive to highlight these processes in a historical perspective by scrutiny of the media technologies arising prior to the Digital Age.

However the main purpose of my study is to examine the scope of possibility of building subjective relations between the users of the various media technologies and the senses communicated through the latter. I attempt to demonstrate that the relationship between the subject defined as the user of the medium and the meanings generated in the various media environments unfolds between the polar extremes of competition and cooperation. I also describe the terms of that confrontation and the protocols of closeness and emotional bond that are built during it. Hence, this is an attempt to construct a theory of intimacy describing processes occurring between a 'human' subject and information creations. In this book I demonstrate in what way and in what phases that relationship is built and what its nature is. I also examine the valency conditions of the instances described, which work out a 'common tongue', positioning themselves between the polar extremes of conflict and collaboration.

Select visual technologies and media genres (in their current shape and historical development), in the functioning (utilization and reception) of which such intimate relationships are observable, will be the subject of the analysis. On the one hand, therefore, media technologies are in this perspective regarded as fora for the construction of protocols for the agreement of the relationship between the subject and the medium-generated meanings. On the other hand, the technologies have the interesting capacity for modifying the status and the ontology of the subject, to which attention will also be given in the present study. The distribution of subjectivity, its hybrid status and its destabilization are frequently the fruit of the decision to become part of the posthuman 'vehicles of pleasure and pain', the mechanism of which will herein be reconstructed. Media mechanisms, as will become apparent, are often at the same time sources of pleasure (often sexual) and simultaneously the apparatus of violence symbolic and physical alike.

The analysis of the above-outlined problems involves several planes wherein the exemplification material was gathered. The project will discuss technologies and genres related to the structure of television content (Teleprompter, interactive television forms appearing in both the analog and the digital eras) composition of the film image and specificity of cinematic technologies (peep show, hybrid animation, digital visual effects). Also new-media technologies and genres will be discussed (e.g. aspects relating to computer games and Web portals making video materials available). This diversity is prompted by the desire to show that on the one hand the building of intimacy protocols is not the domain of the digital era, and on the other hand that the posthumanism of media apparatus is a wide problem, i.e. the area encompasses various vehicles findable throughout various historical periods.

The intersection method

The above-outlined goals related to the need to demonstrate the intimate relationship of a destabilized human subject with the media-transmitted meanings and tendencies towards the multilateral, and, as will become apparent, quite long-lived by now, positioning of information entails the use of several diverse perspectives that partially broach the problem and will together supply a good point of departure for the construction of the analysis schema.

Posthumanism(s)

Several inspiration circles may provide the basis for the construction of the question schema. The first of these is, of course, the emerging reflection on posthumanism, in which the expressly formulated idea of human-informational subjective understanding does not appear with great frequency but which makes it possible to rely on observations relating to the variously defined and ontologically diverse 'other'. Posthumanism, as a critical project with regard to the liberal humanist subject, appears to be the best method for describing the phenomena on which the new subjective instances are founded; besides describing such instances as technological creations (including the computer) or the representatives of other biological species, it is worth emphasizing more clearly the possibility of regarding informational creations as subjects, even though their constitution may be short-lasting and variable, and study them with the use of appropriately developed critical tools.

Posthuman reflection will be utilized here in three scopes. Firstly, it will set out the general scope of the analysis language. Broadly understood posthumanism has already created a certain terminological framework that is based on such newly created or defined categories as hospitality, the other, cyborg, interspecies relations, minority, pro-ethicality, mutation, virality, parasitism and assemblage.[11] They are used in the various areas of posthuman thought independently of the provenance of the 'other' we are facing.[12]

At a certain stage this pan-perspective, however, may prove insufficient, for though many scholars would oppose such a view, the idea of a single posthumanism appears to scarcely be fully defensible if one takes into account the fact that within it there exist so many detailed areas such as artificial intelligence, animal studies, disability studies, cultural imaginations of the post-human, machine–human interaction, the philosophy of the superhuman and transhumanism, etc.[13] Making its appearance within such different 'posthumanisms' is a set of specific phenomena such a unified point of view could fail to perceive, or it could provide only a simplified description of them. On the other hand, it is worth looking to such specific areas within posthumanism with the need to see to what extent the categories and tools developed there could be transplanted to a different specific area.

Not forgetful of the need to 'scan' all such areas of posthumanism where the idea of entering into intimate relationships with a non-human other may appear, I will be paying especial attention to those posthuman contexts in which the category of subjectivated information appears. To Hayles this process is linked rather to the development of artificial intelligence and artificial life, in line with the search for a platform for 'envisioning humans as information-processing machines with fundamental similarities to other kinds of information-processing machines, especially intelligent computers'.[14] Turkle attaches similar significance to AI in her studies, though she notes that the intelligence alone of the robot-companions studied by her is not the only condition for establishing intimate relationships with them.[15] In this connection, I would like in my studies to expand upon this issue to include non-intelligent creations or at least ones the intelligence of which is not of significance to the builder of the intimate understanding. In such a case the subjectivation process is a process of demiurgic creation of new personal instances constituting frequently the negation of the need for intelligent contact or even pronounced interaction.

Mary Flanagan highlights somewhat different contexts of information personas. To her, those are computer-generated 'personalities' constituting the next evolutionary form of the graphical user interface.[16] Hence, at this time they are not necessarily the embodiment of artificial-intelligence scripts, although her examples are equipped with those, but they are purely functional tools, putting on 'a human face on the front of real-time, up-to-date flows of data'.[17] This aspect appears to be promising, as it guarantees the possibility of analysing more that for which we need the subjectivity of informational beings than that what their construction would have to be so we could deem them as such. Flanagan's approach is also in some way non-technological, similarly to the perspective I propose. This means that she concentrates more on the subjectivating potential of information than on such values in the technology generating that information. In so doing she borrows from Barthes with his valuable characterization of reading as an intimate and erotic relationship between the lusting reader-lover and the text, and with such understanding of the text as a semiotic vehicle, which precedes cyborgical creatures and has subjectivation capacity:

> Barthes' effective stretching of semiotics to include images, codes, and cultural systems prefigures cyborg methodologies and allows us to examine this hybrid creature – a creature we can define as one not of materiality or even as a human and machine combination, but rather one of referential and non-referential elements. Digibodies, constructed from text, create a text-based shape: 'the text itself ... can reveal itself in the form of a body, into fetish objects, into erotic sites'.[18]

The third way of employing posthuman thought is the appeal to the historical aspects of the idea, being a development upon Haraway's vocal: 'we have always been cyborgs', or 'we have never been human'. The emerging analyses on the one hand utilize the posthuman thought pattern to analyse historical phenomena,[19] and on the other hand they attempt to find historical sources for such thinking.[20] The reflection presented here will also utilize this historical current in posthuman thinking, which combines the analyses emerging in this circle with the next area to which it is worth turning for inspiration, which is history and media archaeology.[21] This approach, drawing upon to the two above-described historical perspectives, could be called posthuman media archaeology.

Where the presentation requires reconstruction of intimate ways of using media technology, I will often rely on the analysis of archived materials and historical sources. Those will refer to such media technologies as exemplifying the relationship between the human subject and the information being regarded as a subject: *kinetoscope* and *mutoscope, peepshow, Teleprompter, blue box* and *green box*. I would like not only to treat the technologies being here presented by me as proofs of building intimate relationships meaningfully but also to use them as 'meta-metaphors'. This means that in examining historical (and modern) forms of use of media technologies, I will regard the selected examples also as metaphors of relationships between the media user and the meanings generated by the media. This strategy appears to show certain links to Kittler's approach to media history. His gramophone, film and typewriter could be called metaphors of specific thought and historical-cultural formation.[22]

Between psychoanalysis and schizoanalysis of the Other

Lacanian psychoanalysis is a meticulous reconstruction of the dynamics of formation of a subject. This context of his thought is already worth harnessing in the situation of a search for the dynamics of formation of a non-human subject, even though doubtless Lacan's model of subjectivity could be called 'human', as he built it on the basis of his own experience as a practitioner of human therapy. This prompts the question of to what extent this rich theory is a good fit for defining a non-human other and describing construable hybrids built of biological, technological and information elements. Hence, it is a question of Lacan's viability after humanism.[23] On the other hand, we can also encounter criticism of his normative theory coming in the form of the competing model of schizoanalysis created by Deleuze and Gauttari. Perhaps, therefore, one should rather choose that particular route in the quest for a study model for posthuman subjectivity.

Deleuze and Gauttari, due to their interest in assemblage, through the concept of binary machines, bodies without organs, are currently becoming far more frequent guests in the works of posthumanists. Their theory appears more aptly to describe the impermanence of biological–technological–digital market combinations of hybrids subjected to contingencies, which translates into their presence in a great number of works employing the posthuman perspective in the discussion of a whole spectrum of diverse problems, not limited to the body[24] or sexuality,[25] but also involving art[26] or medicine.[27] Deleuze and Gauttari's concept appears, however, to be so anti-subjective as to allow one to trace its destabilization and disintegration rather than even momentary constitution.

It is the opposite with Lacan. Due to the fact that his thought is directed towards the construction of the subject, it inspires numerous scholars who appear to subscribe to the thesis that technology in various ways supports the constitution of subjectivity. One of the core options is discussion about supporting the therapeutic process with information technology, as exemplified by Suler's studies.[28] Such type of lens would subsequently be expanded into the sphere of psychologically understood relationships between a human being and technology. One of the first concepts relating to this area are the oft-cited and commented works of Sherry Turkle,[29] who was one of the first scholars to have adopted the psychological perspective in her study of human–computer interactions. Neither should one forget about the appearance of such type of contexts earlier on within Ihde's postphenomenological current.[30] Studies conducted within this perspective of the study current do not, however, touch upon the aspects of the relationship between the cyberspace user and the information sphere regarded subjectively but are rather (in the technological sense) an analysis of subjectivated treatment of computer devices or robots.[31] They can, however, prove valuable by attracting attention to the matter of intimacy and projection of the mechanisms of interpersonal communication onto the human–machine relationship.

Another place of employment of Lacan's thought in technology-orientated studies is the area of new media and digital technologies. This frame of reference could include Žižek's interpretation of virtual reality,[32] which regards the latter as a frame blurring the previously distinct boundary between the interior and the exterior, or as a reflection of Lacan's idea of truth with the structure of fiction – the true self is revealed in games with identity taken up in the cyberspace. A similar nature belongs to Nusselder's theses of the cyborg nature of our joining of the 'psychological' space that is the cyberspace, understood by him as a psychic sphere showing similarity to Lacan's fantasy world.[33] This current appears to exhibit links to transhumanist philosophy – thanks to technological progress, the place for the shaping of symbolic and imagined structures of our self and the extension of the psychic apparatus capable of forming elements of subjectivity and channelling the libido becomes the cyberspace.

The last plane to deserve attention is the tactics of fishing the various technological aspects out of Lacan's voluminous legacy.[34] On the basis of the latter perspective psychoanalysis appears recently to be becoming a fertile ground for posthumanities (or *vice versa*), the proof of which is a monographic issue of the *Paragraph* dedicated to the connections between the two fields. A certain shortcoming in the texts presented in the collection is the focus mainly on the mechanical aspects of psychic structures. As noted in the introduction to that volume by Dow and Wright, 'psychoanalysis has been exploring the scandalously machinic aspect of psychic life for well over a hundred years now'.[35]

Psychoanalysis is, however, brought closer to the part of posthumanism defined as critical posthumanism by more than merely the examination of the psychic machine park. For as Dow and Wright assert, both approaches focus on the same major categories such as desire, embodiment and representation.[36] When analysing the successive overlapping layers, they point out the similarity in both currents' criticism of rational humanism. In posthuman thought that criticism is grounded in the exploration of artificial and cybernetic foundations of intelligence and the possibility of its recreation in non-human beings, and in psychoanalysis it shows itself through the 'other rationality of the subconscious mind'.[37] Both perspectives also chart a map of the transformation of subjectivity – posthumanism points towards the technological prostheses affecting it, while psychoanalysis focuses on the morphologies of social structures and symptoms triggered by them. Both perspectives also take a critical look upon the limits of embodiment – posthumanism does so by tracing the phenomenology of virtual reality and the complex corporeality of cyborgs, and psychoanalysis by placing emphasis on the symbolically mediated body and permanent rooting of the drives in the space of the real. An important category to both posthumanism and psychoanalysis is the conscious, to which each of them attaches its own concepts.[38]

In Lacan's concept one should look precisely for such places in which an opportunity marks itself to ask questions reaching beyond human psychology and towards the psychology of the non-human, e.g. who can occupy the position of the symbolic great other in the real – only a different human subject and different 'human' sex, or perhaps it could be a different biological being, or perhaps inanimate matter. What if the non-human other is silent, does not use a language? How will the meticulous construct of human subjectivity change if we confront it with the non-human other? These are the questions that the various legs of posthumanism ask themselves within the narrower spheres of the non-human. In my study such a non-human sphere is the media machinery capable of creating new subjects and significantly modifying the 'old'. This is with the proviso that the intimacy protocols developed therein could be accompanied by pleasure and pain both.

Lacanian psychoanalysis sets out an important perspective for posthumanism in respect of defining not only the other but also the complex issues of the visible and of the gaze, which sometimes appear to give his thought an even firmer grounding in posthumanities. Here too one could find a place for Lacan's works, where from beyond the analysis of the complex human psyche thinking about the non-human transpires. Sometimes this will be a reference made to reducing the subject to the eye,[39] sometimes one of defining the subject by gazing at a tin carried by the waves of the sea,[40] but, in reality, the whole concept of the gaze can here be the basis for posthuman thinking. Also Wolfe notes this link between posthumanism and visibility and visuality, dedicating a whole two chapters of his monograph to the matter.[41]

It appears that media vehicles – presented in this work as the locations of assemblage constructs of the subject, constantly forming anew – create spaces wherein a constant oscillation between the polar extremes of psycho- and schizoanalysis takes place. On the one hand, the users of these technologies frequently build the informational other's consciousness upon the familiar patterns of 'human' subjectivity or insert this other into such 'human' ways of being, and on the other hand they themselves are placed in an unstable, discursive position that is violated time after time by the specificity of the *modus operandi* and structure of the media vehicle.

Power

If in describing the specificity of the non-human other we attempt to see to what extent the other's 'human' concepts could be applied here, Lacan's Other immanently linked to the symbolic order is a construct defined by the relationship of power imposed by law. Lacan, building on Levi-Strauss, regards law as the immanent property of a human being, a property that not only penetrates into the sexual order or culture but allows the human being to distinguish itself from other animals, ones not equipped with the capacity for making law. How then should one refer that unique property to the lawmaking of non-human subjects? It turns out that codification of relationships of power is for this purpose a very important element of defining subjectivity. It delimits the right to be a subject across a great diversity of spheres that have been described and established a multitude of times with regard to humans or animals, but as regards the 'non-material Galateas' they still need description.[42]

With the above in mind, should one in turn consider the thought of Foucalt, making as he does rather frequent inroads into new-media reflection, the search would have to be taken to somewhat different places than is usually the case in such reflection. With regard to posthuman intimacy, instead of appealing to discipline, which alongside the development of surveillance techniques and network structures is one of the most rewarding topics borrowed from the author of *Discipline and Punish*, we should rather look for places where we encounter micro-discourses of power, founded in a private environment and in the situation of a continually destabilizing balance of power. This is precisely what my narrative of select media technology will look like. Here they will be the field of negotiation of such a covenant between that which is human and that which is informational, and on the other hand often a type of ally invited into a pact against another party.

Analysis of the relationships of power between that which is human and that which is non-human can also consist in seeing whether certain categories describing interhuman relationships of power could not be generalized to an interbeing level, or whether the founding of such relationships does not happen to have the effect of a configuration whereby the instance being subordinated to authority or imposing its power could become non-human. In other words, as we have crossed the threshold that used to hold us back from employing the same tools to the study of humans and non-humans, let us enter on the path of experiment and employ the theories applied to the 'human' perspective to the study of non-humans. Agamben's thought will in some places of this presentation play such a role. The author of *The Open* is placed within the umbrella of posthuman primarily on account of his study of human–animal relationships and the concept of the anthropological machine suggesting the construability of the category of the human subject that is dependent on historical contexts. I would like to show the extent of the utility of the categories developed by him in reference to biopolitics, such as 'camp', 'outcast' or 'Muselmann'.[43]

Contexts of (post-)anthropological intimacy

This project could be said to be post-anthropological in nature in the sense that subjectivity, so symptomatic of the anthropological perspective, is, can be and should be the subject matter of posthuman reflection. Here, therefore, I have in mind the features of not postmodernist but posthuman anthropology.[44] In reducing the perspective to the narrower scope of anthropological studies into the media, it is worth observing that while the tradition of such studies usually has as their subject of interest the ethnographic aspects and cultural circumstances of the creation and receipt of the media message, which will not be of such great significance to my study, one term that is eagerly used in this area (particularly in reference to new media) is the category of intimacy.[45] It constitutes, as I will show somewhat later on, an immanent element of the construction of protocols between the users of the analysed media technologies and information creations, for this reason setting forth a very significant study perspective.

In connection with how intimate relationships between media users and messages created with the use of media technologies can be founded either at the stage of building such messages or at the stage of receiving them, I am in this case interested in the intimate anthropology of both the creative process and the consumption stage. It is for this reason, among others, that the material I have gathered originates from the analysis of the documentation of the process of creating media messages with the use of various technologies. With regard to film technologies I am, for example, interested in an area that could be termed the anthropology of special effects and composition of the motion picture. In this connection the analysed types of materials include making-ofs, photographic documentation of the film set, interviews with the creators, animatics, concept art and motion capture. On the other hand, I analyse such testimonies of the receipt of media messages as could reveal the intimate context in question (blogs and video records capturing the users' utterances, available on the internet).[46] One of the core anthropological concepts that is the ritual is also a useful element of the studies, since I attempt to show how its repeatability and sanctification can be of use in the fight for the constitution of new subjects.

In asking the question of intimacy, one must not forget that the two essential and even properly defining aspects of this sphere are sexuality and theatricality. As the matter of corporeality and embodiment is one of the leitmotifs of posthumanism, it is no wonder that aspects of theatricality can facilitate its understanding.[47] In theatrical thought, however, aspects of the body interest me less than does the context of performance as the creation of a world; hence, we are coming closer again to the anthropological concept of the ritual. This is an interesting matter in the perspective of the creation of new, non-human beings. In several places I attempt to show theatricality as the potential of not so much being as founding the other (as is the case e.g. in the 'autotheatrical' practices of

Disney's cartoonists), and on the other hand as an opportunity to define one's specificity versus the non-human other, 'who is watching me'.

With regard to the matters of sexuality a great many views describing it with the use of posthuman categories have surfaced.[48] Once again the thought of Deleuze and Gauttari, who point towards the human sexuality (being in their outlook often called the anthropomorphic representation of sex) as a specific case of sexuality in general, is illuminating the path here.[49] The idea of '*n* sexes' assumes on the one hand overcoming the need to be subordinate to societally imposed gender roles, and on the other hand it presupposes valency between desiring machines of different ontologies.[50] A rich typology of post-sexuality is introduced by Luciana Parisi, illustrating also that 'sex expands on all levels of material order, from the inorganic to the organic, from the biological to the cultural, from the social to the technological'.[51] One could assume that the approach presented in my studies accentuates a type of sexuality vis-à-vis information creations that in Parisi's concept would touch upon the biological-cultural level. Media vehicles, which I discuss here, have – as generators of meanings – the capacity for changing the structure of human sexuality on a very deep level. The process of wrapping the most important biological order being the sexual act in an information cocoon will here be shown in detail, e.g. with regard to such apparatus as the peep show or an internet database. Even though much has already been said of the transformations of the sexual sphere in a posthuman view, neither should one forget about Bataille's concept of sexuality, which, in my opinion, could be shown as 'non-human', which will be proved later on. On the other hand, sexuality in Bataille is often grounded in the discourse of authority, which will also turn out useful.

The apparatus as a subject – from new materialism to the cinema-lover

For my studies the idea of new materialism, developing as a result of the efforts of a sizeable group of scholars such as De Landa and Braidotti, is a useful plane of inquiry, though the accent placed on 'immateriality' in this work may raise some questions.

Dolphijn and van der Tuijn note that one aspect of new materialism that is of interest to this work is transversality, which cuts across such traditional dichotomies as nature–culture, subject–object, interior–exterior, etc.[52] Thanks to this potential it is possible to show the phenomena of posthumanism as the effects of a critical attitude towards anthropocentrism, which elude unequivocal classification. On the other hand, new materiality shows itself here also as a critical category, i.e. one that allows disputing the representation-materiality opposition and causes the negative impacts of building a dual approach to be levelled.[53]

It is worth noting that new materialism concentrates also in many cases on the sources of subjectivity transfers and that which Dolphijn and van der Tuijn define as 'duration … inserted into matter'.[54] The media apparatus discussed here will also be shown as generators and simultaneously annihilators of subjectivity undergoing various types of interesting transformations in the technological environment.

One must consider, however, that the media vehicle is a specific kind of mechanism launching the generation of meanings. Hence, my analyses will often start from the material foundation of the vehicles but proceed towards the 'non-material' structure of the agents created through them. Some of the concepts identified with new materialism correspond to this way of thinking. As noted by Dolphijn and van der Tujin, such dualistic thinking appears also in Haraway, who defines bodies as 'material-semiotic agents',[55] and in Braidotti, who defines them as 'texts that unfold according to genetic coding'.[56]

Neither should one forget that the 'informational' character of the 'beings' created in various media environments distinguishes them from non-material objects subjectivated as a result of diverse intimate practices. Though we are dealing here with creations regarded as immaterial, their information status also is a 'fabric' with specific characteristics resulting from the structure of media technology.[57] That specificity will have an obvious impact on the shape of the intimacy protocols built between the medium user and the immaterial 'other' built of meanings.

It occurs from the intimate perspective adopted in this work that the most interesting part of neo-material reflection would be the individual, private and body- or sexuality-related contexts and not the materialistic analyses of social structures (e.g. ANT-type); however, some of the types of media rituals presented in this work must be social in nature to be able to sanction the newly founded entities.

The viewpoint outlined by new materialism would also have as its consequence a search for media-apparatus theories to analyse users' affect vis-à-vis the technologies. Hence, when looking for such non-human instances as could enter into complicated relationships with a human being, it is worth focusing on the current of studies relating to media technology, with the latter being the first to have become regarded as a posthuman vehicle. Here I have in mind the cinema, which began to be so regarded again, thanks to Deleuze. He is, in a way, the double founder of posthuman ideas. This is on the one hand because of his having built together with Guattari an extremely critical – with regard to the liberal humanist subject – idea of a body without organs, as well as desiring machines, and on the other hand because of the concept of the cinema that makes the recipient's and the actor's subjectivities take on a hybrid monster shape and become an assemblage open to affection vis-à-vis technology and message.

Nowhere has the theory of such subjective affect towards cinema been pronounced more distinctively than in the Deleuze-inspired concept of Patricia McCormack.[58] To MacCormack, the cinema-sexuality is a kind of pansexuality that breaks out of the chains of culturally and socially determined sex. It is desire that goes beyond the dialectic formed towards sexual objects. The cinema as lover is not in itself an object of desire, but it disintegrates here into a multitude of individual moments of desire triggered by the act of gazing. In MacCormack's concept we are, therefore, dealing with the creation of intimacy positioned between the cinema apparatus and the film as a multi-layered meaningful creation wherein the various elements and fragments can be the source of desire. This is only one step away from analyses concentrating on the creations of media apparatus as objects of affection. I present them in my study in reference to three areas – film, television and new media.

Terms

The goals set in this place, entailing the study of posthumanism's information facets, grounded in the analysis of the subjective relationships built between media users and information creations or media messages require a set of categories to be built to allow the shape and parameters of such relationships to be determined. This is important in how posthuman subjectivity is in this case determined by negotiation through the construction of *sui-generis* topography (topology) of terms. In other words, that which is human and that which is non-human must be defined by determining the position of the studied phenomenon in relation to these terms and their internal configuration. The purpose of this reflection is to develop such a language for posthuman analysis as would not negate the experience of the studies into human–animal and human–technology relationships, permitting also the formulation of categories specific to the human-information creation relationship. Hence, I intend to build a preliminary terminology for the analysis of such intimate relationships, a terminology I would like to introduce now.

The subject

It is difficult to point unequivocally to a theory of the subject that would ideally match its presentation herein. Taking into account all that which is entailed by the construction of the subject as considered from the posthuman point of view, there are a number of practically opposed judgements here. On the one hand, one can find multiple theses altogether negating the subject. In this way one could regard the multitude of voices in the cybernetics discourse that made a contribution to Luhmann's societal theory. If we take into account Deleuze and Gauttari's desiring machine, we are also dealing here with an approach in which the subject is an extremely functional, elusive and constructed being that comes into existence at the intersection of very different flows. It is very difficult in such a case to determine any boundaries of that which is subjective.

On the other hand, the criticism of humanism is based on the construction of a perspective wherein even though humanism does lose its integrity or dominant position, it still preserves a certain type of 'strong' autonomy and agency. Haraway or Agamben would see the human as a 'responsible' subject that should be moved by concern for other beings in connection with how that is also the path to knowing oneself. In that relationship the human is a type of strong actant who invites. The whole sphere of building the theory of posthumanism, as well as the practice, plays out, in a sense, in between these two polar extremes.

My outlook will be positioned approximately in the middle of this polar configuration, due to how I will be showing on the one hand the ways and protocols of destabilization of human subjects entering the space of the analysed media vehicles, and on the other hand the forms of creating an intimate plane of understanding and competition with 'information entities' built from the perspective of a strong human subject, who 'is capable of that'. As Braidotti writes, such a subject is 'neither a sacralized inner sanctum, nor a pure socially shaped entity, the enfleshed Deleuzian subject is rather an "in-between": it is a folding-in of external influences and a simultaneous unfolding outwards of affects. A mobile entity, an enfleshed sort of memory that repeats and is capable of lasting through sets of discontinuous variations, while remaining faithful to itself'.[59] Memory is in this case as property forming subjectivity in a variously defined and constituted body, or – as one would be wont to say – medium.

I will be using the term 'subject' in reference to information creation, though in this case it is difficult to regard as the best category of all possible. For one could form that impression that a frenetic search for terms to encapsulate humans and non-humans into a single frame is taking place. In ANT representatives that figure is the actor; Haraway uses the terms 'character' (of literary provenance) and 'companion species'. Sometimes a term more proximate to the definitional scope here indicated is 'agent'.[60] The category of fellow species also makes an appearance.[61]

The search for appropriate subject concepts cannot ignore the interesting ideas of new animism. For it seems that a large number of theses pushed forward by posthumanism show a great many similarities to those which appear in new animists. While they usually study indigenous communities, new social phenomena such as the objectum sexuals community discussed in Chapter 8 frequently seem to confirm their outlook. Scholars such as Graham Harvey formulate primarily the pertinent definitions of 'other-than-human persons'.[62] Those are 'beings, rather than objects, who are animated and social towards others (even if they are not always sociable)'.[63] New animists also formulate the important distinction between a person and an object. As Harvey writes:

> Persons are those with whom other persons interact with varying degrees of reciprocity. Persons may be spoken with. Objects, by contrast, are usually spoken about. Persons are volitional, cultural and social beings. They demonstrate agency and autonomy with varying degrees of autonomy and freedom.[64]

Intimacy

Acceptance of the posthuman perspective hinges on two decisions. The former is to depart from the leading role of the human being, that is, the concept of the universal self-determining subject, and in that connection the achievement by it of a certain stage of maturity. It is I, the human being, who become aware of the presence of a non-human other, for whom I take responsibility. On the other hand, the will of becoming connected appears. I will shape my 'self' so as to be capable of connection with the 'other', and find a plane of understanding or ontological integration. I will look for the right interface to enable such a connection, or I will create structures (cultural? social?) enabling such a relationship to be founded. Thus, when discussing the process of posthuman transcendence of the human nature, we must inevitably turn towards intimacy. Intimacy appears for these reasons to be an immanent feature of posthumanism. The intimacy we are speaking about here has a specific nature. Due to how this involves the type of the closest and non-social contact that is largely construed outside the subject in the physical sense (media technology) and in the mental sense (non-human informational subject), the definition of intimacy here is close to Lacan's concept of extimacy.[65] In Lacan, extimacy shows the construction of an 'ex-centric subject'. He invokes the picture of Altamira cave paintings as such an external intimacy based on the projection within the space of the grotto of an irrepresentable and inaccessible Thing.[66] Lacan's reference to the externalizing nature of art and, in a later part of the presentation, anamorphosis as one more vision technology seems to correspond with the perspective present in my studies; for I attempt to demonstrate in what sense the media apparatus that is composed of technology, protocols of its use and cultural and social environment becomes such an external space for the incessant game of construction and deconstruction of the subject. Derrida appears to write about intimacy in a similar way, depicting it as the readiness to build relationships between the living presence and its exterior. This characteristic will be studied later herein with regard to the various strategies formulated in reference to such a subjectivated exterior,[67] ranging from love to cruelty.

Let us see what other aspects of intimacy theory could be of use here. For Turkle intimacy relates to the problem, important in the context of the issues touched upon here, of valency with our creations: 'We search for a link between who we are and what we have made, between who we are and what me might create, between who we are and what, through intimacy with our own creations, we might become.'[68]

More sources can be found that show such an understanding of intimacy that refers to the critical and discursive aspects of the term. To Haraway and the continuators of her thought intimacy will be a form of demystifying the differences and moving non-human others to the centre of the discourse. As Jacqui Gabb writes about the family groups studied by her, 'in pet-oriented families animals often do not exist on the affective periphery, but are included in how intimacy is experienced'.[69] Langan and Davidson, in turn, show that the understanding of intimacy as discourse 'offers an alternative way to approach questions around intimacy', and the more critical theories of intimacy ask 'how, when, where and with whom intimacy can be achieved'.[70] The question of 'with whom?' in the perspective of the posthuman study schema gains prime importance here, although all of the remaining ones direct attention towards the circumstances of the use of the media vehicles analysed herein, as well as their structure.

The interbeing attraction fair

Richard Balzer in his album on the history of peep show outlines in one of the fragments of his discussion of it the background of the functioning of that device within the city space, demonstrating that such virtual shows incessantly had to compete with the other attractions available to the participants of markets and fairs. To quote him directly:

> For nearly two hundred years itinerant showmen hawked their wares in competition with other street entertainers in Europe's great cities. City streets were not quiet places, but more often crowded, bustling, noisy thoroughfares of traffic and commerce where men and women tried to eke out a living selling goods and services, as well as offering entertainments of all shapes and varieties. The peepshows had to compete with dancing bears, learned pigs, jugglers, balancing acts, conjurers, pantomimes and puppeteers.[71]

This scene, scrutinized here in a posthumanism perspective, is a type of symbol of the first competition for attention that takes place between creations of different ontological status, whereby human subjects are gathered on a shared 'scene' with animals and media messages. In my study the category of an interbeing attraction fair will be useful in the search for those spaces in which the human subject is confronted with information creations and competes with them, playing by the same rules.

Instantiation

The term 'instantiation' is the modification of a category known from programming theory as instancing. An instance is the occurrence of an object representing a defined class, while instancing in this case is the process of creating such an object. If we add to this the other definition of an instance as a tier in the structure of the power we are addressing, then the combination of these two understandings will produce a vision of instantiation as an action aimed to include ontologically diverse creations in a single class of subjects, a process that forms in a relationship of power or at least in the discourse. It appears that this process is an immanent feature of posthuman discourse, both in its animalistic and in its technological leg. In the technological leg already Turing notes the necessity of teaching computers, which, like children, require our attention and care.[72] So does Wiener, in creating a common set of instances capable of learning.[73] It is hardly difficult to realize that ANT also is founded on instantiation, even though in that approach we do not actually have to deal with the founding of a subject.[74] In the animalistic leg, on the other hand, instantiation occurs e.g. in Agamben in 'The Other',[75] embodying it through the criticism of the differences between humans and animals, denouncing the historicity of the anthropological categories. One could also assume that the symbol of interspecies fraternity that is Baba Joseph in Haraway, exposing his forearm to mosquito bites in a gesture of solidarity with bitten laboratory animals,[76] is the ideal example of instantiation built on the foundation of compassion.

In my project I will be concerning myself with this moment of invitation to become the subject of the 'information instance'. I will show in what the process of bestowing the status of a subject plays out and what ritual forms it takes. I will also trace the effect of that invitation understood as reaction to instantiation.

The posthuman position

The above-presented concept of an interbeing fair, as well as the instantiation idea entails a type of approach to the phenomena of posthumanism that relies on a topographic configuration of subjectivity. Being or not being posthuman, being or not being a subject, is determined by the position of the being, understood as its place in the sense of a physical or conceptually construed space occupied by beings that differ in ontological status. As Lacan writes, 'everything depends on the position of the subject. And the position of the subject ... is essentially characterised by its place in the Symbolic world, in other words in the world of speech'.[77] Hence the act of 'naming' creations of different ontological status subjects, taking place in the symbolic space, as well as the models for the coming into existence of the 'posthuman position' will be analysed in this work. Here it is worth defining the type of posthumanism that occurs from such 'positions'. It could be called topo-relational, due to how it emerges from the relationships of elements (instances, subjects, apparatus), as well as in their mutual positioning.

Agreement protocol

Taking into account media theory, the category of protocol appears, among others, in Alex Galloway and Lisa Gitelman. Galloway, who focuses on computer protocols, notes that those are 'a set of recommendations and rules that outline specific technical standards'. In his view protocols define 'how specific technologies are agreed to, adopted, implemented, and ultimately used by people around the world'.[78] Gitelman employs the protocol category in reference to the cultural codes accompanying the use of media technologies.[79] In my project the media vehicle will be considered as a place wherein a protocol is developed for agreeing upon the mutual relations between the media user and the meanings generated through the medium. I will show how the properties of the medium define the scope and codify the manner of collaboration of the instances discussed (this model is reminiscent of negotiation-based communication models, but in this case the negotiation takes place not between two medium users who are persons but between the user and the meanings generated through the medium).

Consent

Above, I noted two perceptions of subjectivity. The former entails approaching the subject as a short-term impulse constituting itself at the intersection of different flows or occasionally inhabiting a certain body, not necessarily a biological body and not necessarily an integrated one, either. It is a subject-effect, subject-result, an entity that can be programmed to exist. The latter entails the concept of an affective subject that sensitizes itself to the surrounding beings and gives up its integrity and autonomy for the sake of interspecies or interontological dispersion. In such a case it is an entity that shows decisiveness and has a will of change. This project will analyse case studies that come closer now to one, now to the other approach. In those places, however, when the above-described posthuman position is the effect of a choice, we can speak of an act of Consent unfolding in an interesting way. It is the moment of the human subject's adoption of a dialogical position, thanks to which it becomes the founder of the subjective relationship between it and the sense. The dialogue itself between humans and 'other-than-human persons' is described by Harvey,[80] citing Bachtin's dialogicality concept. The consequence of this attitude is the conviction, very close to posthumanism, that 'humans share this world with a wide range of persons, only some of whom are human'.[81] Once again, therefore, the concept of human subject that is open, sensitive and attentive to otherness makes its appearance here.

Apparatus (of power)

Agamben's apparatus concept is of extraordinary utility to this work in defining the specificity of the media vehicles described herein as machines with the capacity for posthuman repositioning of the user's subjectivity and as an instrument for building intimacy with the message. Agamben, grounding his observation in a Foucaltist understanding of the apparatus, begins from defining it in a way that takes into account its being a network of elements, situated within the power relationship, such as discourses, institutes, buildings, rights and laws, means of keeping order, philosophical determinations and so on. That network positions itself at the intersection of power and knowledge.[82]

Agamben's definition of the apparatus deserves merit first of all by how in his opinion the apparatus is something that creates subjectivity. In other words, the subject is the effect of the apparatus's operation. It is a network structure that has the capacity to impose authority upon a living being and impose thereon a subjective role. The significance of those observations is that the media technologies I describe in this project are such apparatus founding different states of subjectivity occurring in the interaction between the living being – the user – and the informational subjects originating from the substance of the message.

There is taking place here, to follow the train of thought of the author of *The Open*, a specific sort of game between processes that move in opposite directions. Agamben demonstrates that within the apparatus scope we on the one hand have to deal with a process for the construction of subjects and on the other hand a process of their disintegration. He practically attempts to prove that modern apparatus originating from the current stage of capitalism disintegrate subjectivity more than they found it. Interesting within the posthuman perspective are also his judgements of how the currently observed immeasurable expansion of apparatus is the cause of the unbalancing and loss of a cohesive subjectivity. The process takes place, however, not by erasing and overcoming subjectivity but more by disseminating it.[83] Due to the desire to trace in my studies the negotiation processes and the subordination of some instances to others that takes place within the space of the media 'vehicles of pleasure and pain', Agamben's linking of the apparatus to the issue of imposition of authority will prove equally relevant and useful.

Let us also see how the Flusser concept of apparatus could be of utility to the present study. In this case apparatus as devices producing technical images would be specific, somewhat autonomous vehicles, which, as Flusser writes, would only sometimes require players or functionaries.[84] In many places in this work I will discuss how that status of players and functionaries is modified by the structure of the media apparatus concerned. Interestingly, Flusser also writes: 'Even apparatuses that are not fully automated (those that need human beings as players and functionaries) play better than the human beings that operate them.'[85] One could, therefore, refer to this manner of thinking as the inverse of transhumanism, that is transindustrialism – the stage when post-machines appear (at 8).

The will of self-limitation (and reduction to sense)

The above-characterized act of sacrifice is often connected with a will of self-limitation. I limit my self to be joined to the 'informational other'. Significantly, Agamben writes in this case about sacrifice, which – to him – is an apparatus of transition from the profane to the sacred. How the process unfolds, how it ends for the subject, can it cause suffering – these are all questions that will be addressed in this work. On the other hand, it is also worth reflecting upon the inverse process to the act of Consent. The posthuman position under discussion can appear when the conditions materialize for the 'human' subject, who previously had had the will, and power to ordain a new 'non-human' companion has itself been reduced (profaned) to the sense (information, message). As Agamben demonstrates, 'profanation is the counter-apparatus that restores to common use what sacrifice had separated and divided'.[86] It is also worth recalling here Kittler's reflection on the interchangeability of the roles of the psychoanalyst and the gramophone.[87] Both the one and the other 'instances' serve a similar purpose in the recording of memories and night dreams. In the chapters to follow I will describe examples testifying not only to how the human subject occupies the position of the apparatus but rather how it takes on the role of the sense generated by that apparatus and frequently competes with it.

Deep digitization

With regard to the examples of new-media technologies used in this project, I will use a term that defines the modern strategy for intimacy building vis-à-vis the information sphere; the deep-digitization category will be of utility in describing the various types of specific communication and cultural practices constituting the effect of consensus building between the new-media user and the digitally generated meanings. The introduction of this category stems from the fact that the digital paradigm can be understood in a broader context than only the technological. The omnipresence of digital technology may be a symbol of deep incongruity that makes an overwhelming impact on cultural and social behaviours. When Deleuze and Guattari write that 'we live today in the age of partial objects, bricks that have been shattered to bits, and leftovers', then even though the Digital Age has yet to take a while to begin, we can speak here of a prefiguration of the process of adapting to the zero-one paradigm, especially considering how the authors of *Capitalism and Schizophrenia* call their desire machines binary. The era will be characterized by that specific type of intimacy that I will document in my study with examples demonstrating that digital technologies will serve as the forum for the assumption, in a symbolic and a literal sense, of sense 'behaviours' in the digital environment, if such an anthropomorphic term can be used. In reference to the above-presented observations by Agamben about modern technological apparatus of oppression one could say that digital technologies deeply blur and make alike the processes of subjectivation and desubjectivation.[88]

The concept of deep digitization appears to overlap in many places with the category of deep mediatization, the latter authored by Andreas Hepp and understood as follows: 'increasing "entanglement" of our social world with pervasive media technologies'.[89] While the author's orientation for this concept is more towards the demonstration of the social process for digital technologies entering all orders of life, his approach appears to concur wherever he posits the recurrent nature of deep-mediatization process, that is, among other things, the constant production of data from individual and social action practices subsequently contributing to the algorithmization of the processes and imposing deep modifications on them.[90]

The structure of the book

The material gathered in the book is laid out in three parts. In the first part I deal with the technologies that can be termed cinematic. I start from the erotic peep show, which, while it seems to be a technology with more links to theatre than to cinema, I will show to be a product of erotic spectacle, film apparatus based on peeping (kinetoscope, mutoscope) and slot machines. The second chapter in this part of the book highlights the specific elements of the intimacy protocol that is built between creators and characters and shows itself primarily through animated hybrid cinema but also through a variety of other creative practices used by animators, as well as the cartoon structure of the represented worlds. The final chapter in this part will, in turn, be dedicated to posthuman contexts of cinematic special effects. Here I wish to point towards specific subjectivity games relating to the use of modern computer graphical techniques and cyborgical characters of film creations that can be observed in the initial executive stage of production. In the chapters on hybrid animation and special effects I refer both to historical sources and to utterances by contemporary cinema creators, who show themselves to be aware of the deep transformations of subjectivity taking place under the influence of film techniques, even though the latter are not called posthuman.

The second part deals with television technologies and genres. In the opening chapter of this part I discuss the Teleprompter, which appears to be a very interesting vehicle for the blurring of the status of the actors in the communication act. Discussion of the historical and modern aspects of this technology enables the presentation, on the one hand, of the role of text as the subject in this vehicle, and on the other hand the very strong links between the posthuman idea and the philosophy of the gaze (and reverie). The chapters that follow are about interactive television forms. In one of them I discuss the beginnings of television interactivity, noting the posthuman contexts of shared character building in *Winky Dink and You* episodes. The last chapter, in turn, is dedicated to interactive competitions on the television, regarded here as vehicles of uniformization and degradation of the presenters to the status of conversation bots.

The last part deals with select case studies from the sphere of digital media. In the first chapter I focus on the strongly subject-formative and subject-transformative aspects of databases, exemplified by the *BeautifulAgony.com* erotic website. In the following chapter I discuss the relevant manifestos of the posthuman legitimization of non-human subjects in the social sphere taking place during specific wedding ceremonies conducted with both material and non-material objects. The last chapter, in turn, is an analysis of feelings towards virtual characters that are rather opposite to love. Here, I show how the 'other' is defined within the space of The Sims – a computer game in which one of the players' most popular pleasures is tormenting and killing their characters in a variety of elaborate ways.

Part One

Cinematic Intimacies

A kaleidoscope of pleasure:
the erotic peep show as a game of subjects

The two oppositive concepts of posthumanism mentioned in the introduction – disintegrative posthumanism, one that motivates the disintegration of the subject, and 'empathic' posthumanism, one that founds the possibility of establishing a link with informational creations – are joined together into a single appliance I would like to discuss in this chapter. The erotic peep show is a special type of appliance, on the one hand situated at the intersection of the history of the visual attractions and development of the erotic industry, and on the other hand being a space, very rich in social, cultural, technological and philosophical contexts, for the meeting of the various orders of power and creation of complicated relationships among the spheres of technology, information and biology. The erotic booth is also the culmination of the long process of formation of an appliance that can be regarded as a mature example of posthuman space, i.e. space in which the appearing human subject adopts the previously discussed posthuman position.

The peep-show appliance weaves together the long histories of several different orders. The first among them is the one we could symbolically term 'Salome's dance' – the individual erotic spectacle of the dancer's submission to the man watching her. Another is the 'keyhole' case, with the peep show inscribing itself into the history of voyeurism, of which the intimate confines are delimited by the eyehole featuring in a selected range of visual technologies such as the boite d'optique,[1] kinetoscope or mutoscope. The third order is the status of the slot machine, introducing to the erotic peep show the characteristic dehumanized discontinuity, or intermittence, of the dancer–customer relationship.

In this chapter I will embark on a historical reconstruction of this invention as the intersection of the above-described orders, and I will demonstrate in what way the modern peep show bears testimony of the dynamic relationship between that which is human and that which is non-human. My analysis of the peep-show appliance coincides greatly with the critical approach to the male gaze, initiated by feminist film studies, for example, by Laura Mulvey[2] and her successors in thought.[3]

Although multiple posthuman contexts of the gaze in its Lacanian understanding will find their way into the following chapters of this book, in this part the outlook on the peep show will be linking me with the feminist understanding of 'woman as the image and man as the owner of the gaze',[4] which appear to be definitionally inscribed into its operating principle. The study into the peep show will, however, in a way, be an elaboration on this dichotomy, introducing a more nuanced approach to it, one in which the technological appliance is characterized by potential for both the reconstruction of either female or male roles and disruption of the bonds joining the subjects with their biologicity, personality and sexuality. Simultaneously, this disintegration is connected with the transfers of affections and lusts in a technological appliance commoditizing sexuality in a variety of ways. While the skopophiliac dancer–observer relationship is a phallocentric frame and a frame of reference for the violent sexual relationship taking place in peep shows, the technological appliance in which the participants find themselves puts them in the roles of elements of a techno-biologico-informational assemblage. It is a vehicle for the satisfaction of sexual fantasies in which the male dominators themselves unwittingly become a market resource melting down in the mechanical formatting of lust.

The main material for analysis here will be several sources constituting the memories of dancers working in peep shows. It turns out that peep show is a place that elicits such confessions. Interestingly, numerous accounts of this type appear in reference to two famous establishments operating under the name of Lusty Lady, located in San Francisco and Seattle. This is, for example, the case with the blog kept by Pegan Moss, once a stripper at two such places in Seattle[5] (www.peepshowstories.com) or the story told by Julia Query in *Live Nude Girls Unite!*, a documentary on San Francisco Lusty Lady strippers' activism.[6] Another former Seattle worker who has decided to share her reflections is Elisabeth Eaves. In their extraordinarily intimate tales, Moss and Eaves provide a thorough depiction of the technological phenomenon that is the peep show and of the intricate web of dependencies established between the human subjects (dancers and customers) and the technological back premises of the place, as well as between the humans and the pornographic video materials shown at the location. It will also be expedient to invoke John McNamara's behavioural analysis of the visitors of New York peep-show establishments.[7] As it turns out, a convenient methodological base for the analysis of peep show's posthuman aspects can be found in this case in the ethnographic perspective, or one could even say auto-ethnographic, as with Jamie Berger's essay.[8] The accounts I will be drawing upon in this part of the book are either material gathered by researchers (McNamara, Berger) or the dancers' confessions capable of supplying the basis for such analysis.[9]

In analysing the above materials, I will demonstrate on the one hand the distribution of intimacy in the peep-show vehicle and the extent to which the technology disposes of the integrity of that which is human. On the other hand, I will identify the various possible manifestations of the will of self-determination of the human subject negotiating its position in the vehicle and being equipped with a potential for subversive opposition to the informational and technological complex.

The erotic peep show – the 'end of process'

When asking ourselves what orders make up the constitution of the erotic peep show, it will be necessary to realize that some of these orders are technological in nature, while some are the result of a tendency to impose a patriarchal-market power in the sexual sphere. The technological orders are the evolution of peeping appliances and slot-machine technologies. The aforementioned 'Salome's dance', in turn, is the symbolic order of the imposition of sexual power and delimitation of hypocritical sexual roles in which the woman becomes active as a dancer but in reality she is the passive object of male arousal. The confessions of Pegan Moss analysed later in this chapter will, however, demonstrate that this traditional frame of erotic dance is not always accurate for peep show. Moss shows the booth dancer's role to sometimes be that of a therapist and holder of the power that arises from familiarity with the peep-show space with its protocol. This feminist context of the sexual power wielded by strippers is also highlighted by the heroines of *Live Nude Girls Unite!*.[10]

Let us attempt a reconstruction of these three orders having led to the emergence of the peep show as a posthuman vehicle for pleasure. While Huhtamo asserts that the details of the development of the erotic version of the peep show are shrouded in mystery,[11] a functional reconstruction of this pleasure appliance is worth the effort if only due to the opportunity to bring out the posthuman contexts I endeavour to highlight in this part of the book.

The order of the 'Salome dance'

The 'Salome dance' is a Biblical theme, sufficiently attractive in later art history that we encounter a range of its artistic depictions, from paintings, through the celebrated Oscar Wilde drama and Strauss opera based on its text, to cinematic productions.[12] The exotic-dance motif will proceed to become one of the paths in the development of erotic dancing and striptease, eventually leading to the emergence of dancers' performances in erotic peep shows. There are several threads in the order of the Salome dance which are convincing candidates for the original foundations of the peep-show structure.

The first of these threads are the peculiar posthuman accents to be found in Salome's story itself, eagerly seized upon by the authors of the various works (paintings especially) based on the theme, as well as the various interpreters. Another is the petrification of the dancing object of lust, which will be affecting the dancers. It is somewhat closely linked to the fascinating relationships of power forming in this history. Not less important is the separation from this public order of the private reception, which is followed by the gradual and increasingly complex framing of this situation until the arrival of the stage when a glass panel separates the two participants of the erotic act.

The non-human Salome

The motif of Salome's dance could be said to contain considerable posthuman potential. In many takes and representations the heroine is depicted as a non-human form. This is, for example, how she is painted by Des Esseintes in Huysman's *À rebours*, studying the Moreau paintings he had purchased.

In the first one, dated 1874–6:

> In Gustave Moreau's work, conceived independently of the Testament themes, Des Esseintes as last saw realized the superhuman and exotic Salome of his dreams. She was no longer the mere performer who wrests a cry of desire and of passion from an old man by a perverted twisting of her loins; who destroys the energy and breaks the will of a king by trembling breasts and quivering belly. She became, in a sense, the symbolic deity of indestructible lust, the goddess of immortal Hysteria, of accursed Beauty, distinguished from all others by the catalepsy which stiffens her flesh and hardens her muscles; the monstrous Beast,

indifferent, irresponsible, insensible, baneful, like the Helen of antiquity, fatal to all who approach her, all who behold her, all whom she touches.[13]

In other interpretations Salome presents as a non-personal body and a symbol rather than character. As Karayanni puts it, 'the decadent Salomé is an archetypal and notorious "scandalous body".[14]

The erotic dance as a cause of decapitation also provides a clear mark of separation. In the Deleuzian sense, John the Baptist's body, after having the head severed from it, becomes a body without organs, losing its humanity following the loss of its face. On the other hand, Salome's history is usually 'stilled' by painters in the situation after the dance, with John the Baptist's head on the platter, as is the case with Artemisia Gethilesci, Ambrosius Francken or Lovis Corinth's works. The plasticity and the dynamics of this distinctive 'encounter' arise from the fact that the protagonist somewhat frequently attempts to sustain the assemblage dynamics, seeking in the dead head the last traces of vanishing life or regarding the 'organ' as a symbolic representation of the whole. The head is thus more important than the rest of the body detached from it. This is what Huysmans writes about Moreau's second painting, *The Apparition*:

> The severed head of the saint stared lividly on the charger resting on the slabs; the mouth was discolored and open, the neck crimson, and tears fell from the eyes. The face was encircled by an aureole worked in mosaic, which shot rays of light under the porticos and illuminated the horrible ascension of the head, brightening the glassy orbs of the contracted eyes which were fixed with a ghastly stare upon the dancer.[15]

At times we are even dealing with a conflation of the dance and the execution. In Benozzo Gozzoli's paintings the two rituals occur simultaneously, with Salome receiving her gift immediately. Much later, in the erotic peep show, the same festival of separation will be playing out, detaching organs from bodies and depriving the bodies of their constituent parts.

Petrification as the element of a power relationship

The Gospel tale of Salome inspires certain questions about the relationships of power, one of the consequences of which is the definition of a subject and of an object. This is because on the one hand Salome dancing in front of Herod functions as an erotic stimulus and is thus reduced to an object of lust, in the sense in which Bataille describes it, viz. in the sense of a human subject being regarded as a thing.[16] Karayanni demonstrates that to the decadent Europe of Wilde's time the entire Orient was such a petrified object of lust: 'Salome incites the need for control, in the active and the passive, is a body of which the movement and sound are more of a theatrical incarnation of our phobias, lusts and fascinations.'[17] Meltzer, in turn, interpreting the second of the Moreau paintings purchased by des Essaintes, *The Apparition*, notes that the Salome presented in it is almost void of life, depersonalized, static, equated with inanimate objects. Salome even presents as a naked body the elements of which are turning into heavy items of ornate jewellery.[18]

In this process description of the petrification of the subject, it will be expedient to pay some attention, however, to a different type of popular nineteenth-century shows – so-called *tableaux vivants*. Those are spectacles of unmoving silhouettes appearing at certain point in time, in the form of erotic shows shaped by the censorship regulations introduced in England and in the United States. The rule was that nude dancers could appear in a scene only if they were standing still. Sometimes the movement was animated by the spectators themselves turning them around their axis.[19] In this perspective, the *tableaux vivants* become an element of the peep show's prehistory, demonstrating their capacity for the reduction of the female subjecthood submitting to the male gaze. As the Hovets demonstrate, the idea of the *tableaux vivants* was for the dancer to 'freeze, become an inanimate object, as though a monument or painting, a lifeless doll, forced at the same time to put on a coagulated wooden mask'.[20]

This matter of the objectification of the pleasure object is a prominent motif not only with Bataille but also with Lacan; in this study it will resurface several times, being characteristic of the various technologies discussed herein. Elisabeth Eaves, confronting in her confessions time after time the fact of having been a pleasure object in a peep show, describes the problem in a similar way.

On the other hand, Salome's erotic dance is part of a masterful intrigue woven against John the Baptist. Things being as they are, one could say it is Salome who holds power over Herod, using her sexuality as an instrument of execution. This sort of imperiousness sometimes marks its presence in peep-show performance, though previously the truly spectacular example of a performance exploding the established relation between the observer (usually male) and the observed female object of lust was the bold dance shows for which Oscar Wilde's drama and Strauss's opera laid the canvas. Toni Bentley demonstrates how the performances of the early twentieth century's four female celebrities – Maud Allan, Mata Hari, Colette and Ida Rubinstein – provided the forum for the manifestation of female non-conformism and emancipation.[21] This liberative-emancipative model will subsequently become dynamically popularized in the form of demand for such type of spectacles along with what had been an aggressive model of femininity for the era. As Petra Dierkes-Thrun observes, one could speak of a sort of Salomania in the United States at the time.[22]

This model, however, gradually becomes distorted, and the liberating dance eventually becomes one of the popular types of striptease. According to Deirkes-Thrun, parodies begin to abound, with subsequent Salomes constituting an imitation of the great creations of their predecessors becoming only the more undressed. One of them, Daisy Peterkin, nicknamed La Belle Dasié, even established a school of seductive dance, from which 150 new Salomes would graduate every month.[23]

There exist, therefore, two oppositive tendencies in the development of the erotic shows – the tradition of the *tableaux vivants*, the *comédie en vaudevilles* and itinerant circuses, out of which striptease and pole dance evolved, and the other, liberative tradition connected with the emancipationists, whom Bentley dubbed the 'daughters of Salome'. It is worth noting, however, that her histories of famous women who decided to perform in the nude are a history of women's liberation from the shackles of the patriarchal culture at the turn of the nineteenth and twentieth centuries, while the later mechanisms, culminating in the erotic peep show, exhibit the opposite process that is the petrifying impact of the emerging capture apparatus. The dynamics between the two models will, however, subsist in peep shows, as I will demonstrate in the later part of this train of thought.

The one on one

From the perspective of the erotic show's path to maturity the circumstances of the reception of the above-described Gospel example are also important. In the dance for Herod they have a less than fully determined character, resulting in the different artistic visions of the locations where it took place. On the one hand we are dealing with a public performance – a dance during a feast. On the other hand, though it is the 'chemistry', full of a dirty fascination, between Herod and Salome, which in this case marks the scene's constitutive element. Hence, although the performance is public, in reality it resembles the peep-show dance – a dance for an individual spectator. For the time being, it is closer to the stripper's lap dance, with her rubbing against the man's thighs, than the spectacle of a peep-show dancer isolated and separated by a glass panel. Thus, it can be concluded that the space in which the Gospel tale of Salome plays out is not yet a technicized space. There is not yet a sublimated apparatus enabling the formation of a certain protocol and imposing a suitable frame on the dancer–observer relationship (apart perhaps from the architectural setting of the hall and the arrangement of the participants).

In the history of the erotic dance this process of the gradual transition from public to private performance, all the way to 'one-on-one' performance is worth tracing. The aforementioned Maud Allan will dance for King Edward VII in 1907 in a private performance with an audience of 'only' 27.[24] With time, high-profile striptease became a one-spectator show. Between the private striptease in which the participants remain in direct physical contact and the eventual peep show in which there is a glass panel and other elements of advanced apparatus of capture there remains plenty of room for experimentation.

Jamie Berger highlights such an early, transient stage in the development of peep shows. In his youth (the 1980s) touching the strippers in peep shows was allowed for an additional fee because behind the sliding curtain there had been no glass panel yet. Of course, that involved a different type of interaction. The dancers offered their bodies to be touched by spectators for an additional fee, something which nowadays increasingly draws objections from the unionizing dancers in the United States.[25] One concludes that in open booths of this type the process of establishing a frame has already completed – the sexual relation or interaction has been put in a frame. Thus, the next stage introduces the glass panel as a mark of separation and at once 'screenization'. The dancer becomes suspended in the space 'between', where she is and is not a subject and at the same time is and is not an object.[26]

The slot-machine order

Amid the rich history of slot machines it will be worth distinguishing several threads potentially relating to the adoption of this solution by erotic peep shows.

As David Nasaw has it, the first public entertainment machine operating on coins was Edison's phonograph.[27] Accordingly, it can be inferred that slot machines have always been involved with not just the sale of goods but also entertainment services. This model finds confirmation in one of the first patents for vending machines. According to Segrave, an 1867 machine selling omens is one such device.[28] Later solutions included, among other things, paid opportunities to show off one's physical strength. John Milo developed a testing machine taking the shape of a pig or cow. The tail acted as a lever representing the user's strength.[29] It will be expedient to emphasize the later use of slot machines in the first erotic peep shows displaying film materials. Amy Herzog demonstrates that such appliances were often hidden behind a gallery of other forms of entertainment with coin slots, such as flippers[30] which marks them as a consistent continuation of entertainment vending machines.

To Klein, in turn, entertainment slot machines will be the ideal illustration of devices intended for the creation of special effects.[31] Many modern machines outright copy the special effects from films and television, with their visual abundance, specific varieties and use of licensed Hollywood characters and plots. In his opinion, both the first machines of this type, which dispensed food, and the later gambling and video-game machines create a labyrinth effect – they provide pleasure with no exit.

The coin mechanism analysed in reference to the peep show marks a direct reference to those concepts of capitalism which highlight the disintegration of the subject arising from the appropriation and commercialization by the market of the various components of the subject's unique identity. Here I am referring primarily to the machine and assemblage concepts of Deleuze and Gauttari.[32] No wonder that this exact economic aspect also surfaces in the discussion of the peep show. Jagodziński demonstrates that in this way the act of gazing becomes appropriated:

> The peep-show *vitrine*, in reality collapses the distinction between looking and buying, window-shopping and shopping *tout court*, by making the act of looking itself conditional on payment: the peep-show shifts the act of consumption one step back, to its preliminary stage, as it were, making the act of looking itself, rather than what is looked *at*, the object of purchase, as if a department store started charging its customers for browsing; it turns the image displayed in the *vitrine* itself into the commodity, thereby displacing the 'actual' commodity which ostensibly displays. In effect, the image of the commodity *becomes* the commodity.[33]

Klein also observes that the entertainment slot machine constitutes, as it were, a metonymy of the globalized digital economy.[34] What is equally or even more important from my perspective in the discussion about slot machines in the erotic industry is that when entertainment contents are commercialized in this manner we are usually dealing with a grant of temporary access and not a transfer of goods. This difference shows that the temporally conditioned access evokes a binary situation. The binary operation of the machine either enabling or blocking the service is conducive to the fragmentation of the experience. This marks another example of this deep current of binarity anchored in access mechanisms.

The peeping order

Towards the end of the nineteenth century works on motion pictures had led, among other things, to the evolution of such devices as Edison's kinetoscope or its improved version, the mutoscope, constructed by Herman Casler. The latter will extend the popularity of earlier devices providing a visual attraction such as the raree show, *boite d'optique* or *mondo nuovo*, showing still picture (though some relied on a simulation of three dimensionality). Their career had begun in the seventeenth century. Shows of this type would become popular in both Europe and Asia, where even until the present day one can still meet itinerant artists with their peep shows (See Figure 1.1). In the nineteenth century the hand-painted slides shown by such devices will slowly begin to be replaced by photographs. With time, one part of those will be erotic photographs. An interesting aspect of the functioning of all these devices is the reception situation. The latter shows a characteristic duality entailed by the simultaneous peeping and being in a public situation.[35]

The mutoscope (Figure 1.3) and the kinetoscope (Figure 1.2) appeared merely a couple of years before the Lumière brothers' cinematograph and, as Richard Balzer observes, had to compete with it by offering an erotic selection (such as the *What Butlers Saw* series popular in England). Initially, the reception conditions were similar to those offered by the classic peep show presenting still pictures. On account of its reception conditions, this invention, therefore, provided the ideal setting for the pursuit of one's sexual needs, especially considering how, after a time, increasingly comfortable versions would come to life, enabling greater degrees of separation from the environment. The introduction of coin slots doubtless marked an important milestone in the 'erotic' history of such machines. The idea of coin slots thus accompanied motion peep shows since the onset. According to Quigley, kinetoscopes with a slot mechanism appeared already in 1894, that is, in the year the invention premièred before the New York audience.[38] Nassaw, in turn, reports that both kinetoscopes and mutoscopes fitted with coin slots began to appear in male-dominated peep-show establishments appearing briefly in the United States near the end of the nineteenth century. The mutoscope, being a device outfitted with a handle to move the film forward,

Figure 1.1 Public peep show in China (*c.* 1871–2). Public domain. From J. Thomson, *Through China with a Camera*; Westminster: A. Constables Co., 1898.

became the ideal appliance for erotic films such as *The Birth of the Pearl*, showing partial nudity for the first time ever.[39] This is because the machine's user has full control over the speed of the film and can stop freely at selected moments appearing as individual photographs – 'stills'.

The automation of the sexual experience, coupled with the assistance-free payment option, increased the user comfort by providing a greater sense of safety due to eliminating the need for contact with staff.

A video-booth boom came with the 1960s and 1970s of the twentieth century.[40] Herzog reports that the first erotic peep shows had the shape of rear projection.[41] This peculiar phantasmagoria, originally frightening at the turn of the eighteenth and nineteenth centuries, here adopted the form of rear-projection pornographic film. Rear projection provides the type of experience describable as perception from a partner-like position. The spectator's silhouette does not enter the light stream or interfere with the projection; instead, the spectator

Figure 1.2 Kinetoscope (exhibit from Kodak Museum in Rochester, NY).[36]

meets the projection on the screen level. It could be said that this image of the pleasure object heralds the arrival of a live dancer to take the same position. This again is a moment of posthuman bringing together of the subject with the image.

The same sequential order as described above dominated the erotic business unfolding in the United States – besides the booths presenting first erotic

Figure 1.3 Mutoscope (*Carnival attraction at the Imperial County Fair, California. El Centro, California.* Russell Lee, 1942).[37]

material and then erotic video, booths featuring live dancers made their first appearance.[42] Erotic shows consisting in a striptease or seductive dance in front of the spectator were nothing new at the time, of course, but the situation of having this act inscribed in the technological order, with the dancer becoming 'visible' after inserting the coins, was a new development. It is noteworthy that in this case the erotic order appropriated the very name 'peep show', nowadays mainly in reference to erotic shows.

Humanity and the booth – the human subject as an element of the pleasure vehicle

The specific effect triggered by this vehicle in the congregating human subjects and the positions taken by the subjects regarding the technology sphere and the information sphere will both be important here in the posthuman take on the peep show. Thus, the overview of the various accounts of the peep show highlights the following main aspects: reduction of the subject(s), assumption of the posthuman position, resulting from the attraction fair playing out therein, entering into the centre of the binary system, subversive action against the Deleuzian machine and dismemberment spectacle.

Reduction of the subject

The peep-show technology has reduction potential; the human subject found in this space becomes divested of a number of elements of its identity, and on the other hand the vehicle has the power of channelling that subjecthood in select limited directions. This is the way Moss describes the functional (existential?) conditions faced by the dancer in the booth:

> The booth is a 3 x 3 ft (approximately) box, in which we perform our job.
>
> There are three fantasy booths in addition to the stage. The booths consist of one wall, two windows (one facing the hallway, and one facing the customer), and one door that opens to the dressing room.
>
> On the left side of the window, facing the customer, there is a speaker through which you can talk to the customer. Fortunately, the customer can hear you even if you are away from the speaker. On the right side of the window, there is a screen that displays the first four letters of your name. It is great if your name is four letters. I go by Natalia at work, so my name reads Nata on the display. I probably would have changed by name if I knew this beforehand, because I constantly have to explain that my name is Natalia, not Nata. Then there are those guys who just can't get Natalia ... so they end up calling me Natalie or Natasha.

I've known several girls who had really great and original names, but the customers could never pronounce them, or would get tongue tied, so the dancers would end of changing them. Sometimes, the simple ... girl next-door names work the best. Also, if a customer calls from work to see if his favorite dancer is working, they can ask for Sara instead of Star.[43]

Eaves, on the other hand, demonstrates the schematic nature of the dancer's activity, reduced to a dozen-odd poses. Here too this posthuman reduction happens – the stripper becomes an automaton performing several sequential movements:

My dancing settled into a routine: Window opens. Start three feet away. Turn, twist, bend. High kick. Sink to floor. Approach window on knees. Stand up. Raise foot to bar, show pussy. Crouch down, show face, lips, tongue. Stand up, turn, bend over. Sometimes they were done in one minute, sometimes it took half an hour. I could do this consciously, which I often did at the very beginning of a shift, or right after a break, or if the customer piqued my interest. But I often did it mindlessly. The stage could be relentlessly monotonous.[44]

Eaves is aware of this reduction subject to the laws of the market:

For a price, a stripper will pretend to be a kind of woman that doesn't exist outside the imagination—the naked, adoring, one-dimensional sex object. She creates the idea that a woman's appearance, behavior, and sexuality are for sale. For a few dollars, for a few minutes, she will be nothing but tall, busty, and blond.[45]

Here enters a reference to the reductive act of the categorization of the dancers at the beginning of their work in peep shows. This is a reduction of the dancers to operation within the frame of several bodily attributes only. They thus have specific attributes assigned to them so as to provide the customers with a suitably diverse assortment of dancers for their shared performances – blonde, brunette, athletic, curvy, sensuous, ginger, tall, curly-haired, thin, petite, tanned or busty.[46]

Another fragment from Moss's diary elaborates on the description of the condition of this reduced entity, which, due to the clear technological characterization, could be termed 'cyborgical'.

Below the display, there are some buttons. When you show up for work, you enter a code with these buttons so that your name will come up on display. The booths are hooked up to a computer program that keeps track of the money going into the machine. The computer is on the counter out front and the clerks monitor it. At the end of the day, the clerks pay us out. They look at the computer and see how much money is under our name. (...) There is also a button to clear the time, should the customer finish early, and a button to close out the booth at the end of the day.[47]

Eaves also describes the deep process of the adaptation of the dancer's body as a system having the purpose of causing sexual satisfaction.

If I liked another dancer's step, I would copy it, practicing over and over until it was polished to perfection. I could see exactly how I looked at all times. I could fine-tune moves, making quarter-of-an-inch adjustments to hip or shoulder or chin. What was sexier, leg forward or back? Right side or left? Flat foot or tiptoe? I had hours to contemplate these questions. I noticed minute changes in my body. I saw it swell with salt and water every month, then recede. I came to understand high heels. They made my legs and ass rise up, taut and tight. I watched muscles appear on my thighs.[48]

Elsewhere she terms the dancer's status as 'inhuman'.

She knew the men didn't really see her as a complete human being, but even if all they saw when they looked at her was a sex object, at least they saw a sex object who was well organized and in control.[49]

This reveals the important imperative of non-human transformation arising from the peculiar posthuman power of the male libido (and perhaps also the female). The dancer, in turn, submits to this imperative, taking care of herself as an efficient and coherent sexual mechanism.

Sometimes the customer manages to take direct technological control of the dancer despite the glass-panel barrier between them. Eaves describes how one of her colleagues performing in private booths consented to performances featuring a vibrator remotely controlled by the customer who had built it.

While the above quotations illustrate the dancers' cyborgical status, the fragment below highlights another, somewhat different dimension of this posthuman reflection based on putting the dancer's status on a level with her image:

Sometimes the monotony had a surreal effect. We weren't supposed to wear watches, so our only indication that a clock was ticking somewhere was the ten-minute span in which people came and went for breaks: April is on her break; April is back. Charlotte is on her break; Charlotte is back. That's twenty minutes

I've been here. Maria is out; Maria is back. That's thirty minutes. Cassandra's shift is over. Blue is on break; Blue is back – forty minutes. Candy is on break. I'm next! But it was easy to lose track. It would have been rude to ask customers what time it was, but we often did ask them other things: Was it still raining? Was the sun out? The game over? The traffic okay? Girls in boxes couldn't be expected to know such things. Fantasies didn't have such mundane concerns; we didn't even have clothes. **We were no more than a suggestion of humans; we were images hovering in a shiny red vacuum**. Time, traffic, weather – these were beyond our world.[50]

Thus, the dancers, suspended in a vacuum and outside of time, explicitly refer to themselves as images. In this perspective we are dealing with the perception of the subject not only as a technological automaton but also as a being with a purely informational ontology.

The attraction fair

In the above-presented reminiscences by the dancers, the peep show presents as an extremely technological pleasure vehicle delimiting, or even imposing, a strict frame for the subject's functioning. Analysis of the machine's operation, however, provides us with an opportunity to make inferences not only on the subject-technology plane but also on the subject-significance plane. The peep show points towards the possibility of the existence of a technologically shared plane on which the sense generated by the medium can be brought together with a living and acting subject. Thus, we are dealing with a highly distinctive fruition of the idea of an interbeing attraction fair. The dancer is competing for attention with the pornographic video message. This competition can be direct, as Moss demonstrates:

There are at least 10 video booths … possibly more. I should have counted them before I made this post, but … oh well. (…) The video booths are private … very similar to the peep show booths. They cost $1.00 for a few minutes … less than five. When you walk into the booth, there are two television screens; one on top of the other. Once the video starts, the screens are split into several sections … so you are actually watching several videos at the same time. I found this to be a little distracting … until I found out that there are some buttons below that you can use to highlight the section of the split screen that you want to watch. You then push another button and that video comes up on the entire screen. They periodically change the movies to ensure the customers aren't watching the same videos over and over again.[51]

Thus the enthusiast of this type of sexual experience can choose between two mechanisms of sexual satisfaction – now the live dancer, now the video (see Figure 1.4). Both of the competing instances are assigned a specified and often identical market value. In Amsterdam's Sex Palace, an outdoor advertisement shows that video booths cost the same fee as live performances (2 euros).

The ritual described by McNamara can be interpreted in the same context – the men prostituting themselves in New York, looking for homosexual customers in peep shows (here understood as points of sale for pornographic cassettes and magazines, where video booths can also be found) often turn out to also be the actors in the films displayed in the booths. In this way they attempt to encourage the customers to engage their services. Here too the attraction fair taking place in the peep shows offers the mischievous choice of the pleasure object from between the character in the video material and/or its real counterpart. The competition is, however, even more fierce. The male prostitute must compete against his own image, losing when the customer is terrified by the prospect of physical contact with a biological object, as opposed to 'safely' masturbating to the film character(s). On the other hand, if the sexual act takes places in the booth, it becomes the impossible act – the pleasure object is at once a real and a mediatized object.

Figure 1.4 Entrance to the Lusty Lady peep show in San Francisco with live dancers competing against the video. Photographer: Nick Gripton.

The binary-discontinuity system

The third aspect of the relationship between the subject and the digital sense manifested in the functioning of the peep show should be termed as the discontinuity of the communication activity. The peep show with the slot machine is a peculiar vehicle of digitality breaking the reception situation into a part relating to performance (existence – digital one) and a part containing no activity (non-existence – digital zero). The dancer can be said to 'come to life' only for a couple of minutes paid for by the inserted coins – this binarity applies to both the customer and the dancer. The dancers from the Lusty Lady in San Francisco emphasize that the customers they see in the unveiling windows, reminiscent of low-hanging paintings on a wall, look like puppets on a spring, jumping out of a box at a specified time. The binarity of the customers' sexual experience is founded on the rigid timeframes determining the presence or absence of the object of pleasure:

> When a customer gets a show, the amount of time he buys shows up on the display where your name normally is. This way, you can keep track of the time and remind the customer when his time gets down there … especially if he hasn't come yet. There's a real art in bringing this up. You don't want to be too blunt about it (or matter of fact) because the guy is likely to lose his train of thought … or even his erection.[52]

Here, therefore, sexual satisfaction is inscribed into the binary order. Peep show, however, is digital in the sense of zero-one fragmentation of everything the vehicle has subsumed. A whole complex system of varied oppositions appears – doors opened versus doors closed, part of the body versus the whole, object versus subject, activity versus passivity, the watcher versus the watched.

The panopticon and the binarity of watching (whom I watch and who can see me)

In peep shows and erotic shops with video booths one observes dynamically changing relationships between subjects and objects arising from a variable looking perspective. In such changing relations, that which can be seen can be assumed to become the object and he who looks becomes the subject. This distinction, however, is not so obvious and is renegotiable, being affected by such factors as the architecture of the place, the relationship between the gazing situation and the fact of being watched, as well as the type of spectacle (porn film or stripper's performance).

McNamara describes the rich ritual and elaborate strategies for the utilization of the booth as a place for having sexual intercourse.[53] The customers employ sophisticated strategies for entering them with their paid or unpaid partners. They watch the films in their solitude, waiting for the partner to arrive, and so on. In this ritual once more the echo of the Derridean cat and of the Lacanian 'boat' is heard in the video booth in which the porn film is a mute witness to the sexual act, itself having previously been the watched object, just a moment ago.

Visibility is a very significant aspect of the shaping of the dancer–customer relationship and the entire peep-show economics. At Eaves's workplace one half of the booths was caption 'we see you' and the other 'we don't see you'. In this case visibility separates the 'common', cheaper booths, opening themselves to a joint scene (Figure 1.6), from the private booths – exclusive and expensive.

The Lusty Lady girls' complaint is that in those 'private' booths, in which the glass or rather mirror does not allow them to see the customer, their performances are often recorded without authorization, to be later uploaded and publicized on the internet. One could say that here, directly, takes place the process of 'stealing the soul', so feared by primeval cultures with the advent of the photo camera.[54] Eaves thus describes this panic and fear of loss of control over their image (and even perhaps, in a sense, their soul):

> I thought I had a uniquely female fear, this ever-present sense that my sexuality could be used against me. I didn't know what I was afraid of exactly. (...) Stripping was nothing but a moment in time, but photos were permanent.[55]

The process of instantaneous mediation of the sexual experience will take place here. In the peep show we are dealing with the mischievous panopticon idea, which, when considered from the dancing stripper's side, contains some hidden depth. Its uncertainty involves the show's recipient – is this a performance for the customer or for the customer and his camera (and a larger group of voyeurs). Following Lacan's understanding of the mirror, one could say that the dancer who looks into it defines her own subjectivity in the face of a true 'Great Other'. A complex relationship between the subjects begins to be built here, one which I would define as secondary aggressiveness. Lacan discusses this aspect in reference to the formation of a child's personality, where the child is frightened by the fragmentation of its own body seen in the mirror. In the booth space, aggression can be evoked by the dancer's own image, being the sign of the Other concealed behind it, both in a narrower sense the customer, more powerful than she is, who sees her, and in a broader sense the great Other being the world watching her on the internet.

At some point in the book Eaves identifies this question of the variable nature of the watched-watcher relationship:

> They had weird wants to be negotiated, mental trip wires that made them desire more than just visuals. They wanted to tell a girl what to do, or they wanted counseling, or they needed her to playact. **Maybe they wanted to be looked at themselves.**[56]

Moss's memories support this assessment. Pegan describes numerous unusual behaviours undertaken by the customers during her shows, including defecation on the glass panel. In such a scenario the roles become inverted, with the customer satisfying his sexual deviations by seeking the expressions of disgust, fear and dread on the dancer's face; she is now the spectator in his own perverted show.

Figure 1.5 Formatting elements of pleasure appliances: entrances to the cabins of the Lusty Lady peep show in San Francisco, closed in 2013. Image courtesy of Kevin Warnock.

Figure 1.6 Formatting elements of pleasure appliances: the peep-show dancing stage. The frequent laying of the walls with mirrors deepens the sense of losing oneself in the appliance. Image courtesy of Kevin Warnock.

Subversive action

Of course, one has to realize that the dialecticity of the space that is the peep show extends between the complete dissipation of human subjectivity in the vehicle and attempted self-definition in the face of it, sustaining the vitality of the assemblage. This sense of disintegration compels self-organization and a desire to sustain integrity by domesticating or criticizing the space. Testimony of the desire to domesticate and transcend the frames imposed in the vehicle is found in the fragment below:

> The maximum number of girls working a shift is three as there is only three booths. (...) There are days when we are quiet and just keep to ourselves. Most of us bring in books and read in our booths. I used to light a candle and read and write next to it. Unfortunately, one day I lit my wig on fire when I leaned across the flame to talk to a customer through the speaker. (...) On the days when the girls are feeling social, we talk to each other either through the walls of our booths, or we poke our heads out and talk that way, while our ass is facing the window to the hallway. (...) Sometimes (when it's slow) we will climb into a booth together and play games. We play cards, mad libs, or just color with

crayons. (…) There are other times, when Girl will ask if I'll rub her neck or back. I'll climb into her booth and give her a nice massage. (…) Overall, I prefer the quiet moments in my booth. I like to bring things from home (blankets, pillows, etc) to make it more comfortable.[57]

The cited passage highlights the great need to domesticate the unfriendly technology but also the movement between the booths and the leaving of the booth, discussed by the author in a different post on her blog, for the purpose of assisting one of the customers with the selection of his 'transvestite' wardrobe from a shop nearby, could be termed as a need for the restoration of the digitalized analogism (i.e. discontinuity) of the interpersonal human interaction. This action, therefore, contains subversive potential. The deep digitization taking place here refers to the typical situation in which a spectacle of discontinuity plays out. Sometimes, however, there is an attempt to hack the code, with the dancers succeeding at breaking out of the algorithmic loop in which they exist.

It seems that in this perspective of a defence of humanity as a non-petrified assemblage attention could be drawn to a specific moment in the Seattle Lusty Lady's operation being the so-called Play Day. That was a day of attractions specially designed for promotional purposes, which one could regard as a sort of carnival-style inversion of the regular time of the place and the established frames of the space along with the roles assigned in it. During the meticulously prepared event a show took place in which the customers had the freedom of the establishment, so they could move around freely, without having to observe their distance from the dancers, even take an active part in the attractions, often switching roles with the staff. That was, therefore, a once-a-year time of 'irony' (this ironic approach was also continued by The Lusty Lady in all famous puns on the marquee above the entrance, referring to current holidays, events or film premières, see Figures 1.7 and 1.8).

The dismemberment spectacle

Analysis of the video-booth spaces, whether those densely populating (American, especially) sex shops or those located in such erotic 'theatres' in which they compete against live dancers' performances, brings out altogether different contexts of the peep show's inroads into posthuman optics. Here too a festival of relationships among subjects, technology and video materials plays out. The first matter is the presence of so-called glory holes in some of them.

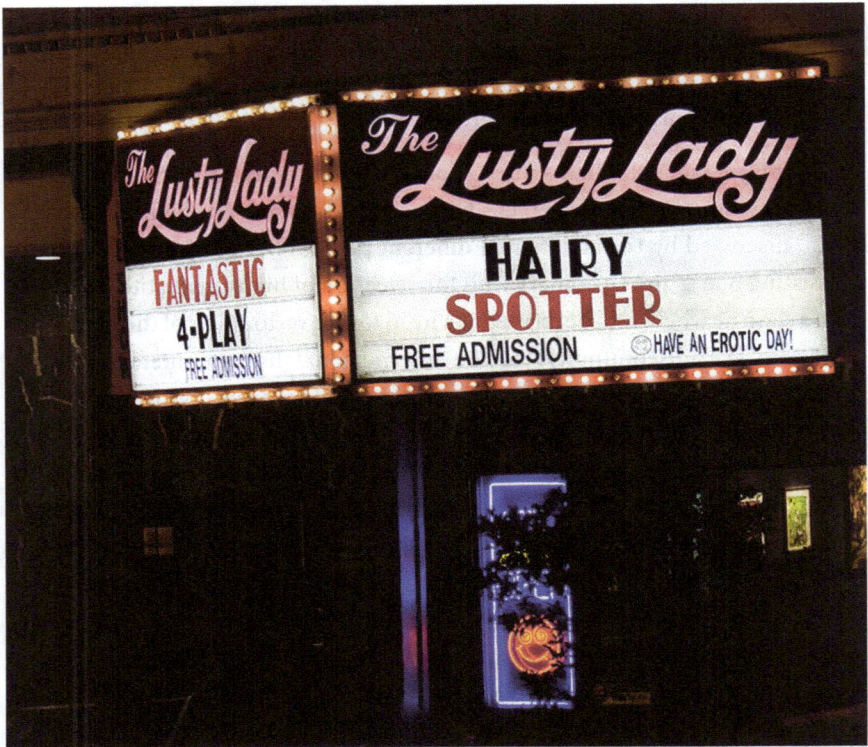

Figure 1.7 The Lusty Lady's word games: reference to *the Fantastic Four* and *Harry Potter* movies. Photographer: Seth Anderson, CCBY-NC-SA 2.0.

Openings in walls, allowing one to watch the customers sitting in other booths or, more frequently, have sexual intercourse with random strangers, marks a characteristic element of the technological entourage affecting the shape of the game forming the subject relationships. Dunlop[58] records that the first glory holes had appeared already in the nineteenth century on passenger ships, where the men drilled them on purpose so as to spy on the ladies in their cabins. Modern glory holes are an architectural element of public toilets, baths and, precisely, video booths.

Authors researching glory holes in public baths indicate that the users go there to build new assemblage connections between genital organs in order to break with the stratification of traditional sexuality, while making a conscious sacrifice of their own autonomy.[59] With equal strength, the glory holes in peep shows stimulate the dynamics of the process of disintegration of the traditionally

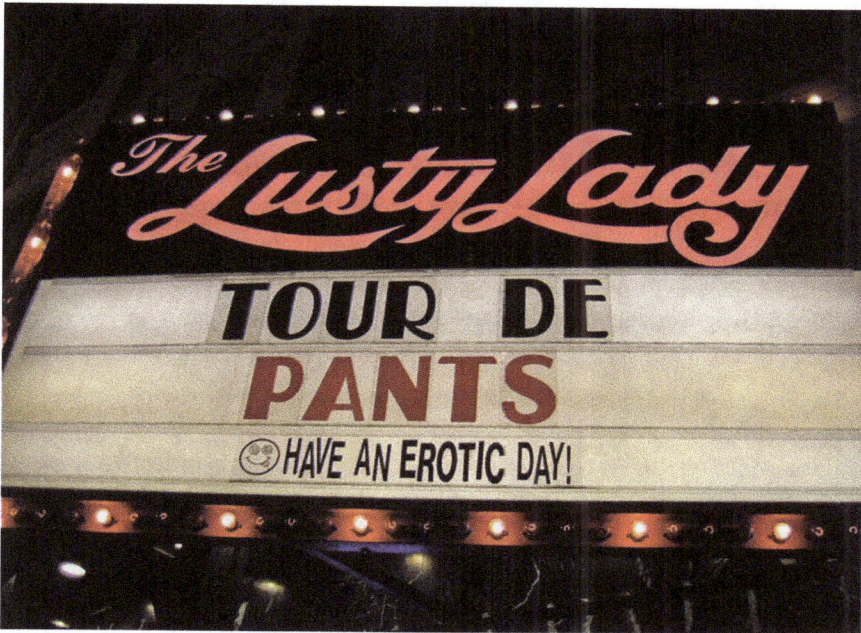

Figure 1.8 The Lusty Lady's word games: reference to the Tour de France. Photographer: Chas Redmond, CCBY 2.0.

understood subject, as well as the object–subject game. Here, it must be observed that, in peep shows, what the authors of the study regard as the assemblage freedom of disintegration and joyful submission to the emancipating ethic of non-autonomy can transform itself into a classic example of the Deleuzian–Gauttarian machine, with the technology and architecture of the place taking the shape of the apparatus of capture. The authors of the text demonstrate that in baths the moment of the petrification of the assemblage to the machine comes with the development of a dependence on that 'sex without a face'. In the peep show, where masturbation is the main form of sexual satisfaction, glory holes are what expands the offering of sexual range of options and develops on the game of subjects and objects. This will be worth noting in those sex shops in which so-called buddy booths appear. In that case the subject–object game is joined by the visible–invisible game. Buddy booths have glass panels on the sides, so that the visitors can watch the actions of their masturbating neighbours.[60] Here the process of dynamization of the actor–spectator relationship begins, with the visitor turning into both an actant and an observed target. The same context appears in atypically constructed peep shows. Due to the round shape of its stage where the strippers dance, the one in Amsterdam's Red Light District, the only to have remained, invites the casting of furtive glances at the other spectators.

As a result of the application of technology, the glory hole turns what is real into what is imagined. The imagined can turn into the real when the booths' side windows are lowered by the joint decision of the neighbours.

In addition to all of the above-discussed dismemberment processes there is also one entailed by the architectural design of the booths themselves. In a sense, it is legislated. Each cabin, just as is the case with toilets, must have a see-through area of significant height at the bottom (Figure 1.5). For this reason the customers' legs are largely visible. In this way they become a separated element, organs without a body. Here, the legislature joins the fragmentation discourse and the visible–invisible discourse. In extreme cases, such as in the city of Ventura in the United States, the doors in video booths are required to be absolutely removed, in order to stop illegal sexual acts from taking place in the public space. The peep show's absorbing force, however, makes that not a great trouble to the customers. According to the *Los Angeles Times*, the municipal police in Modesto, where a similar solution has been imposed, complains that 'lewd acts have not ceased and the customers have even on occasion groped plainclothes officers sent to the scene'.[61]

The dismemberment leads to new configurations of biological, technological and informational elements. This mechanism is perfectly oiled and economically efficient. The customers, in the act of digitized pleasures, divest themselves of genetic material which rather serving procreation ends up on an automated conveyor belt. From the floor the sperm is removed by staff. After a busy day of monetization it is no longer needed.

***

In analysing the motivations of peep shows' returning customers, Eaves employs the characteristic topos of biogenetic provenance. In her view, something in the customers' sexuality has gone awry. 'Somewhere in the circle of sex, love, and society, something had broken down and tangled.'[62] So they come to the peep show because there that broken sexuality can find satisfaction. This motif is close to the mutability idea. Errors in the sexual DNA can be eliminated only in the peep-show space. The appliance becomes a therapeutic tool. Wes Goodman even refers to the booths as 'confessionals'.[63]

Here, the choice between a video record and live participants of the spectacle of the sexual act is a gesture of invitation to build a plane for joint action –

the lust and search for the unachievable, in the Lacanian sense, is an act of decentralization of the biological subject in favour of more nuanced subject games. The simultaneity or asynchronicity of the orgasm, the role of an object of the sexual act or its subject, or both, the game of the imagined and the real, these all are the different pieces of the puzzle. Let us add to this the fragmentation of the perception of the body – shoed feet, visible from the corridor, penises in glory holes, and so on.

Characteristic of this digital approach to subjectivity will be the discontinuity of the existence of such a subject (the diaphragm covering the stripper when the paid time runs out, the booth sides that be lowered or pulled up) and its fragmentation (glory holes).

In the perspective of the above analysis, the peep show presents as an idiosyncratic kaleidoscope iridescent with the various posthuman glass pieces of sexual nature. On the other hand, it is precisely in this vehicle that the distinctive 'digital' characteristic of the intimate relationship between the immersed subject and the database that reconstructs this order comes to the fore. One could conclude that the peep show is an example of a vehicle enabling access to the *jouissance* which is unsufferable. Having access to the notebook kept by a different dancer, Eaves calculated that Zoe must have witnessed masturbation by 1392 men before turning nineteen.[64] Here is created the all-encompassing database giving access to 'non-possible' experiences, to the 'augmentation of the same thing'. To the customers, as Eaves notes, it is a search for augmentation and an attempt to reach the limits of the *jouissance*:

> These men wanted, simply, to see more. More body, more tongue, more tit, and especially more pussy, as deeply as they could behold. Sometimes I laughed out loud at this. I wasn't mocking them; it was just that I found it so absurd. More was never enough. You could have your labia nearly planted against the window and they still made 'spread it' motions with their hands, bending and peering to get a better angle.[65]

The disintegrated subject entering into new relationships with the sphere of technology and information can become in that space a *modus vivendi* of the posthuman complex stretched between the two polar opposites of the submission pole (the machine) and the pole of sustained dynamics (assemblage). Submission entails the acceptance of the reduced position, while the subversive, liberative moments of the fight for the preservation of integrity and diversity allow the assemblage dynamics to be sustained. The posthuman body which enters this apparatus is suspended between the diverse successive binarities. The Krokers observe that we are dealing here with suspension between fantasy and psychosis, hyperexteriorization (of the organs of the body) and hyperinteriorization (of the projected subjectivities).[66] Accompanying this game between embodiment and subjectivity is a never-ending recursion of the body, multiplied in a 'never-ending labyrinth of media images'.[67]

Animation and the origins
of interbeing intimacy

There is scarcely any kind of cinematographic art nowadays lending itself more to the discussion about the posthuman relationship between humans and their visual creations than animated film. Donald Crafton thus writes about Sullivan and Messmer's character, Felix the Cat:

> Intelligent and mature adults could participate in a ritual wherein a pen-and-link representation of a cat is endowed with 'real' status at least as great as that of the screen images of human actors. Clearly, audiences recognized their own behavior in Felix's and attributed to him the foibles of the human species. Moreover, they perceived in this animated drawings a personality – not just a character or a type, but an individual with his own quirks of appearance and behavior that distinguished him from all the others.[1]

Alan Cholodenko, in turn, posits that the essence of the art of animation is to bring or restore life.[2] For his part, Norman M. Klein analyses the destabilizing character of the structure of the animated film with regard to species or biological ordering:

> In the midst of a walk cycle, a creature changes species. Its body a proportions become exaggerated, with 'extremes' on either end. But the frames inside, called 'in-betweens', stabilize the action, make the switch more convincing; and also balletic, rhythmic.[3]

Further Klein:

> For a few frames, the object – the body in this case – does not look like what it was, nor what it will be. This pause is a mode of Artifice, similar to Perspective Awry in the Baroque, a glitch that reveals the apparatus of filmmaking.[4]

On the basis of these and many other statements from cinema creators and researchers, we can assume that even before the posthuman perspective made its permanent home in academic discourse, this type of intimacy involving animated characters, along with discussion about their status, had already resounded heavily in the opinions of animation practitioners and film theorists, even though they had not yet come across this current of research.

The purpose of this chapter will be to gather such testimonies up together and analyse selected films from the posthuman perspective. The discussion will cover both the content layer and the production stage with a succession of various aspects of visual technologies manifesting themselves as the formative apparatus for various protocols of posthuman intimacy. The construction of this intimate plane in animation, besides, expands into additional fields. A total of four such fields will be characterized.

The first part will contain the description of a broad set of posthuman contexts relating to the production of hybrid films connecting the live actor's stage with animation.[5] This part will come in two stages. The first stage will describe the historical period in which one can speak of the practice of this type of combined film art as the binding paradigm for the first animations. Therefore, we are dealing with interbeing communication in its definitional sense. Of course, these beginnings of animation coincide with the first stage in the development of cinema at the turn of the nineteenth and twentieth centuries. In a certain sense this means a period of emergence of different types of film art from a yet underdefined magma of creative substance. Hence, the use of the term 'hybrid film'[6] is completely appropriate and yet somewhat misleading in how this hybridity was a sort of beginning out of which the typical animated film had yet to emerge. The second stage in the development of hybrid cinema was the period in which the hybrid effect went on to become a consciously used tool. It will be worth tracing the way in which this tool contributes to the construction of a series of new protocols of intimacy and in which films this happens.

The second foundational field for posthuman relationships in animated film is the production stage. This part of the analysis will refer directly to hybridity as a consciously employed production effect, although it will also turn out that during the production of typical, as one could say, ontologically homogeneous animated films, too, such contexts can appear.[7] This unveils a very important context of posthumanism we are going to refer to, for the purposes of this book, as 'topo-relational posthumanism'. Across the various examples of film art, the above-discussed 'posthuman position' can appear in specific circumstances. It begs notice that in the end stage of the activities of cinematographic creators that is the ready film work we are frequently dealing with a sort of homogeneity of such a picture. With things being that way, the game of instances and subjects can be challenging to perceive. Often, it can only be captured at the production stage. I will re-address this in a later chapter, applying the same perspective, which one could term 'making-off methodology', to the analysis of the cinema of the Digital Age.

While the production stage is a convenient time to trace the agreement process of the actor-animated character relationship,[8] whether we are dealing with their combination on the hybrid-film plane or with the animated character substituting for the human in a manual pencilling process or mechanical rotoscopic ritual, the animators' work product can itself serve as a medium for posthuman contexts spanning the content layer or the structural layer (animation effects and procedures). This will be the subject-matter of the third part of this chapter. In other words, I will endeavour to show that it is possible to develop a typology of animation motifs and effects based on the adoption of posthuman optics.

The above-introduced sections will make a reference to two strategies for the building of an animated picture – two strategies which, while being polar opposites, in both cases provide an opportunity to trace posthuman threads. Michael Barrier observes that beginning with Snow White Disney changes the animation-building optics. 'It [from then on] regarded its characters not as an assemblage of detachable parts but as organic wholes.'[9] Thomson and Johnston confirm this change of style, while placing it a bit earlier, near 1930, which is when Disney begins to depart from cartoons composed of gags alone towards the telling of complete stories.[10] They point out that Disney was one of the first who began to ask for realism.[11] Thus, this is about a situation in which we either decide to delineate the relationship between the real world and the animated world, sparking intimacy and affect involving the created characters, modelled after the real,[12] or toy with the plasticity of our characters and our ease of constructing them. The application of both of these strategies can later be traced in many other creators and other historical periods. Both give a sense of possibilities facing the creators of animated films in the creation of the cartoon *diegesis*.

The last part will explore the field for intimacy creation lying beyond the work itself and outside of its production process. What I mean here are such social and cultural acts as attest that the creators of animated films themselves and other 'insiders' have an ambition to treat animated characters as partners and peers, or they create a plane for such treatment by the audience (whether the plane connotes sympathy or antipathy).

The beginnings of animation – interbeing communication *ex definitione*

Hybrid film in a historical view

Film historians are not of one mind on which production should be regarded as the first animated film in the age of cinema.[13] Difficulties arise from the fact that intermediate forms – hybrids precisely – occurred in numerous places in the world, hence the differences of opinion on the subject. On the other hand, some types of animation then arising coincide with a full range of experiments with the first special effects, hence another area of non-distinction.

This is the case, for example, with Blackton's *Haunted Hotel* – a 1907 production employing stop-motion animation of objects. The highly impressive scene in which the table sets itself, the knife cuts the bread on its own and tea and wine pour themselves into cups on their own is anchored in the complex plot of a haunted house abounding with tricks and featuring a character played by an actor. Similar doubts arise with regard to Blackton's 1908 film, *Thieving Hand*. It is the tale of a poor man missing a hand who is gifted with a synthetic limb. The prosthetic device appears to be suffering from kleptomania. Its user gets rid of it, but it comes back and does so with loot taken from a jeweller's shop display. The unfortunate fellow ends up in prison. Here too the stop-motion animation of the hand is inscribed in the broader context of live action with real actors.

Blackton's chronological first – *Enchanted Drawing* of 1900 – is, by contrast, an example of the attempts at cartoon animation which were frequent at the time. The significance of this example lies in showing clearly how the idea of intimacy between the creators and the animated character was guiding the precursors of this particular film form. The cartoonist in the film enters into an interaction with the character drawn by him. The character smiles when given a cigarette and drinks a cup of wine, it frowns when having its hat taken away, etc. Blackton's other production, of 1906, *Humorous Phases of Funny Faces*, is similar in character, as is Emile Cohle's *Fantasmagoria* of 1908. Sometimes the whole artist is shown in them, sometimes just his hand, but at all times we are dealing with a combination of real action with cartoon drawings.

Two outstanding examples in this group, encrusted with a wealth of diverse interpretations, are *Gertie Dinosaur* by Windsor McCay and *Out of Inkwell* by Max Fleischer. McCay's film exemplifies two traditions from which hybrid films borrowed. The first tradition is the near-documentary nature of the actor's stage, serving simultaneously as the film's metaset. Not only in *Gertie* but also in *Little Nemo* does McCay illustrate the circumstances of animation creation as the result of a process of thousands of drawings. Interestingly, the plot axis in both films is a bet on whether or not McCay can put life in his drawings. The animation is the fruit of that wager.

The other tradition, described in detail by Nathana and Craftona,[14] is the vaudeville tradition. It turns out there were two versions of the film about Gertie the Dinosaur. It is in the latter version in which the paradocumentary context appears, with McCay presenting the result of his work to his colleagues who had made the wager with him over dinner. The former version makes a reference to the frequent circumstances of the demonstration of the film art in theatres and palaces of magic. Not only in the case of films produced in the United States but also, for example, Melies's films displayed in his Robert-Houdin theatre we are dealing with the inscription of films into the frame of what we could call a broader multimedia spectacle, featuring elements of magical illusion and theatrical tricks. This is also how things were with McCay's film, which had originally been framed not as a paradocumentary tale but as McCay's own on-stage performance. McCay would face a real audience and, alike to a circus handler with a whip, he would present his dinosaur's performance on the screen. As we can see, this example features a complicated system of dependencies and relationships in which the film's creator and his animated character find themselves. The vaudeville stage provides here a perfect example of the 'interbeing attraction fair'. The film's latter version is an equally interesting example of the plane's interplay. McCay is a pseudo-real character participating in a paradocumentary with a longer play time than the animated scene, similarly to *Little Nemo*. In the animation he attempts to impose his will as the handler on the dinosaur, an attempt that is not quite successful. He too ends up inside the animated picture as a rotoscoped cartoon character, which appears to bear witness to the ultimate 'triumph' of animation over live action.

Out of Inkwell, in turn, is a series that builds in a sophisticated sphere of tensions between the live character and the animated clown, Koko. Fleischer, having himself starred in the cartoons as Koko's main antagonist, usually has plenty of trouble with him. An important motif is the clown's reactions to changes in the live-action plan. In the *Modelling* episode (1921) Koko caricaturizes the big-nosed gentleman in Fleischer's studio. In *A Trip to Mars* (1924), before the launch, he manages to set off an explosive charge that launches Fleischer himself into space (Figure 2.1). In later, 1934 film (*Ha! Ha! Ha!*), Betty Boop and Koko evoke hysterical laughter from all objects and people by letting out laughing gas. In *Earth Control* (1928), Koko and his dog, Fritz, even bring the entire 'live plan' to its demise. In the context of the construction of intimacy with an animated character, it is remarkable how the character recorded in rotoscope sessions was Max's brother, Dave.

A great number of productions of this type could be regarded as the incarnation of the hybridity imperative, for example, *Artist's Dream* by J. R. Bray (1913) – a film about a cartoonist falling asleep and having his sausage eaten by the cartoon dog, an idea repeated in Lantz's *Lunch Hound* in 1927. We also have hybrid episodes of *Animated Grouch Chaser* (1915) produced by Raoul Barre for Edison. The year 1916 saw the creation of Wallace Carlson's series of films pairing cartoonist Harry Dunkinson with the drawn character, Dreamy Dud. Otto Mesmer also produced his own hybrid films (*Trials of the Movie Cartoonist* 1916). And then there is *Colonel Heeza* of 1923. There is also a large body of European projects based on the so-called 'lighting sketch' idea, with political ideas communicated by live-animated sketches of famous politicians. This was also the guiding idea for the creators of the interesting, if odd, 1924–5 series *Animated Hair*, with sketches of often famous people change into portraits of others through migratory elements of the hairdo suddenly turning into other parts of the face.[15]

In all of these films interaction between the live plan and the animated plan presents differently, with varied degrees of sophistication. In the 1923 *Forbidden Fruit* interaction between Colonel Heeza and Lantz and the other cartoonist features only at the beginning of the film. *Lunch Hound* (1927) contains masterful live and animated inserts and makes use of combined frames. In one of Raoul Barre's films, *Cartoons on Tour* (1915), animated inserts do not interact with the live plan; instead, they complement it, such as in the scene with the just-married bride's father not accepting the marriage watching, in a book(!), an animation titled *The Pleasure of Being a Grandpa*. Disney's series of fifty-seven cartoons about Alice (*Alice Commedies* 1923–7) is a good example of the animators' sinusoidal development of models for masterfully combining the plans, eventually to shed the burden of the live plan altogether. Tellotte[16] also demonstrates that the Alice series was a sort of testing ground for Disney's experiments with changing the degree of plan integration, constructing a history between the planes and the manner of interaction between live actresses and animated characters.

In the search for a cutoff point marking a break with hybridity, as the legacy of the first animated films, our attention should focus on the time when Disney abandons the live Alice (the series end). That is a significant moment for two reasons – on the one hand, the financial expectations of the little stars impersonating this character were growing, and on the other hand, remarkably, the idea of the 'live' Alice was becoming increasingly formulaic and unoriginal.[17] In the posthuman perspective one could say Disney and crew's technique had matured to a point where the live actor could no longer suffice, became redundant and only filled the subordinate role of a 'drawing model'.

While it is true that Fleischer continued to create hybrids well into the 1930s of the twentieth century, it seems that what we have in this case is the conscious use of a technique that may well appear in an animated film but does not necessarily need to, *Betty Boop* being an example of this, with some of its episodes being animated and some being hybrids.

The decade that followed coincided with what was dubbed the golden age of animation. This means the triumph of pure animation and a quest for as complete and lively characters as possible, based on a diligent study of reality. Here, realism is a subordinate project to the animated picture, but let us not forget that animation must then compete with live action, translating into the emergence of an 'interbeing competition' plan. Later, I will demonstrate, for example, how this process went with such productions as *Snow White*. Despite the triumphs reported by homogeneous animation in the 1940s, a certain group of hybrid films appeared in the 1940s, such as *Anchors Aweigh* (MGM 1944) with a song sung by Gene Kelly, the mouse Jerry in the *Tom & Jerry* series, as well as Disney's *The Three Caballeros* (1946), where the 'American' Donald Duck is joined by the Brazilian parrot Jose Carioca and the Mexican rooster, Panchito Pistoles. The characters experience various adventures across Latin America, interacting with live bandstand stars from the various regions. In *Songs of the South* (1948) Disney includes three sequences featuring animals, with a bear, rabbit and fox as protagonists, as well as a final scene with the live plan slowly transforming into the animated plan. In *Melody Time* (1948) a combined sequence appears, for example, in the *Pecos Bill*. The Warner Bros.' romantic comedy, *My Dream Is Yours* (1949), features the hybrid sequence of a boy's night dream accompanied by the song, 'Freddy Get Ready', performed jointly by Doris Day, Jack Carson and Bugs Bunny.

Hybridity begins to be revisited in the latter half of the 1950s of the twentieth century – a period of dynamic growth for television and abandonment of cartoons in cinemas. Walter Lantz combined the audience's familiar characters with real-action film in his series, *A Moment with Walter Lantz*, directed by Jack Hanna. When following the various episodes of the series, one gets the irresistible impression that the animated characters play better than the actors, i.e. the animators and producers playing themselves. The cycle showed the backstage of animation creation, thus making a meta-reference at least at the beginning of each film.

A great triumph of the idea of hybrid cinema begins with the popularity of *Mary Poppins*, of 1964 (dir. Robert Stevenson). In the 1980s this motif gets a refresh in *Who Framed Roger Rabbit*. Robert Zemeckis's film proved itself to be a work of innovation and attracted a diverse body of interpretations. Later productions included *Cool World* (1992, dir. Ralph Bakshi) with two versions of Kim Basinger and *Space Jam* (1996, dir. Joe Pytka) with the Michael Jordan and Bugs Bunny duo. Around the same time *Evil Toons* (1992, dir. Fred Olen Ray) – a very weak horror film featuring a cartoon monster – and *Rampo* (1994, dir. Rintaro Mayuzumi, Kazuyoshi Okuyama) are produced. In Poland, one of the animators who often refers to the hybrid film convention was Witold Giersz, the author of *Little Western* (1960) or *Red and Black* (1963).

The idea of hybridity was appealing to and used by television productions, from the Italian *La Linea* of 1972 to *Doodlez* (2001–4), of which the latter could scarcely be called a hybrid but it does employ a similar convention with the cartoonist being present and intervening in the animated characters' world. The hybrid convention also appears in music videos, for example, Paula Abdul's *Opposites Attract* (1988).

At some point 3D animation enters the hybrid world, with such productions as *Scooby Doo* (2002), or the *Smurfs* (2011). In this case, however, the idea of presenting two ontologically different plans is diluted by the use of motion tracking, making it possible to blend the plans seamlessly rather than highlighting the connections.

Theoretical concepts

Several different theoretical concepts are used when describing the idea of combining the plans in animated film. In a very exhaustive way, Erwin Feyersinger puts hybrid films in the perspective of Gennette's narrative idea of metalepsis.[18] On this basis he goes on to develop an extensive typology for such pictures, depending on the direction of the jump between the worlds and planes. Metalepsis categories allow him to transparently categorize the numerous examples of hybrid films produced in different historical periods. Still, the conclusion can only be that Feyersinger's narratological perspective restricts hybridity to the film creators' decision about the narrative structure of the history being created. By contrast, hybridity on the one hand extends beyond the limits of narration, towards the structure of the film picture and narrative decisions,[19] and on the other hand it should also encompass ontological aspects, which for the purposes of the analysis present here means the question of the status of the subjects and their mutual relations. Another problem is the fact that the examples invoked by the author from the beginnings of animation are not the effect of a conscious choice in their creators. Animation had first to emerge out of the live-action film and leave it behind in a period when the creators had access to tools sophisticated enough as to invite the conclusion that live actors were no longer really necessary. Hence, one could desire for the metalepsis idea to here be a broader construct fit to cover the full spectrum of problems also in the area of posthuman intimacy. This category has the great advantage of enabling transgression between the worlds to be defined in keeping with their specificity.

Crafton, on the other hand, employs in this case the term 'self-figuration', defined as follows:

> Early animated film was the location of a process found elsewhere in cinema but nowhere else in such intense concentration: self-figuration, the tendency of the filmmaker to interject himself into his film. This can take several forms; it can be direct or indirect, and more or less camouflaged.[20]

If we look either back at the earlier or forward at the later examples of the trend for animators to appear in their films, the desire for stardom in one's own animated picture has a diverse range of consequences. For example, Crafton notes that Fleischer, by acting in his own animated films, himself became a celebrity.[21] Apparently, in such films we have to do with a meta-level existing in parallel to the storytelling level; the ability to call animated characters to life gives a twofold power: demiurgy and actorship potential. Out of this mix the possibility of creating a plane for negotiation and intimacy emerges.[22] The act of Genesis is here repeated in the micro-scale.

It is worth noting, however, that while the self-figuration category describes a process – similar to metalepsis – of jumping between worlds, in this case the process is being examined from the perspective of creative decisions, as though

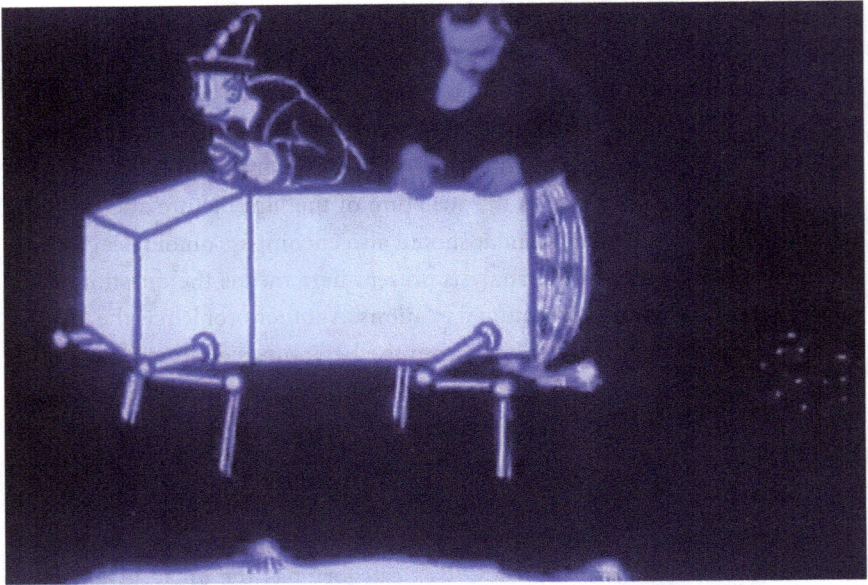

Figure 2.1 Fleischer and Koko. A frame from *A Trip to Mars* (Fleisher Productions, 1924). Image courtesy of Ray Pointer, Inkwell Images, Inc., 2003.

the animator's external world had been the origin, which is different from metalepsis as a process that starts on the storytelling level. Of course, in both cases one has to bear in mind that we are not dealing with a total freedom of such jumps or leaps. McCay and other creators who decide to cast themselves in hybrid films become elements of the *diegesis*; they cease to be realistic characters and instead they become intertextual characters. Nonetheless, the essence of hybrid films is the preservation of the ontological separation of the two plans within the film world and the interplay between them, and the essence of many of the first hybrid films is such staging of the live plan as to resemble the documentary plan.

Alan Cholodenko, by contrast, describes the specificity of hybrid films using categories borrowed from Derrida. Cholodenko studies one of the most expressive examples of this current, being *Who Framed Roger Rabbit?* (1988, dir. Robert Zemeckis). In his opinion, the use of the equivocal word 'framed' in the title already is a potential reference to the Derridean frame and framing. Consistently applying the deconstruction method in his analysis of Zemeckis's production, the Sydney academic proceeds to demonstrate that hybrid film constitutes a deconstruction of cinematography's basic opposition between film as the dominant category and animation as a frequently marginalized film form. In his opinion, 'animation would no longer be a form of film or cinema. Film and cinema would be forms of animation.'[23] *Who Framed Roger Rabbit?* deconstructs the historical and ontological differences between live action and animation. To Cholodenko, this is also a good example of Derridean supplementation in hybrid film. The interchangeability of roles, co-appearance of live actors and animated characters, as well as the interplay among the various forms of being in *Something's Cookin* (animated film produced inside the film world) are all examples of how such supplementation – having a powerful critical function – takes place. Later in this train of thought references appear to Derridean concepts of the *pharmakon, hymen, peregron* and contamination logic.

Hybrid film inscribes itself into Manovich's concept of layers of the composite picture, derived also from historical examples.[24] Taking him up on this proposal, we could conclude that layers in hybrid film are not 'anchored' in the image, that their borders are still visible, their separate ontological status is not lost, and thus they bear testimony to the game played between the anthroposphere and the sphere of cartoon creation.[25]

The topic of the character's acquisition of independence is eagerly explored by animation creators themselves, whose films appear as though they were a critical commentary on this aspect. One of them, Nathan Gilder, the creator of an animation of this type (titled *Vessel of Wrath*), refers to the idea of compatibilism,[26] which defines the relationship between God and man in the perspective of free will and determinism as discussed, among others, by the Stoics, Christian theologians (Augustine of Hippo, John Calvin, Martin Luther), and Thomas Hobbes and David Hume. Here, the posthuman context pushes the limits of analysis further, to also include the relationship between the animation creator and the animated character. In his essay, Gilder not only illustrates this divine agency on the example of his own film but also references the aforementioned hybrid films, as well as the highly expressive example of one of *Looney Tunes* episodes, *Duck Amuck* (1953), wherein Daffy Duck is humiliated and even tortured by the unseen cartoonist who time after time changes the duck's background, erases parts of his body or inserts items that are harmful to him in the scene.

The above concepts taken together make it possible to define hybrid film as that type of the film art in which the metaleptic interbeing intimacy plays an important role. The posthuman contexts inscribed in this genre arise firstly from the structural properties that such a work has – the matter of negotiation and creation of a platform form understanding at the stage of adapting the actors' play to the cartoon picture or *vice versa*, i.e. adaptation of animation technique to the existing cartoon plan and the matter of being a layer in a film work. With feature films, in turn, this is about a narrative construction that enables on-screen interaction, with the live plan serving as the feature frame for the disjoint animated tale, the jumping in of actors into the cartoon world and jumping out of cartoon characters into the live plan, and so on.

Production of the animated picture as a process of relationship agreement

Both in homogeneous animated films and in hybrids the posthuman perspective appears to be a very useful method for the capturing of the intimacy between film creators and their characters, as described here. The above, however, manifests itself primarily at the time of construction of the film work, since the end effect, even though it may intentionally preserve the stylistic separation of the live plan and the animated plan, operates from a common *diegesis*. Therein one cannot see such a stage of negotiation and agreement of roles and autonomy spheres. Such an opportunity is found only in step-by-step analysis of the materials documenting the work on the film. Here, I will provide several examples of how this commonalization protocol is being built, drawing from creators' statements, making-ofs and other testimonies of this work.

In typical ('homogeneous') animated films the idea of substitution – fundamental to animation – manifests itself in the idea of the faithful emulation of the real world, as regards the specific method of construing cartoon characters on the basis of observation of real animals and people, propagated by Disney. This way of thinking about animation involves, in turn, the desire to compete with live-action cinema, appearing with *Snow White* in 1937. In *Animated Man* Michael Barrier describes this process of construction of a competition platform through Disney crew's examination of similarities and differences between character creation in animated film and the creation of roles in live-action film. Till the present day, Thomas regards *Snow White* as the production with the richest character personalities in Disney's oeuvre.[27] Together with Johnston they signalled, for example, that actors can operate on emotions in building their on-screen portraits, while animators have to be objective and analytical if they want to reach and move the audience.[28]

Some interesting posthuman contexts appear already at the stage of such analytical creation of *Bambi*. The process could be said not to be an example of simple anthropomorphization but to be broken down into a multitude of different orders. It was noticed that the further the animator headed towards the caricaturization of animals, the more precisely the animal's nature could be captured and actorship opportunities created for the animal.[29] Thus, by definition, the process of creating credible characters is a process of constructing hybrids – entities vested with a personality modelled on the human personality and reflecting the specificity of animal movement and typical animal behaviours.[30] The goal was to portray the animal so that it would look not like it does in reality but like humans imagine it.[31] The drawing of animations appears here to be a process of mediation between the animal nature and its anthropologically 'twisted' perception by humans. Nor is it by accident that Thomas and Johnston begin their book about Disney animations with reflection on animal emotion and communication. The indirect suggestion is even made that because animals' emotional states are communicated by their entire bodies, the creation of animated characters' emotionality looks the same even where those are human characters.[32]

In itself, the stage of studying animal movement obviously falls within the subject area of interspecies studies and instrumental treatment of animals. Live, often wild, animals were brought to the plan for this and other films. During the production of *Bambi* (1942) a fawn was brought to the studio and reached maturity in captivity as the production went on; animal carcasses were studied and autopsies performed on them.

According to both creators, the process of animation preparation is a mixture of intimacy building between the audience and the characters and amplification of the impression of reality of that which is being watched.[33] The degree of the characters' 'humanity' is, in their opinion, the measure of the animation's credibility (*he has to be human enough*).[34] It is not far from here to Sherry Turkle's 'sufficiently human' robots requiring care and thus becoming close to their human caretakers.[35] In a different place they note that the basis for character creation is the intimate relationship between the animator and his character, consisting in designing oneself inside the character. In this case the leap happens on the level of emotions and feelings, and the animator must live in that little person from his or her drawings.[36]

Barrier observes that due to Disney's desire to compete against live-action productions, the basic problem for the crew creating *Snow White and the*

Seven Dwarfs (1937) was the preservation of the characters' consistency.[37] This is yet another interesting posthuman thread. In the other chapters I attempt to demonstrate in what way, through the application of the various media technologies, this collective process of subject creation can take place. Here, the effect in the form of the animated character, too, is such a negotiation of its final shape, personality, and so on, as a work product of an entire team of animators and actors either playing some elements of the scenario or voice-acting. All such persons project elements of their personalities or lend select qualities to the characters. The end effect is cohesive but internally we have a hybrid structure.

What is also worth noting is that the animators working on *Snow White* modelled their creation of the characters and their movement on methods of actorship. For example, Tytla relied on Richard Boleslawski's book importing Stanisławski's actorship method to America.[38] One of Disney's animators, Hamilton Luske, also looked to that philosophy, stating:

> Our actors are drawings. (…) We cannot risk ruining a sequence or a good characterization with some mechanical imperfection or jitter that reminds the audience that we are dealing with drawings instead of real beings. The success of *Snow White* was due to the public accepting our characters as living beings.[39]

Luske would go on to specialize in directing actor scenes for Disney's later films, while bearing in mind that actorship had to look completely different in this case, with subjectivity and scenic movement being here subordinated to animation.

Very frequently, this process of thinking about animation in theatrical categories also included a strategy of 'self-analysis'. Animators often made use of the mirror to draw their own facial expressions. From the posthuman perspective this could be regarded as another form of distribution of subjecthood and another manifestation of Craftonian self-figuration transpiring at the production stage.

Thomas and Johnston note that *Snow White*, precisely, made the breakthrough when it came to the use of actors' scenes as inspiration in animation creation. Somewhat by accident, Disney's animators stumbled upon an opportunity to leverage this powerful tool that allowed them to infuse their creations with subtlety and appreciate the whole spectrum of sublimated phases of movement and mimics, of the existence of which they had previously had no idea or could only surmise it. It is also a noteworthy finding that the mechanical drawing of post-frame scenes in live-action films had yielded unsatisfactory results in the form of highly artificial sequences wherein the characters would lose the 'illusion of life'.[40] Hence, the animators were forced to learn to use live action as a source of reference and not as a film to copy into their drawings. They had to give their own personalities to the motion picture and yet deform the characters in the animation sufficiently to avoid an artificial appearance. Thomas and Johnston call this process 'caricaturing'.[41]

The film made use of a great many scenes played by live actors, whose body postures and facial expressions became the building stuff for the animation. The scenes themselves bear witness to live actors' adaptation to animated film. The teenage dancer, Margie Bell, impersonating the Princess, recalls, for example, the adaptation of her silhouette to the proportions of the animated characters in order to make the scenes look more credible. Snow White's larger-than-real head was simulated by putting a football helmet with hair painted on it on the actor's head.[42] The girl would sweat and suffer in it, so the idea was eventually given up on, but it continues to bear testimony of the sacrifice of the actor's subject potential for an animated character, which Disney's and other cinema creators' productions often required.

Disney's subsequent productions reveal increasingly sophisticated ways of combining the animated and the live plans. A September 1944 article in *Popular Science* describes the complicated apparatus for the recording of such scenes, used in 1945's *The Three Caballeros*, employing rear projection (see Figure 2.2).[43]

Another hybrid produced by Disney at a significantly later date but making a new opening for this type of productions was *Mary Poppins*. It both is and is not a good example of the relationships, as examined here, between actors and creators on the one hand and animated characters on the other hand. While

Figure 2.2 Creation of *The Three Caballeros* with rear projection. Image from "How Disney Combines Living Actors with His Cartoon Characters", *Popular Science*, September 1944, 106.

the film does not have an animated protagonist, let alone one as expressive as Roger Rabbit, the interaction between the live and the animated plans is so sophisticated and subtle that the industry continues to recognize it as a model example of such integration. The film itself was well-liked enough to earn as many as five Oscars.

The creators' opinions show a characteristic pattern we can also trace in observations pertaining to the production process of later hybrids, namely, immersion in the game with animated characters. On the one hand, the actors note that sometimes it was difficult to adapt to the imagination of an animated character they did not have right next to them to see. Simultaneously, they were instructed by directors to make their actorship and movement style more similar to the behaviour of cartoon characters. On the other hand, the animators complained that the live-action plan was not specifically prepared for their needs. For example, Dick Van Dyke would step on the penguins in the dance due to not having left enough space for them on the stage, so they had to perform incredible feats of acrobatics in order to make the sequence look credible. Negotiation of common space built inside the film *diegesis*, therefore, takes place here. As Thomas and Johnston observe, 'the characters come from a different worlds, and need special consideration to make them compatible'.[44] Elsewhere they enumerate a set of qualities having the greatest impact on this compatibility, such as weight, texture, shading, colour and perspective.[45] One could say these factors are what makes a successful 'posthuman position' in hybrid cinema.

In one of the most mature cinematic pictures of this type, Zemeckis's *Who Framed Roger Rabbit?*, the creators attempt to facilitate the process of negotiating the common space by the insertion of a partially 'human' substitute. In rehearsals rubber dolls moved by persons on the plan were used. In the shots for the live plan Bob Hoskins, impersonating Detective Eddie Valiant, heard the live recording for Bugs Bunny by Charles Fleischer as the voice actor. In this case the actor himself speaks of the necessity of launching a transprojection, for he had to empathize remotely with the bunny invisible from the plan and react just as if Bob Hoskins had been tugging him in that scene. During the first days of the shots, Fleischer asked for a bunny costume in order to better submerge himself in the role, even though he was only providing voice-acting. The whole production revolved around the pursuit of the highest fidelity possible in the simulation of the presence of cartoon characters on the live plan. A large number of animatronic arms and limbs were made as prostheses of the various elements of the bodies of cartoon characters for realistic effects on the live plan. This was the case, for example, with the remotely controlled arm of baby Herman, in which he held a cigar, or with the arms of his ruffians holding weapons.[46]

Bob Hoskins completed special mental training to enable him to assess the invisible Roger's body weight, to which he had to adapt his moves. Zemeckis notes that the film's credibility was mainly built around Hoskins's play. In the director's words, 'he was the one who had to believe the rabbit was there.'[47]

The above backstage story shows how an entire festival of the various relations among the human sphere, material mechanisms and cartoon animations plays out in the production space. This festival (or fair?) also reflects a variety of models of perception, contact simulation and acrobatic play. Here too a connection between the activity of watching and the construction of a posthuman relationship appears. Nick Ranieri, one of the animators, states that the crew had followed previous hybrids but in all such productions there was the problem of the live actor's gazes all focusing on the same point. According to Ranieri, previously, one did not look at animated characters at all. Looking at cartoon characters had always been looking through them, not at them. The actors had found it difficult to focus on a single point located precisely where the cartoon character's head and eyes should be.

The film turned out to be such a marvel of innovation that it went on to become the subject of much academic study. It is thus worth examining in a little more detail by tracing the posthuman contexts therein. Telotte identifies such threads indirectly, asserting that the dual construction of the film's presented world is a symbol of criticism of racism and other forms of segregation. He compares the situation of cartoon characters in ToonTown to black musicians performing for a white clientèle in Harlem's Cotton Club (with the memorable 'for humans only' at the entrance). He also draws from the idea of a ghetto for animated characters living in 'a separate, chaotic, and even frightening area.'[48] This brings to mind somewhat the plot of *District 9*, with aliens locked in such a ghetto.

Susan Ohmer also discusses the Roger–Eddie relationship in the categories of a changing relationship of power. On the one hand, the animation is subordinate to the live plan, marginalized and placed in opposition to the dominant human. On the other hand, animation can be something more than humanity, with its practically infinite range of possibilities to transform and potential for reviving a human being.[49]

In the aforementioned text by Cholodenko, the latter notes the intimacy between Eddie and Roger symbolized by their accidental kiss. He even suggests that the categories of an unconsummated marriage could be applied to that relationship (in reference to the Derridean *hymen*). The characters, in his opinion, try to exchange and saturate their subjecthoods to 'humanize rabbit' and 'rabbitize human'.[50] Elaborating on this, one could say Roger is a character doubly referencing the interbeing level. On the one hand, he suggests interspecies relationships, considering that his wife is the cartoon woman, Jessica, who, in her own words, loves Roger more strongly than any woman has ever loved a rabbit. Zemeckis himself claims Jessica was to have been an intermediary between the cartoon plan and live actors' plan. On the other hand, Roger and Eddie's relationship is an intimacy of beings that hail from different ontological orders (actor versus cartoon) but, mischievously, are of the same sex.

Who Framed Roger Rabbit? is unique in how it references a variety of posthuman contexts both on the production level and on the level of the creation of the presented world and plot. Its hybridity and the role of a negotiation protocol between the live-action actors and the animated characters are thus visible across all of the film's planes and all of its production stages, hence perhaps its popularity as an object of academic analysis.

Typology of posthuman effects

The previous section showed the animation-creation stage as an agreement process of the intimate relationships between the creators and their animated characters. It is based on the creation of the presented world on the basis of the *per-caricatura* principle. This means that the posthuman threads discussed by me here resulted from a strategy of thorough study of realism and its transposition onto the animation field with strict accounting not only for the specificity of the medium but also for the affection 'shown' to the cartoon world. There is another strategy, one which Disney gives up in favour of the suggestive and imitative animation ushered in by *Snow White*. It is a historically prior strategy but one that will always remain present in other creators' films. I would like to discuss it in this section.

What I refer to here is the freedom of character creation in animated films, based on a critique of realism and on leveraging the medium's plasticity. This freedom, of course, inspires the creators to reach for motifs and effects very clearly describable in the familiar categories of posthuman reflection. Many of the popular currents of this reflection – the transformation of the body, its technologization, hybridity, anthropomorphization of nature (biological organisms) and technology, critical approach to anthropocentrism, interspecies relations and more – mark their presence in ambiguous and mischievous ways in the animated space. Mischievous because they either solidify the pre-critical approach to interspecies relations or they become, on the level of the creation of the presented world, unwittingly critical by reference to the meta-cinematographic and meta-humanist sphere, thus affirming the 'we have always been cyborgs/posthuman' concept.

For example, Kozlenko says: 'The uniqueness of the animated cartoon lies in the fact that, of all film forms, it is the only one that has freed itself almost entirely from the restrictions of an oppressive reality.'[51] This passage appears to be a live transplant from some posthumanism or transhumanism manifestoes, if compared, for example, to Kurzweil's claims that humans will transcend the 'limitations of our biological bodies and brain' or to the following excerpt from Humanity + Declaration: 'We envision the possibility of broadening human potential by overcoming aging, cognitive shortcomings, involuntary suffering, and our confinement to planet Earth.'[52]

In this part I would prefer not to concentrate on a holistic analysis of plots in which threads connected with the posthuman idea could be sought,[53] for I am interested first of all in the context of the possibilities opening themselves before the animators in the field of posthuman character creation and creation of the presented world itself as a locus for the fruition of the idea. As Barrier writes, 'in some of the Oswald cartoons, machines and animals are all but interchangeable.'[54] Especially Disney or Fleischer's early cartoons are a festival of such motifs and operations testifying to the joy in overcoming the limitations of that bounded reality with posthuman potential.

Bearing the above in mind, I would like to propose a sort of simplified typology for posthuman effects in animations relying on the freedom of deconstruction of the characters' and the presented world's consistency, illustrating it with examples drawn primarily from precisely the early cartoon works by Disney, Fleischer and other animators. This typology will be based on a distinction between motifs and figures. I understand a motif to mean a narrative operation in the content layer and a figure to mean an operation dealing with character structure or the structure of the presented world.

One must remember, however, that some of the operations are not specific to film alone. We can find a wealth of similar figures and motifs in different presentation systems, such as literature or painting, but some of the solutions appear to be characteristic of animated film.

The specified motifs and figures were selected on a posthuman basis – they contain references to reflections in this field. Those are usually matters relating to the body's conventionality and impermanent limits, the construction of hybrids and 'cyborgs', but elements referencing interspecies relations can also appear.

Figures:

a) Anthropomorphizations
   - Of machines, devices, tools or parts thereof – a car, for example, is a frequent object of anthropomorphization, and a characteristic, unforgettable example is the cutlery and tableware in *Beauty and the Beast* (1991); so many elements of cartoon characters' material surroundings undergo anthropomorphization that it would be difficult to suggest any that had never been anthropomorphized; in Fleischer's cartoons, for example, a popular motif is the anthropomorphization of frankfurters that begin to behave like disciplined soldiers.
   - Architectural objects – in the *Ha! Ha! Ha!* episode in which Betty sprays laughing gas a bridge is among those ending up laughing. In *Swing You Sinners* (1930) with Bimbo the dog, the cemetery gate eats the key, the tombs sing with their own mouths or dance, and even a patch of dirt under a tomb or grass near it is anthropomorphized. Bimbo enters a shed by a door which is the shed's mouth.
   - Plants – trees are very often objects of this kind, becoming the characters' antagonists. In *April Maze* (1930), with Felix, walking trees appear, as well as flowers with dancing legs and inflorescence turning into hands.
   - Animals – a great number of species, from large animals to bacteria; in *Ha, Ha, Ha* with Betty Boop and Koko the Clown bacteria are presented as workers driving a pile into Koko's tooth (of course, the entire concept of Barille's *Once Upon a Time... Life* (1987) is also based on this idea).
   - People changing into other people – a frequent operation is to equip characters, for a time, with the heads of other characters, animals or fantasy creatures – for example, Koko the Clown's head in *Bed Time* turns into the devil's.
   - Total transformations into human form – for example from a butterfly into a fairy in *Flying Mouse*.

b) Transformations into animals or their parts
   - Machines – Oswald's mechanical cow; in *Trolley Troubles* (1927) with Oswald the tram behaves like a horse pulled by its tail by one of the rabbit children. In *Through the Mirror* (1936) the armchair is a lady setting her footrest after Mickey as though a dog; in *One Good Turn* (1929) Felix is chased by barking frankfurters.
   - Plants – in *Flowers and Trees* (1932) the Christmas tree fleeing the fire turns into a hen protecting small Christmas trees from it.
   - Humans – the boy from Disney's *Babes in the Woods* (1932) is turned into a spider; one could also mention several other examples arising from the use of the transformation trope, but we more frequently come across a local attribution of animal characteristics to human characters which arises from the immediate context of the story, such as humans fawning like dogs to get what they want or behaving like predators when attempting to scare or defeat someone.
   - Other animals – in *Mechanical Cow* (1927) a falling Oswald and his paramour, as well as the kidnappers are presented as nose-diving birds. The cow in *Trolley Troubles*, offended by Oswald, leaves pulling up its tail as though a dog's. In Disney's *Merry Dwarfs* (1929) a grasshopper is shoed like a horse. In *Hot Chocolate Soldiers* (1934) the Easter bunny is a beast of burden. The full gamut of fish and other sea animals pretending to be different animals, such as tigers, elements or a giraffe, appear in Disney's *Merbabies* (1938).

c) Transformation into plants – it is a difficult challenge to find such examples – in *Flowers and Trees* in Disney's 1932 *Silly Simphonies* series the lizard becomes the tongue of an anthropomorphized dry tree trunk; examples of transformations of animals and people into plants are difficult to find, primarily due to the fact that such transformations do not open suitable possibilities for the demonstration of movement or creation of subjecthood; at times such operations can be perceived in a situation in which temporary immobilization of a character is necessary, but that happens rarely, as immobilization is more expressively demonstrated by reference to inanimate objects (rocks, walls, etc.).

d) Transformation into machines or inanimate objects or parts thereof
   - Humans – one of the emperor's servants in *China Plate* (1931) becomes his tablet; the witch in *Babes in the Woods* becomes a rock.

- Animals – in the *Oswald* episode with the mechanical cow, the feeding of the little hippopotamus resembles the pouring of gasoline into a car gas tank, with Oswald measuring the fuel level in the hippopotamus's belly with a special gauge; in *Felix in Hollywood* (1923) the cat first pretends to be a cane, then a travelling bag, and then, showing off before the studio boss, he detaches his tail as a case and mimics Chaplin, who accuses him of having stolen his idea of himself as a character.[55] In *Astronomeus* (1928) on one of the planets a great walking hammer changes him into a nail. In *China Plate* a Chinese fisherman uses a cormorant as a fishhook.
- Plants – in *Comicalamities* (1928) Felix uses a small Christmas tree changing it into an umbrella, which then returns, on its own, to its place when it stops being needed. In *Flowers and Trees* one of the trees changes into a harp, and flowers change into fire alarm bells and extinguishing tools.
- Other inanimate objects; in *The Mechanical Cow* (an *Oswald* episode) the ruffians' car turns into a dustbin.

e) Transformations into non-material objects – a poignant example here is Felix's turning into his own name communicated in Morse code. In *Doubles for Darwin* (1924) the cat first literally enters the transatlantic cable and leaves it as his own name written in dots and dashes.

f) Bodily deformation and detachment of organs – no matter which animation type or technique we are dealing with, deformations of the characters' bodies are commonly consistent with the idea of caricaturing the basic rules of animation such as anticipation or reaction of the body to kinetic changes caused e.g. by physical impact, penetration, etc. – the characters' bodies often coil into a concertina fold, flatten or elongate as a result of pulling, become red with heat or blue with cold, and so on. Elements containing potentially strong references to posthuman conventions involve the detachment of organs with their fluid transformation into new objects; this is where Felix the Cat excels, detaching and turning his tail into a variety of useful tools in the majority of the episodes. Oswald, in turn, in *Trolley Troubles*, is seen scrubbing the tram with a brush that turns out to be his own tail. A frequent element animators like to detach from a character's body is the nose – it can be pulled as though on a spring, it can fall out, it can be wound up, and more. Sometimes total destabilization of the body may occur. In *Flowers and Trees* (1932) a caterpillar fleeing a fire breaks into segments that later arrange themselves into a different order, with the head being the last.

g) Organs acquiring new functions or autonomy – sometimes the characters are equipped with organs that are given new functions; for example, Roger Rabbit's ears became an independent channel communicating his emotions – curling into a coil when he was thinking about something, drooped tellingly when he was sad, etc. In *Swing You Sinners* Bimbo's ears similarly enjoy a life of their own, and in Disney's *Busy Beavers* (1931) the beavers' tails are, for example, hammers used for driving piles in the river. Sometimes parts of the body even turn into separate organisms. In one of the episodes Koko the Clown's hair turns into an independent human-like figure.

h) Hybrids
   – Biological hybrids – the cannibal in *Cannibal Capers* puts on the lion's jaw and becomes a dangerous predator threatening the lion, peeling the lion's skin off, etc.; in *Swing You Sinners* Bimbo's violent altercation with the chicken has them swapping heads for a while;
   – Biologico-mechanical hybrids – characters often join their bodies briefly to a mechanism; in *The Inventor* (1922) Felix gets inside the cannon and for a moment they form an inseparable whole.

Motifs:
a) Animal inequality (companion species or production species for animals)

This motif highlights the internal rupture in numerous animated films, where part of the animals are anthropomorphized and part are not, or only in a minor degree. In copying the *status quo* of the human–animal configuration from non-film reality, creators of animated plots subordinate some animals to others. This motif is especially visible in the pairing of Goofy and Pluto – both characters are dogs but only one of them is sufficiently anthropomorphized to speak and act like a human being. Sometimes one can even see unequivocal exploitation of some species by others; for example, hunting is a ritual frequently portrayed in animation. In *Felix goes Hunting* (1923) the cat hunts on behalf of his human head of household. His attempt to kill a bear leads to the bear's reciprocal assault on the human's house. 'Fortunately', the latter's wife is so anxious to get the bear's fur that she herself overpowers the creature. A hunting scene appears

in *Comicalamities* too. The activity of scalping is a characteristic element of
such hunts, with the animals subsequently disappearing from the screen,
naked and thus unattractive to the plot, no longer tempting objects for
exploitation.

b) Interspecies rivalry or cooperation (small scale)

In a multitude of films we encounter conflicts playing out on an intimate
level between two characters, customarily put in antagonistic positions,
such as cat and mouse, cat and dog, and so on. In such small-scale frames
species can ally for a short time; for example, mouse and dog against
cat or mouse and cat against an overwhelming common enemy that is
more important to defeat than their daily squabbles. This small-scale
perspective can accompany entire series, such as *Tom & Jerry* or *Wile E.
Coyote and the Road Runner*. In *Comicalamities*, in turn, Felix is assisted
by Messmer himself (or rather his hand); when the cat fails to capture
the bear, he is the one helping him get the fur. Mechanical characters
sometimes participate in the conflict. For example, *Mickey Mouse's
Mechanical Man* mischievously draws from the interspecies idea. Here,
Mickey is coaching a robot who is to fight a boxing match with a huge
ape named Kongo the Killer, the latter being the audience's favourite. The
robot is largely portrayed as a subject sympathized with by the audience
and contrasted with the ape's character, almost anthropomorphized at all.
The entire plot culminates in Minnie and Mickey's kiss in the boxing ring
– a triumph of humanized animality over non-subjectivized animality
and over the subjectivized mechanism scattered in parts across the ring.
The small scale in this interspecies tales makes it possible to look for
pictures of interspecies intimacy, as in the example with the robot. Mickey
weeps, empathizing with the floored robot. In a different film by Disney,
Flying Mouse (1934), the murine protagonist kisses the hand of the fairy
from whom she had received a pair of wings. Such manifestations of
interspecies intimacy are not a frequent structural axis in animated plots,
because intimacy within the same species is the prevailing norm (such as
the elaborate arboreal courtship in *Flowers and Trees*), but they do happen
from time to time.

c) Interspecies rivalry or cooperation (universal scale)

Sometimes, however, apart from small-scale portrayals of interspecies
relationships, we will encounter plots featuring conflicts on a species scale.
The Inventor (1922) features a war between cats and mice. Thanks to Felix,

the cats have an alliance with humans. His carer, the butcher, sends an army of combat frankfurters to his aid. The battlefield with bodies of cats and mice strewn on it evokes a mental association with images of mass-killing of animals, which the film's creators probably did not consciously intend. War is also the structural axis in *Hot Chocolate Soldiers*, featuring rivalry between chocolate characters and a biscuit army. *Doubles for Darwin* is another peculiar example of relations between entire species. Here, Felix tries to find hard evidence of man's origin from ape. The film begins with a humour reference to reverse-evolution, with a shark using a fishing rod with a fish to catch Felix. More such references follow. The cat challenges the radiotelegraph operator to stand and fight like a man. In the ape city Felix finds different examples of advanced ape civilization, but showing them a newspaper with pictures of humans and asking if they are related results in the apes going berserk and chasing him all the way to America. The *Felix* episode in which the cat goes to Mars can also be counted among such 'species-wide' panoramas. After surveying the ground and the creatures living there he calls his kin from Earth to invade.

d) Disability

Three Blind Mouseketeers (1936) is an example of how a character's disability is usually exploited as a narrative opportunity to negate the disability. The plot with the crippled mouse heroes denies the existence of any handicap by generating a success story for the character on the basis of a series of coincidences. In Disney's film the mice manage, by miracle, to avoid traps and defeat the cat, and their disability is in no way a hindrance.

e) Hybridity as maladaptation

We can find a lot of films about maladaptation in the animated oeuvre, but a good example of the use of hybridity is Disney's *Flying Mouse*. The protagonist – a small mouse – wants to fly like birds do. The good fairy grants the wish, but the mouse fails to become any happier for it, as the birds have no desire to befriend her and instead she attracts the attention of bats, presented as a gang of unsympathetic cut-throats. In the end, the fairy takes back the wings, counselling the mouse to enjoy her harmonious specieity.

f) The meta-critical punishment

In a lot of hybrid films, but also formally homogeneous productions calling upon the idea of connecting the drawer's and the character's world, we encounter the motif of the imposition of punishment on animated characters, usually assisted by the omnipotence of the cartoonist inserted into the plot; this is the way of Daffy Duck's torment in *Duck Ammuck*. In a similar fashion Fleischer punishes Koko the Clown, whose sleep is disturbed by a figure coming out of the inkwell. The cartoonist has Koko spend the night on a tall and pointy mountain, from which the clown eventually falls. Sometimes this meting out of punishment takes the opposite direction – the aforementioned *Out of the Inkwell* ends with a monstrously enlarged Koko chasing Fleischer all over New York. Scenes of this type could in some way be regarded as symbolic representations of a rebellion against the torture and torment of animated characters. Sometimes such oppressive treatment of characters happens on a character-to-character level. Felix, disappointed in the passivity of the female cat for whom he kept procuring baubles throughout the episode, literally tears her from the page on which they are both drawn and shreds her into tiny pieces.

To each of the above-presented figures and many of the motifs a handful of additional parameters could be assigned. The first among those would be time. Modifications can be either permanent or temporary. In the former case they may provide a structural axis for the whole plot, such as in the story of the winged mouse. Temporary modifications, by contrast, are specific dramaturgic effects, ways in which to manifest emotion or the dynamics of the scene. The time parameter also encompasses the distinction between reversible and irreversible transformations, each of them having a different dramaturgic significance of the effect. For motifs, the time parameter will be important in determining the durability of the represented relationships and in portraying the dynamics occurring between the different states.

The next parameter could be the degree of transformation. Sometimes the anthropomorphization effect is barely pencilled in – the object is given, for example, just one human trait. In the *April Maze* episode of *Felix*, the bird playing the tune on the electrical wires remains a bird. In *Astronomeus* Felix ends up in a boxing fight with a non-anthropomorphic comet – the latter's anthropomorphization consists solely in the capacity to box. Anthropomorphized trees can be either rooted in the earth but have moving branches and even faces, or they can have full freedom of movement. Hence, the degree of transformation ranges from 'acting like' to a complete morph into something else. However, we usually face intermediate forms. This parameter, the degree of advancement, also includes proportion. If, for example, a hybrid character, i.e. a non-homogeneous creature, appears in the film, we need to bear in mind that one of the elements dominates unless their proportions are equal.

Another parameter is the driving factor behind the transformation. This makes it necessary to trace the plot motifs leading to the transformation. In *Ha, Ha, Ha* anthropomorphization results from the fact that the inanimate elements begin to react to the same factor Koko and Betty are influenced by – laughing gas. In *Doubles for Darwin* the use of the telegraph makes Felix dissolve into Morse code. Sometimes basic emotional states or conditions of the body will suffice. In the case of the frankfurters taken by Felix to his picnic, the fear of the storm animates them to attempt escape. Hunger prompts Felix to undo his fur coat as if it were human clothing in order to expose his thin ribs.

We could also define the transformation's territorial extent as a parameter. Its essence shows itself in, for example, the comparison between the small scale and the global interspecies cooperation or rivalry. The idea is to specify whether the transformation affects a single character, or an entire group or collective. Sometimes this will be just the one changeling character, and sometimes the whole presented world, such as in a good number of *Silly Simphonies* films in which the plot axis is the animation of entire 'micro-worlds' in shops, animated during the owner's absence. We find this concept in *The Clock Store* (1931), *The Bird Store* (1932), *The China Shop* (1934) and *The Midnight in a Toy Shop* (1930).

The character's response to the transformation can be an important parameter, as well. This usually means acceptance or rejection, evoking subsequent narrative situations. The characters show emotion in connection with their malleable bodies. Sometimes that is joy, as with Oswald's horse, with legs ductile enough to reach a runaway stage-coach, and sometimes it is rage, as with Daffy Duck tortured by the drawer, who turns out to be Bugs Bunny. Body modifications can evoke other complex emotions changing during the action, such as with the mouse being gifted a pair of wings.

Analysis of animated films in the perspective of the proposed typology of posthuman effects shows a large group of cartoons – whether those analysed by me and mostly predating Snow White or many of the later ones – is supersaturated with effects relating to subjectivation. In those animations the space is filled with various types of objects and instances being given the status of subjects. Betty Boop spraying the laughing gas and 'infecting' the entire presented world with laughter, including cars, bridges and buildings, is a fitting symbol of the universal strategy of animation of cartoon-film spaces by bestowing it with the character of a subject. In Klein's words, 'but animation is shapeshifting not only of the body, but of the space as well; as if body and space were scripted and breathing together. They are multiple (...) phantom limbs.'[56] This introduces thinking about the animated creature as a complex entity, an ecosystem of sorts, wherein technological and biological elements and physical phenomena blend together and act together. It is no accident that the most perfect illustration of this independent hybrid organism is animations by The Brothers Quay, with Klein finding interontological games among meat morsels, dolls, screwdrivers, mannequins, dust and air, as in *The Street of Crocodiles* based on Schulz's prose.[57]

Another distinctive characteristic which makes it possible to trace relations between animal protagonists and humans in animated plots is the introduction of a non-distinction sphere, with the animal protagonists helping their human carers out with thankless tasks and showing the same type of lack of sensitivity to the species rivalled or exterminated by them. Also the signs of cartoon characters' identification with humans are quite distinctive. Felix, who in one of his travels was tasked with proving the human origin from apes, changes his opinion and explains that it is apes originating from 'us', where 'us' means both humans and thinking cats.

Familiarity and the public backstage in the creation of new subjects (or platforms for communication and competition)

In the case of animation, the creation of a platform for understanding can also take place outside the film work's structure. It turns out that the Craftonian self-figuration process often took place outside of its confines in the public space. One such example is the animation creators' frequent inclination to appear together with their characters in all sorts of manipulated photographic materials (Figure 2.3 and 2.4). The animators would hold their charges in their arms, include them in photographs of themselves at work, and so on. The audience of the time were sometimes witnesses to a subtle interplay between the animated world and the producers' reality. Crafton, for example, mentions a cartoon that was supposed to advertise the live-action film, *The Great White Way* (1924). This is Little Nemo and Flip's dialogue: "Flip: I say, Nemo, I dreamed last night, that Winsor McCay was an actor!" Nemo: "He i san actor! He may be a bad one, but he is an actor, Flip".[58]

Voice actors who felt a particular bond with the character also could resort to a similar convention. For example, when describing his father's work, Richard

Figure 2.3 Walter Lantz and his animated characters (Everett Collection/East News).

Fleischer mentions him receiving wishes from Betty Boop's voice actor, Mae Questel – 'Love from Betty Boop, alias Mae Questel'.[59] This example illustrates Questel's attachment to the cartoon character, but there are also examples of rivalry. The younger of the Fleischers notes that Betty represents a certain popular type of femininity which a number of then-famous women identified themselves with, including actor Clara Bow and singer Helen Kane. The latter

Figure 2.4 Walt Disney and Mickey Mouse (Everett Collection/East News).

Folks, meet Betty Boop (right). You'll be seeing a lot of her because she is the new animated cartoon character who is trying to cut in on Mickey Mouse's popularity. Does she look familiar to you? Now look at little boop-a-dooper Helen Kane. Helen was the cartoonist's inspiration for Betty, the first time a real life character has been used for the popular jumping comics

Figure 2.5 Helen Kane and her stage competitor, Betty Boop. Published by *Photoplay Magazine* just before the lawsuit in May 1932.

sued Fleischer for the appropriation of the phrase used by Betty Boop on-screen (Boop-oop-a-doop). During the hearing, the court, among other things, asked Kane to remove her coat and hat, so as to make it possible to assess the similarity of her silhouette and face with Betty Boop's, and she intentionally adjusted her hair in order to make the similarity even more evident (Figure 2.5). The court eventually dismissed the suit, but the hearing itself emphatically demonstrates the possibility of collating a live actor with a cartoon character in a posthuman position, which in this case plays out in the court space.

Betty Boop's character is also the focus of several more controversies suggesting an equal footing between cartoon characters and live actors in the public space. Richard Fleischer shows how Betty Bop faced similar repercussions as one of Hollywood's most provocative actresses, Mae West, following the introduction of Hays Code:

> Fleischer Studios was hounded and even threatened until Betty started to change. Just as she changed at the beginning of her career from a dog to a person, she now had to change from a mini-sexpot to a sort of schoolmarm.[60]

The drawers had to make the character more decent by making her dress longer, losing the garters and the deep cleavage. Because of such operations, however, she lost her unique style and with it her popularity.

Going back to Disney, his statue in the Magic Kingdom Park, holding hands with Mickey Mouse (see Figure 2.6), could be said to be the most distinctive symbol of crossing the boundary between the human person and the sense created by it, or rather the gesture of inviting it to be a subject. It is of no small significance that the statue, placed in 1993 in California, appears amid a growing global awareness of the posthuman idea, thanks to the popularity of Donna Haraway's *Cyborg Manifesto* published in print in 1991.[61] The statue is

Figure 2.6 The interbeing union in its Disney iteration (*Partners* statue by Blaine Gibson).

named *Partners*, similarly to Charles Boyer's 1981 lithography showing Walt and Mickey holding their hands for the first time. The artist who designed the statue, Blaine Gibson, used to say that underlying his concept was the thought of Walt telling Mickey: 'Look at all the happy people who have come to visit us today.'[62] The creation of the statue also led to the establishment of the exclusive prize, Partners in Excellence, awarded to a small number of Disney employees for their contribution to the corporation's development. A while later a small version of young Disney and Mickey, named *Storytellers*, was inaugurated in the Anaheim theme park in California in June 2012. While the former sculpture symbolizes the triumph of the mature Disney and his animated partner, the latter tries to capture the young animator's arrival in Los Angeles.

***

The posthuman contexts of film animation discussed in this chapter demonstrate this area of cinematography to have been one of the first to develop a grammar for the creation of interbeing intimacy. This appears across a number of fields in animation. The point of departure here is the process by which animation was separated from live-action cinema. The first hybrid films were, in a sense, a testimony of the growing independence of this form of film creativity in the process of negotiating the rights of animated characters. Somewhat frequently, on the plot-line level, the characters do something contrariwise, they 'intentionally' break elements of their surroundings, they escape the confines of the screen, sketchbook or inkwell. On the other hand, the creators are not always entirely confined to any one defined ontological plane – McCay penetrates into the dinosaurs' world, and Disney almost marries Mickey in a symbolic fashion in entering the public space together. These metaleptic leaps bear witness to the establishment of rules of co-existence, borders and demarcation lines. The art of film appears to be full of this type of negotiation apparatus, and on this idea I will elaborate in the next chapter. Finally, while it would be difficult to attribute free will to cartoon characters, the following strategy makes itself apparent – 'let's act as if they did have it'. This gesture of invitation signals the acceptance of one's own projection in the role of the Other and is Disney's taking of Mickey's non-material (cartoon) hand in a handshake.

The cyborg-cinema and the layer-man: film technologies as vehicles of posthumanism

If we realize that in Ang Lee's 2003 film version of *Hulk* the scene of scientist Bruce Banner's first transformation into the green monster is the transformation of a human being placed in the presented world into a comic character, the scene will be the testimony of a process definable from the posthuman perspective as the human subject's difficulty adjusting to being distributed and morphed. To the character, the transformation entails physical suffering and different forms of limitations. He is not accepting the power he has gained. This is a discursive configuration. What we are dealing with is the struggle playing out between two instances in a single body capable of transformation, or in two opposing worlds, such as in the dream scene with Banner confronting his monstrous *alter ego* in the mirror. Hulk steps out of that mirror, seizing scientist and drawing him into the creature's own world. The effect of such negotiations is not always suffering or limitation, but it is only natural that entering into another posthuman position like this one triggers a variety of anthropological consequences.

In the chapter on animation, I endeavoured to demonstrate the way in which the production process fits within the canon of building an intimate relationship with a visual cartoon creation. When tracing the history of a different area of film production, namely special effects, we will encounter more vehicles for the construction of such intimacy vis-à-vis film fabric not necessarily personified into a specific character the way this was done in the cartoon world. They also make it possible to demonstrate how posthumanism's significant idea of the distribution of subjecthood places itself in another sphere of cinema. This distribution is focused around several categories.

The first one is the layer, understood as an element of film compositing, which, if referred to the subjecthood of actors and other 'live' characters creating the film plan, produces a number of anthropological consequences. The theory and history of analogue composite cinema are already well-reported in historical sources[1] and have been described in terms of the concepts defining the modern CGI age.[2] The posthuman perspective, however, allows us to focus more on the anthropological consequences of 'being a layer' and accordingly to identify the ways in which composition technologies destabilize subjecthood and reconfigure the subject's position.

Another important category is the figure of the cinema cyborg, understood as the heterogeneous assemblage product of the production stage, as opposed to the 'homogeneous' final character presented on the screen. The production stage provides a good opportunity to trace all the 'seams' and connections in the hybrid constructions of beings presenting homogeneously in the finished film picture and often 'pretending' to be human, and the impact such constructions have on the subjecthood of the actors who constitute an element of this patchwork and the final shape of that subjecthood as observed in the film.

The third category will be the interbeing fair of cinema attractions. What I mean by this is the understanding of the film plan as a place constituting the product of decisions about the status of the beings shown on the screen and their place in the film frame. Nowadays, film creators, taking a significant variety of conditions into account, can somewhat freely choose among live participants in the action (humans and animals), dolls or dummies or puppets, and animatronic mechanisms, computer-generated, 'manually' animated and AI-scripted pseudo-independent agents. The assurance of continuity and homogeneity between such ontologically different instances is one of the main challenges facing the creators of special effects for films.

This chapter will identify the main anthropological consequences of the operation of the above categories in film production. The sources providing the relevant examples will first of all be the history of special effects narrowed down to the evolution of compositing and hybrid constructions of film characters, as well as analysis of selected production materials of CGI cinema. Hence, I will be relying on the optic previously referred to as the making-off perspective. Making-off is a supporting film form that, while being created ex-post in relation to the ready film, reaches back to its production stage, thus providing an opportunity for analysis of the hybrid structure of the film image even before it becomes a homogeneous ready product.[3]

The human layer

The history of special effects underlying the development of composite cinema is teeming with inventions intended to separate the acting subject from the rest of the film plan as best as possible. We can assume, therefore, that from the very beginning we have been dealing with the process of formation of a separate 'human' layer that will later undergo various types of analog and digital processing. There exist a whole range of keying technologies having in the past allowed the actor playing the relevant role to be extracted from the background and re-embedded elsewhere. The posthuman context of such technologies is the product of the fact that being found in a chromatically homogeneous film space puts the human subject on an equal footing with the other layers of composite cinema. The space itself, here in the function of a territory without properties, also has its own characteristics and forces the actor to take a defined position. This non-being space housing the subject is also an area changing its location, shape and size, one that can turn from an absorbent territory into a spot travelling on the actor's body, sometimes crawling onto the actor's face, sometimes a different part of the subject's body or surroundings, or it could itself become a subject.

Historical reduction games and colour games

The evolution of keying technology could be identified as on the one hand a tale of the systematic reduction of the screen's signifying elements all the way to an all-encompassing nothingness, and on the other hand the history of the 'pinpointing' of colour to allow the fullest possible coming into existence of the posthuman position to create the ideal harmonization protocol.

This reduction becomes perceivable when we realize that the invention of the blue screen and the green screen goes back to a variety of techniques relying on the masking of elements of the set with the use of matte planes and objects painted on glass. So-called grass shots and, later on, first forms of matte painting used by Norman O. Down since 1911 were the first forms of such reduction. Here, the creation of multi-layer moving pictures involves separation and limitation. A camera largely but not completely masked by the shutter would record picture fitting within a small part of frame. The rest, unlit, would be used for the recording of other objects so as to create a fantasy picture.

We can find a lot of anthropological contexts in the historical but still very popular technique known as matte painting. The principle of a separate space comes into the spotlight here, with the artists first painting complicated sceneries leaving out black, unpainted holes into which the miniature action will subsequently be 'pasted'. Matte painting is a technology that depicts the interesting tension between the active subject and the frame space. Here, each of the instances has its own separate place negotiable during the production according to the latter's important priorities. These must be followed both by the actors, who are not allowed to venture beyond the precise and absolute demarcation line for action, and by the matte-painting artists leaving for them a space to act in the picture. The place or space for the actors is mostly decided by the perception capabilities of the spectator's eye – for example, how the spectator begins to trace a vast panorama from left to right or focuses on a central location within the frame, etc. The topography of the frame thus also becomes a topography for the allocation of life and subjecthood in it. Hence, the peripheries of the frame will be reserved to inanimate and static objects, and the centre to the acting subject, such as in the masterful last scene in *Raiders of the Lost Ark* (1981) playing out in a huge warehouse, wholly painted and not recorded. In the centre of the frame, the sole place that is lit, a wooden crate with the Ark inside is rolled on a cart by a warehouse employee. The scene is so suggestive that it might as well take thirty seconds, though matte-painting shots normally do not exceed ten.[4]

This unique interplay of nothingness and existence in composite cinema, which initially had only been the elimination of individual elements from the recorded picture, ultimately led to the 'depletion' of the scene, with only the actor being filmed in a homogeneously coloured space remaining. Such was the price to be paid for the total freedom in creating the surroundings, although the opinions of specialists suggest that the free building of a new world also has its own specific limitations, which I will be visiting in a moment.

The pinpointing of the 'colour of nothingness' begins, in turn, from the black background having, as the 'female matte', constituted part of the process referred to as 'travelling mattes'. Through a different invention, one he patented in 1918, Frank Williams improves keying on a black background, although white backgrounds were also occasionally used with this technique. One of the best examples of successful application of Williams's technology was *The Invisible Man* (1933, dir. James Whale). By then, the technology developed by Dunning and improved by Pomeroy employs also the blue colour, although orange is used in order to differentiate the background and the foreground. The whole invention, however, served its purpose only in black-and-white cinema. Thanks to the experiments initiated in Technicolor's lab in the early 1930s, the blue screen could be used for the first time in *The Thief of Baghdad*, in 1940 (dir. Ludwig Berger et al.). The blue screen also appears in the much later invention by Petro Vlahos, for which he received the Oscar in 1964 and which saw significant use later on. The basis for his invention was found in the much earlier technique utilizing sodium lamps emitting yellow light; in this case, however, the light is white. Vlahos patented such a system in the United States in 1963,[5] but sodium lamps had been used before in France and patented for the purposes of composite cinema by Jean Kudar in 1949 in the United Kingdom.[6] The yellow-lit sodium vapour was used, among others, for Hitchcock's *The Birds* (1963) and Disney's *Mary Poppins* (1964). Vlahos himself in 1987 patented another compositing system, support different background colours – blue, red and green.[7] Of those colours green is currently the favourite, as it is the best fit for digital cameras, though blue is regarded as superior when filming human skin or blond hair. Other colours are sometimes used, for example, red in the long shot with the blue-and-white US presidential jet in *Air Force One* (1997, dir. Wolfgang Petersen).

The blue box and the green box – games of subject and space

While looking for an answer to the question of what the anthropological consequences are of residing in the empty single-coloured space of the blue box or the green box, one cannot avoid putting this technology in the broader context of such categories as nonexistence or nothingness, nor comparing it to other empty spaces in which the performance is placed. The blue box, understood to mean the space of nonexistence, holds multiple connotations from very different orders – from the Biblical, through the philosophical to modern popular culture.[8]

The philosophical codifier of nothingness, Jean Paul Sartre, notes that it is a substrate on which the formed world appears, thanks to the human potential for lifting it out of nonexistence:

> In the movement of turning inward which traverses all of being, being arises and organizes itself as the world without there being either priority of the movement over the world, or the world over the movement. But this appearance of the self beyond the world-that is, beyond the totality of the real-is an emergence of 'human reality' in nothingness. It is in nothingness alone that being can be surpassed. At the same time it is from the point of view of beyond the world that being is organized into the world, which means on the one hand that human

reality rises up as an emergence of being in non-being and on the other hand that the world is 'suspended' in nothingness.[9]

This passage appears to be the ideal match for the description of those subtle games between the space and the subject that manifest themselves in the theatrical space. The Brookian empty space is a demiurgic space – it allows the world to be constituted on the scene, as long as the actor stands in it. The actor, therefore, fits here within the Sartrean concept of a subject wielding free will and the potency for the creation of the world.

If in Sartre's concept the point of departure is that world-creating existence in the world, the blue box may appear as the ironic negation of this basic assumption. In the blue box or the green box, we encounter a change of roles – by this vehicle, the actor placed in the space ceases to be a subject vested with full agency and capable of world creation, instead turning into a malleable layer. The world, on the other hand, turns into a nothingness that could be 'different being' – being somewhere else,[10] and on the other hand the space itself can be world-creating and subject-creating, as I will demonstrate shortly.

A discussion on this subject in the forum of renowned visual-effects specialists organized on the centenary of the journal, *Cinefex*, saw a whole set of arguments confirming this anti-world-creating and 'un-theatrical' character of the blue box or the green box.[11] In the opinion of Rick Baker, actors need to have some visual elements with which to play. Phil Tippett emphasizes that working only with the blue screen all the time would doubtless result in a very downtrodden actor. Tippett could not quite imagine a way for the actor to muster the same enthusiasm with which one would be ambling around a pleasant plan or gorgeous landscape. John Knoll notes that actors complain about the blue screen because the essence of actorship is reaction, which is hardly possible where no one or nothing exists. Craig Barron points towards the blue screen's one more 'anthropological' affliction – the invention makes the actors' eyes look like glass since they do not know in which direction to look or what is truly happening in the scene. Paddy Eason, on the other hand, addresses the body language of the actors being filmed against the blue-screen background, which, according to him, is altogether different in the forced space of the studio compared to a realistic location. He believes the actor's looking direction and overexpansive motions to be subliminal signals capable of making the audience realize that the actor was being filmed on the blue screen.

The above remarks failed to discourage a varied group of film creators from heeding the temptation of the all-encompassing blue or green screen. The

Figure 3.1 The absorbent apparatus of the green screen: Kristen Bell in *Pulse*, 2006. Dir. Jim Sonzero. Everett Collection/EastNews.

actors' environment in *Captain Sky and the World of Tomorrow* (2004, dir. Kerry Conran) was wholly computer-generated. The majority of the scenes in the new *Star Wars* series were shot on the blue screen. *The Matrix* (1999, dir Lana and Lilly Wachowski) alone consumed eight square kilometres of blue screen. The goal of the procedures on the plan, however, is to eliminate the blue-screen or the green-screen ironic twist by providing the actor with a stimulus to exist in the world, due to not creating it like in theatre. At least some token elements of the set do appear – outlines of equipment, body parts, elements having some palpable weight and so on.

Such efforts being made on the film set when working with the blue box or the green box would tend to attest to a desire to restore the actor's world-creating potential, the demiurgic power the actor holds in theatre. On the other hand, Sartre himself infers that the human subject at once has the ability to dispute and tear away from the world towards nonexistence, hence having a quality that could be termed 'neantization'.[12] His suggestion is as follows:

> Being can generate only being and if man is inclosed in this process of generation, only being will come out of him. If we are to assume that man is able to question this process – i.e., to make it the object of interrogation – he must be able/to hold it up to view as a totality. He must be able to put himself outside of being and by the same stroke weaken the structure of the being of being.[13]

In this case the blue box or the green box would be a doubly ironic invention. On the one hand it would confirm – on the whole vehicle's ontological level – the anthropocentric potential for problematizing the idea of being and of the world, and on the other hand in itself it would undermine that anthropocentrism. The following juxtaposition presents two empty spaces (see Figure 3.2), which could appear similar in their expression, guided, however, each by a wholly different conception of the subject. In the Brookian staging of *A Midsummer Night's Dream* (1970), the reduction of the space to an undecorated two-colour stage is an act of demonstration of the potential for the creation of stage reality by the actors. The green space of the green screen used in *The Matrix* formats the actors to the form of a layer, which then causes them to cease to constitute an anthropocentric point of departure for the reality that is being created.

Functions and places of nothingness

In cinema the green or blue nothingness becomes a synonym for places of instantiation, a being in its potency stage. Nothingness takes on a variety of functions on the plan and takes different places in it, which I would like to describe in this part of the chapter.

Figure 3.2 Competing models of the 'empty space'. Upper panel: a photo from the 1970 staging of *A Midsummer Night's Dream* under Peter Brook (©Donald Cooper/ PhotoStage); lower panel: a frame registering green-screen work on *The Matrix*, 1999. Dir. Lana and Lilly Wachowski (Everett Collection/EastNews).

The all-encompassing nothingness

Sets for the various shots or whole films produced in one-colour spaces setting the ground for computer graphical artists' unbounded creativity provide an example of a type of totality that the production crew in general and the actors in particular must face. A good illustration for this totality is *Sky Captain and the World of Tomorrow*, where all scenes were shot on blue and green boxes, with only several minor elements of decoration appearing. This assumption resulted in a total of 2,031 computer shots, distancing the previous record-holder, *The Lord of the Rings: The Return of the King* (dir. Peter Jackson) with its 1450.[14] Such a large number of scenes shot with a green-box or blue-box background in this film and many other films take its toll on the actors. In the words of Ken Ralston about the actors' feelings during the staging of Tim Burton's *Alice in Wonderland* (2010), 'the intense green of the shooting environment was exhausting'.[15] The creators planned to use the blue colour, potentially more psychologically tolerable, but with Alice dressing in blue that idea was discarded.

Focusing on the consequences of entire films being produced with the use of the green box or the blue box, we will primarily realize the above-mentioned need for providing the actors and the director with the support (technological again) they all need in order to gain greater awareness of what is currently happening on the screen. In such cases, various types of previsualization systems can be of assistance; in simplified animation those can show precisely what the action is going to look like. A three-dimensional (3D) animatic allows the actors to feel more confidence in the one-coloured nothingness. The watching of a simplified models has a peculiar temporal context in animatics. The actor is supposed to copy a role played by a digital character, not creating the world anew but replicating it, following virtual alter ego; by definition, therefore, his or her job is 're-creating'. Therefore, systems generating simplified live graphics have a different positioning. Such a technology was used in Burton's *Alice* and, of course, in *Avatar* (2009 dir. James Cameron).

Another important element of the all-encompassing nothingness is also the matter of the placement of the 'traces of being' therein. Numerous holistic locations filmed with the blue box or the green box can contain outlines of the material plan. The nothingness in production thus has, although not always, certain indicative outlines of 3D shapes, architectural elements or different characters for subsequent instantiation in post-production.

'Marked with nothingness'

Single-coloured nothingness, such as I am here describing, has the potential for being placed in different locations on the body that, when masked, enable the introduction of new virtual elements. This 'touch' of nothingness in cinema begins long before the blue-box era. In 1933 *The Invisible Man* takes a form that is somewhat oppressive to the actor. Claude Rains, in the titular role, had to put on a special black velvet costume because of the need to mask out the body parts supposed to be invisible in the frame. The costume tightly covered all 'invisible' parts of the body, including the head and mouth. The production was an arduous process, for little could the actor hear, even though the director was standing several metres away with a megaphone. Rains, moreover, had to learn a special way of moving so as to avoid his masked palms appearing against the backdrop of the 'donned' body.[16] This effect returned in a similar shape in *Memoirs of an Invisible Man* (1992, dir. John Carpenter), for which Chevy Chase wore blue costumes concealing the parts of the body that were supposed to be unseen.[17] In newer productions the 'green nothingness' is a convenient substrate for digital make-up, including prosthetics. In the third part of *Terminator* (…), casting Arnold Schwarzenegger in the lead role, the damaged left side of the titular robot's face was digitally generated in a place in which the actor wore green prosthetic make-up.[18] In a newer version of *The Invisible Man* (*The Hollow Man, 2000*. dir. Paul Verhoeven), watching Kevin Bacon's entirely green face leaves an eerie impression.

In modern productions the green colour covers a number of different parts of the body, and not only human body at that. Green-masking of parts of the bodies of the creatures serving as the characters' mounts is a frequent procedure. In Jackson's *King Kong* (2005) the huge paw in which he grabs Naomi Watts is a gargantuan green cast (see Figure 3.4). A great number of green-masked prostheses can also be encountered, which will be discussed below.

Nothingness as a subject

The phenomenon of the blue screen and the green screen consists in the masking out of not only parts of the body but of entire human silhouettes with a uniform colour. In this case, however, the actors or, more often, assistants do not lose the sort of agency that allows them to affect the screen reality, even though they themselves may remain unseen. They become a sort of transparent layers in the film's composite structure, its disappearing *spiritus moventes*, a nothingness imbued with subjecthood.

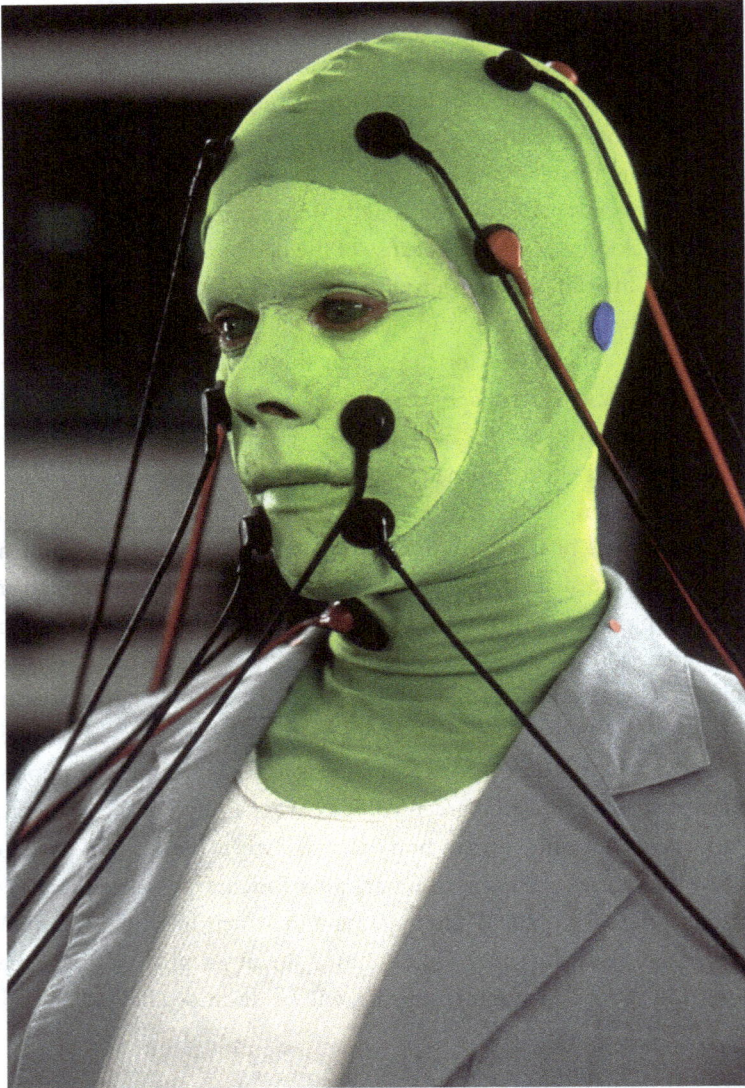

Figure 3.3 Kevin Bacon marked with 'green nothingness' for *The Hollow Man*, 2000. Dir. Paul Verhoeven. Photo from Alamy Collection.

Ron Burnett is the author of the concept of thinking digital images, which it will be expedient to recall here. He notes that current digital technologies permeate the picture to such an extent that it becomes, in a way, an intelligent image. This intelligence can be derived from saturation with AI technologies,

Figure 3.4 Companion species of the CGI cinema: Naomi Watts in a digital paw of titular character in *King Kong*, 2005. Dir. Peter Jackson. Everett Collection/EastNews.

which we will be discussing later on, but also from the activities of the human subject itself, who, thanks to technologies such as keying, can 'transplant' his or her actions into the film action.[19]

One could say that this method of bestowing subject-like characteristics on the film picture begins already at the onset of cinema. Erik Barnouw describes how Albert E. Smith and Steward Blackton, when creating *The Battle of Santiago Bay* (1899), simulated cannon shots from the vessel – cut-out of a photograph – by blowing cigarette smoke through tiny openings in the cut-out.[20] The manual moving around of starships by *Star Wars* crew has become a legend. Until the present day there has probably not been a single film without some variety of invisible assistants helping the movement of either vehicles or characters on the screen with the strength of their own hands.

In modern digital composite cinema a green outfit covering all of a person's body is a frequent prop when the film plan needs a human being to propel movement or operate a prosthesis. A large group are characters whose only the outline is needed for further digital processing. In such a situation they are invisible in the final version of the movie.

In *Superman Returns* (2006, dir. Bryan Singer) invisible helpers animate Superman's cape by pulling strings.[21] In *The Last Airbender* (2010, dir. M.

Night Shyamalan) a green helper swings one of the fighters on a rope.[22] In *Source Code* the duties of invisible helpers belonged to blue-clad mannequins of the two protagonists, making it possible to generate the effect of the actors being licked by tongues of flame when they themselves were being recorded on the green screen.[23] In the second part of *The Chronicles of Narnia* there is a green-clad operator of Aslan's head. In *The Lord of the Rings: The Return of the King* a blue helper operates Sheloba's head in her fight with Sam Gamgee.[24]

In Tim Burton's *Alice in Wonderland* we can find a whole train of characters wholly enveloped in green costumes.[25] Part of them provide the substrate and outline for virtual characters such as Tweedledee and Tweedledum (see Figure 3.5). 'Disappearing' helpers also abound. One of the scenes requires a piggy footstool for the card queen. Here, the helper acts as the force pushing the virtual animal under the queen's feet, replaced on the plan with a green roller. In one of the scenes with Jack of Hearts, a total of five invisible helpers are animating the horse for the character to ride on the plan.

A suggestive example of invisible helpmanship on the plan can be found in one of the most poignant scenes in *Avatar*, that of Neytiri's first meeting with a truly crippled Jake Sully. The scene, referred to as 'Pieta' in the production, demanded the actors to be aware of the spatial dependencies resulting from the difference in structure and size between human and Na'vi bodies. The scene was put together from two different shots with Sadana and Warthington acting each alone. In Saldana's part, she was holding a girl in her lap, simulating the much smaller hero. Warthington's part needed two green helpers and a prosthetic head. One helper supported the actor, simulating Neytiri's long arm's embrace, and the other moved a green prosthesis of her head, so that the actor could gaze directly into the eyes of his beloved.

In *I, Robot* (2004, dir. Alex Proyas) we again have green creatures, though at this time they act as human proxies for digitally generated robots. An interesting secondary character of the live characters on the plan emerges here. In this case we can speak of a reverse situation compared to the digital doubles I will be discussing later in this chapter.[26] Here, actors are not being replaced with their digital copies, but instead they themselves become copies of digital characters tasked with providing live actors (primarily Will Smith) with the opportunity to interact with the robots in a way that will be credible in the end effect.

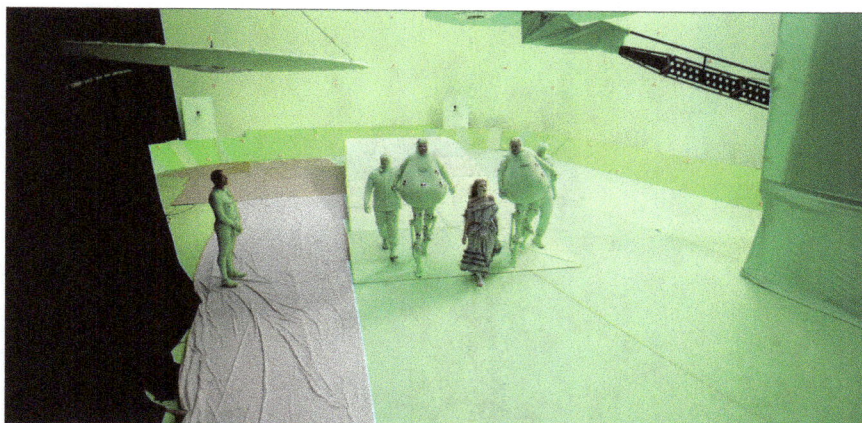

Figure 3.5 Alice's green companions on set of Tim Burton's *Alice in Wonderland*, 2010. Kobal Collection.

The pre-screen cyborg

The history of special effects, as well as select aspects in the history of animation, highlights a number of tools lending themselves to Agamben's concept of the anthropological machine, understood in the strict sense as the effect of technological action. One could write a separate history of animation and effects, one structured around the anthropological consequences of their use by actors or, better still, the use of such solutions 'on' actors. Film technologies have often been an example of the formatting, limitation and adaptation of the actors' bodies, as well as other items to the final cinematic effect, from the moon's dough-coated face to the most modern prostheses used in modern special effects. If we recall the circumstances of the production of *The Vanishing Man*, we will see the poor actor sweating in a costume clinging tightly to his body. Actors being suspended on ropes are something that happens in probably every film in which humans can fly.[27] Film make-up, especially of the kind employing digital additions and other elements of facial prosthetics, requires quite some patience and can sometimes take several hours to apply. In other words, constructing the film's illusion machine often requires a diverse range of acrobatics and unnatural positions of the body. The price to be paid for the transhuman end effect is submission, at the production stage, to a variety of procedures adapting the actor to first the analog and then the digital film fabric.

To repre
ror, an
covered

Figure 3.6 Oppressive apparatus of cinema: helmet used in the recording of the dialogue line for the talking mirror in Disney's *Snow White*.[28]

Whether these vehicles modify the actors' scope of action in a significant and 'hard' way or affect them a lot more subtly, one can conclude that the creation of opportunities for the emergence of cyborgical structures is an immanent property of film tricks. Below, I discuss a varied range of strategies for the construction of such cinematic cyborgs. They show themselves mainly in the

Figure 3.7 Oppressive apparatus of cinema: retort used in the making of *Eternally Yours*.[29]

Figure 3.8 Oppressive apparatus of cinema: testing of cinema loudspeaking systems by US Standards Bureau.[30]

production stage of a cinematic work. I will demonstrate the main directions and forms of distribution of human subjecthood in these vehicles.

Prosthetics

One of the principal elements of the creation of film illusion involving the body is the creation of prostheses with various different functions to serve and placements throughout the body. Although prostheses have matured into an interesting subject of posthuman reflection on disability and transhuman reflection on the imperfections of the human body only lately, film prosthetics is already a field rich in tradition, albeit a field not yet placed in the broader area of reflection on posthumanism. And yet it abounds with interesting contexts.

Concerning the current state of the art, it is worth noting two mutually opposed strategies for the creation of cinematic cyborgs via prosthetics. The first is the creation of additive prostheses. Their purpose is to be used in a variety of procedures allowing actors to play beings with non-human body structures, from animals that exist in reality, through anthropomorphic and non-anthropomorphic fantasy creatures and creatures of fairy tales, to robots

Figure 3.9 Examples of film prosthetics providing the foundation for post-processing, turning actors into machines or animals, *Guardians of the Galaxy*, 2014. Dir. James Gunn. Everett/EastNews.

and androids. The actors are equipped with stilts, orthopaedic crutches and prosthetic arms they need in order to play apes, wolves or bears. Some parts of the body are expanded on in order to simulate a different silhouette (such as in *Real Steel, 2011,* dir. Shawn Levy) and so on. Nowadays, a character's ultimate look usually depends on meticulous computer post-processing, but on the set

John Carter (2012)
Directed by Andrew Stanton
Shown from left: Unidentified, Willem Dafoe, Director Andrew Stanton on the set.

Rentals grant one-time, EDITORIAL use only, unless otherwise negotiated. Please inform us about usage or non-usage as soon as possible. Research fees may apply if no images are used.
© Walt Disney Studios Motion Pictures

Please Credit:
PHOTOFEST
(212) 633-6330

Figure 3.10 Examples of film prosthetics, *John Carter*, 2012. Dir. Andrew Stanton. Photofest Digital.

the prosthetics have a number of important tasks to do. For example, they allow the body's limits to be set so as to make it more easily computer-editable (the actor is usually plugged into a mocap system) and to allow the actor concerned, as well as others playing in the same sequence, to better identify with their roles.

One characteristic feature of the additive use of prosthetics will often be injecting human subjecthood in on-screen monsters that are not necessarily perceived as 'human' by the audience. A frequently used tactic is to build their credibility by incorporating elements of actor's play. One could say that this is a type of action reminiscent of Disney's strategy of caricaturing the world. In animation animal characters were supposed to be saturated with 'human' subjecthood because that was what made them appear more animal-like to the audience. The same is supposed to be the case with additive prosthetics. This type of strategy seems to be derived from all manner of animal and fantasy costumes donned by the actors of pre-digital cinema. The same principle will apply to the most recent productions as well.

In *Rise of the Planet of the Apes* (2011, dir. Rupert Wyatt) the majority of the apes were played by stunt performers outfitted with limb extensions and dressed in mocap costumes with markers. In *Avatar* many of the creatures inhabiting Pandora were 'played' by members of the stunt crew equipped with a diverse assortment of prosthetics forming the specific outline of a creature such as the banshee being tamed by Jake. The significance of the playing of animals by stunt performers was incredible also due to the composition of the scene and the animals' interaction with the actors. Animator Richard Baneham recalls that he often had to compete for space and time for virtual animals in the various sequences filmed with live actors because there was not enough room for the animals in the frame or the scene was too short.[31] In this connection the crew began to record mocaps with 'prosthetically enhanced' stunt performers in order to organize the scene around the animal so that the animal really was there. Some other time, in the scene with viperwolves, stunt performers wearing costumes with markers were running around the set with weighted training sacks, so the actors could feel the actual weight of the creatures they were interacting with. Such physical parametrization of a virtual animal through the mediation of an actor equipped with prostheses also took place during the production of *The Golden Compass* (2007, dir. Chris Weitz). The latter film's bear character, Iorek Byrnison, was filmed with the use of an exquisite prosthetic structure handled by an operator with stilts and the animal's green head grafted on a long jib.

A different optic in film prosthetics is the reductive model linked to the above-discussed blue or green keying technology. In such a case the purpose of the reduction of elements of the body is to demonstrate their absence from the final body appearing on the screen. Thus, only the screen body is missing any

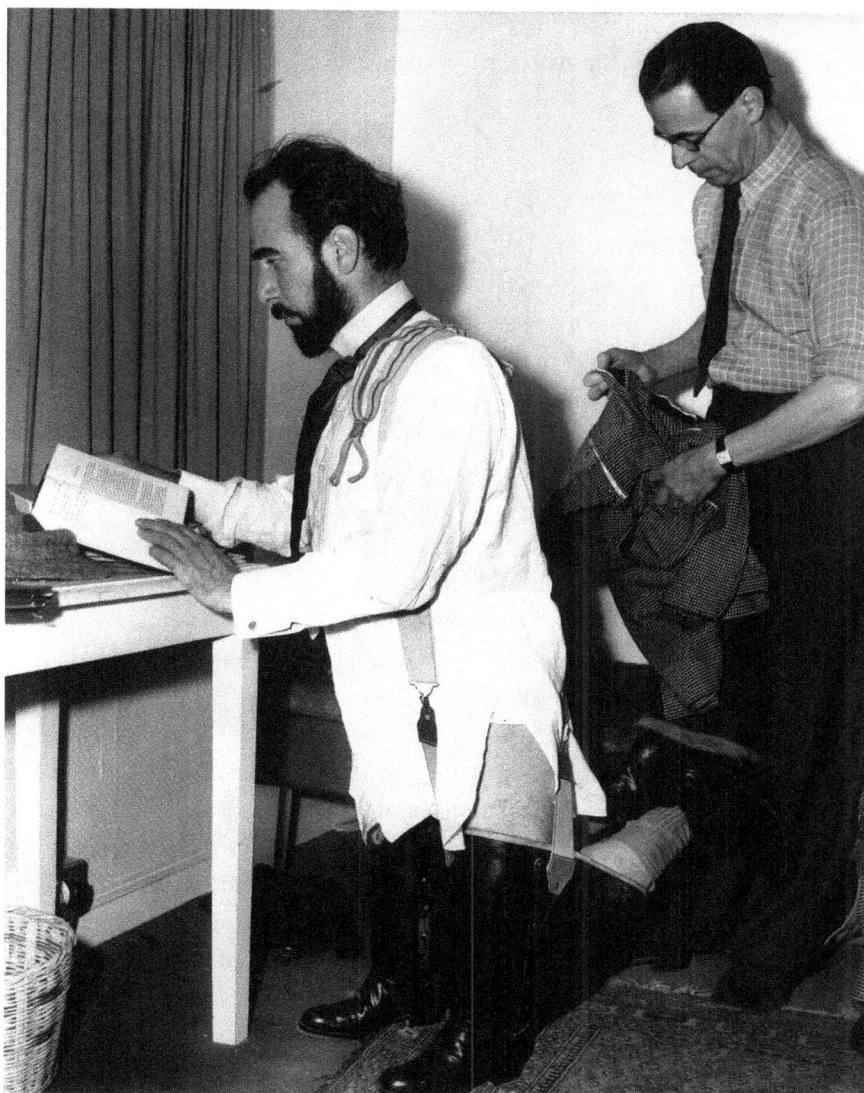

Figure 3.11 'Reduction' prosthetics: Jose Ferrer's knee shoes shorten the legs of Toulouse-Lautrec played by him in *Moulin Rouge*, 1952. Dir. John Huston. Everett Collection/EastNews.

parts or is a hybrid body with visible prosthetics. Gary Sinise's blue stockings concealing his legs while playing the disabled Lieutenant Dan (*Forrest Gump*, 1994, dir. Robert Zemeckis), or Asa Butterfield's green ones in *Hugo*'s (2011, dir. Martin Scorsese) night-dream scene, the one with the majority of the character's body other than his head turning into an automaton, are spectacular examples of this. In this case the nothingness of the blue box and the green box becomes the ground set for the elimination or prosthetization of limbs, visible, of course, only on the screen.

Formatting by grid-snapping

The above-mentioned mocap techniques, referred to – in their developed form – as performance capture, constitute in themselves a form of formatting of the actors for the film's purposes. In a variety of image-capturing systems the actor's body and especially the face is outfitted with a plethora of markers. The purpose of the latter is to allow the computer to 'see' the actor's motions and facial expressions well. Consequently, one could say that this type of formatting resembles snapping elements to a grid – a familiar function of graphics software and word processors. This snap-to-grid metaphor, utilized by Peter Lunenfeld in his 2001 book,[32] here shows another condition for the establishment of a harmonization protocol between the live actor and the digital fabric. Even those systems which do not use markers appear to subscribe to this model of creation of a protocol enabling the computer to 'understand' a human character. The precise, laser-targeted stop-motion-based system used for the first time for the 'bullet-time' effect in the Wachowskis' *The Matrix* provides a good example of this. It is worth noting that the goal here is to maximize the information status of the actor's body. To source information about the actor's position, motions, skin texture, facial expressions and muscle movement becomes the most important task during the production of scenes played by actors and during the various additional sessions employing a 3D scanner, facial mocap, etc. Here, one could invoke N. Katherine Hayles's category of virtuality, defined by her as 'material structures [being] interpenetrated with informational patterns'.[33]

Mocap too is a system in which interesting 'interbeing' contexts transpire. During the production of *Hulk* a number of people contributed captured movement for the titular character.[34] Stunt performers, body builders and even Ang Lee himself were among them. *The Polar Express* (2004, dir. Robert Zemeckis) saw the reverse situation, with six roles – including the protagonist role of the boy who lost faith in the Christmas spirit – being played by a mocapped Tom Hanks. The question is what makes the character's integrity such as in the Hulk situation, or the character's uniqueness such as in *The Polar Express*, if everybody is played by the same person.

A very special type of mocap is the various systems for facial motion capture – special because it largely defines the options available nowadays to animators for the creation of believable digital characters. The face constitutes the most important element of the scanned actor's body, for it is the carrier of emotion and the most important place enhancing the credibility of the digital presentation. It is symptomatic that the majority of studies into animation and effects used in the creation of film monsters, fantasy creatures and often even 'regular' animals reference Paul Ekman's facial-action coding system (FACS). Its value lies in parametrization, easily transferable to systems controlling the facial expressions of digital characters. It would seem that the use of such a system facilitates the work on the physiognomy of the digital subjects, given how the grid-snapping has already been taken care of by Ekman and reduced to a finite number of facial expressions and positions of facial muscles. Nothing could be more wrong! It turns out that the face is the most challenging territory to capture, demanding the largest investment of labour and a great deal of creativity from the animation artists.

These digital face-building efforts strongly correspond with the meaning Deleuze attributes to this 'organ' in his film theory. Not only does he believe the face defines subjecthood, he also points out its typical structural aspects – it is never a partial object the way the other parts of the body are; on the contrary, it stands for the whole subject, it is a being in itself, but it is also in itself a close-up.[35] The opinions of special-effects creators confirm this special status of the face. In the words of Steve Begg, 'human beings are very aware of subtle details in the face – and if those details are not present, or not carefully placed, people can detect artificiality'.[36] Eric Barba concurs, turning particular attention to the eyes: 'We knew that if we didn't get the eyes right, it wouldn't matter how good the rest of it looked.'[37]

Special-effects creators appear to venture beyond such a concept of the face as would entail the traditional, one could even say, anthropological, close-up in the films analysed by Deleuze and instead to be headed towards the praxis of building it again from scratch. It is thus no longer a human face. Granted, Deleuze himself regards the face as not necessarily a human-only attribute. Being a close-up, it is placed between two characteristic polar extremes. As Deleuze puts it, 'each time we discover these two poles in something – reflecting surface and intensive micro-movements – we can say that this thing has been treated as a face [visage]. It has been 'envisaged' or rather 'faceified' [visagéifiée]'.[38] On the side of the polar extreme linked to the surface one could place all of the efforts and constant shortcomings in the area of face lighting.[39] A great number of effects creators note that much has yet to be refined in this area. Micro-movements, on the other hand, involve yeoman's work on the animation of the complicated construct that is the digital face. Quantitative data from a number of different projects demonstrate the great effort currently being put in its creation in film production. In *The Lord of the Rings: The Two Towers* (2003, dir. Peter Jackson) Weta Workshop used 675 sculpted images of Gollum's face, for which 9,000 muscle shapes were created.[40] One of the animators for *The Curious Case of Benjamin Button* (2008, dir. David Fincher), Karl Denham, was sent to work for a whole year on the main character's eyes only.[41] Facial mocap is a very useful tool in this arduous process of face construction, but it alone will not suffice. A huge amount of work has to be done by the animators themselves, such as Denham, for they are capable of bringing emotion to faces captured by a mechanical and thus dehumanized system.

In this perspective Deleuze also puts the emergence of the paroxysms appearing to fit squarely within the 'non-human' nature of the film face. The study of the human face for the purposes of digital mapping often ventures beyond natural states. For example, the creators of Gollum's face took advantage of materials showing the facial expressions of people subjected to electrical shock.[42]

Incoherent cyborgs – coherent characters

Modern film techniques also give us the opportunity to watch patchwork structures of characters appearing coherent in their final shapes but resulting from a collaborative effort in production. Collaborative character creation by two actors took place, for example, in *The Curious Case of Benjamin Button* and the cinema version of *Captain America*. A head swap evokes the patchwork construction of Frankenstein, although the film does not show such a sewing together of the monstrous body.

In Fincher's film sequences with the child born as an already old man and getting younger were based on the physiognomy of Brad Pitt and the bodies of several different doubles.[43] Due to as many as 329 scenes involving head replacement, totalling more than an hour of play time, it appears to be justified to speak of body actors and a head actor. Sessions with Brad were filmed after the scenes with Benjamin's 'bodies' from his various developmental stages. Brad was adapting to the doubles' body languages and synchronizing his head with their bodies.[44]

The same concept was applied in Joe Johnston's *Captain America: The First Avenger* (2011).[45] Here, the main character rejected by one military draft board after another for his frail frame decides to enrol for a medical experiment allowing him to become stronger. In the producers' view Chris Evans, the actor playing Steve Rogers – the future Captain America – was too muscular for the first part of the film, showing 'Skinny Steve'. Accordingly, the feeble youngster's body in those sequences was supplied by Leander Deeny. In each of the combined scenes Evans wore oversize clothes or uniforms and helmets in order to have a better feel of the frail hero.

Digital face replacement is a similar collective creation. It was first used also in the tale of the comic-book superhero, *Captain America*, where the emaciation was amplified by sometimes placing Evans's digitally scanned face over Deeny's face. This effect is often used when a stunt performer is replacing the actor for scenes in which the face needs to be visible. This was used, for example, in *Event Horizon* (1997, dir. Paul W.S. Anderson), where Lawrence Fishbourne's face was 'transplanted' onto a burning body provided by his stunt double.[46]

The cyborg as a distribution of subjecthood

Another technique, used in such productions as – in a chronological order – *The Polar Express*, *Beowulf* (2007, dir. Robert Zemeckis), *Avatar* and *Tin Tin* (2011, dir. Steven Spielberg), highlights the current trend for the distribution of subjecthood through the use of complicated mocap techniques for the creation of unique characters that on the one hand reflect a great number of their actors' characteristics in the form of facial expressions, behaviours and simply actor's play, and on the other hand the whole entourage is transferred onto a virtual body that may well not resemble the real one at all. Here, the impressive animated characters on the screen are in reality informational-human hybrids. As shown on the screen, they appear to be animated, but the actor's *animus* is moving them. The actor thus distributes some of his or her characteristics to the hybrid character.

Jody Duncan, who wrote an article on *Beowulf*, asks, 'what for?'[47] Why use such laborious techniques as the scanning of the actors' entire bodies and generating their digital images from scratch, putting on the skin, adapting the light, etc., just to create an effect that is very credible but resembles live-acting shots?

Jerome Chen, the creator of digital effects for *Beowulf*, demonstrates that the answer revolves around the degree of control – with live acting the director has to take all sorts of compromise into account, for example, being unable to get the ideal shot because out of two takes one has great actorship but imperfect photography and the other the opposite. With the system used in this film the whole actor's play could be recorded with no fear about the other aspects of the end effect and with full freedom for the director to build the picture out of raw material from a session with sophisticated mocap incorporating 228 cameras and electro-oculography capable of capturing even the tiniest eyeball movements.[48]

Avatar brings the technology for the creation of such a digital body capable of 'carrying' the actor's subjecthood transferred to it to a whole new level. As Joe Letteri lets on, 'in the past CG character "muscles" have been like baloons under the skin that move based on joint movement and so forth. What we did was simulate real muscles, fat and tissue.'[49]

Work on character models serving as objects for the distribution of the actor's subjecthood often resembles searching for an opportunity for the 'posthuman position' to come to the fore. In this case it would mean such a shape of the model as to provide at once the best transmission of the actor's qualities and the opportunity to create a new being. In *Avatar* the initial Na'vi models had been different. They were replaced after the first tests with live actors and facial motion capture, however. For Na'vi eyes turned out to seem too far apart, the mouth too drawn out in the form of a snout and a myriad of other discrepancies.[50]

The aforementioned strategy of injecting non-anthropomorphic creatures with 'human subjecthood' in the area of prosthetics also appears in the area of creation of informational-human hybrids that, in turn, end up being animals in the final picture. *King Kong*'s production employed a specially developed facial animation system combining the expressions of Andy Serkis (the actor playing the giant ape), captured with the use of a special system, with models of gorilla facial muscles, developed by Weta Digital.[51] Here, we are thus dealing with attempts at creating systems to simulate animal–human hybrids through the use of digital graphics. By necessity, therefore, all such creatures have a human element to them, enabling the audience to better empathize with them but also perpetuating, in a way, the anthropocentric way of thinking about them.[52]

Production hybrids

The quintessential cyborgs of the production stage are creatures, created on the screen, whose cyborgicity results from the combination of human, technological and informational (i.e. graphical and animated) elements (see Figure 3.12). Already in Disney's *Mary Poppins* the scene with the main characters, Mary and Bert, floating on the shells of animated turtles was made with the use of a special blue trolley.[53] *The Chronicles of Narnia: Prince Caspian* (2008, dir. Andrew Adamson) employed special blue-masked self-propelled amphibious vehicles from which the upper halves of centaur bodies played by live actors could 'protrude'.[54] In *John Carter* (2012, Andrew Stanton) the eight-legged animals called thoats and used the characters as mounts were 'played' by electrical off-road vehicles. Special frames were put on top of them to mimic the creatures' backs, being rocked by an operator seated below together with the driver. In both cases rounding out this screen-action framework are 3D graphics completing the creatures' bodies as shown on the screen.[55] These examples

Figure 3.12 The various incarnations of the pre-screen cyborg: hybrid combination of elements of machinery, human body and digital models in blue- or green-masked places in: King Kong (dir. Merian C. Cooper and Ernest B. Schoedsack; p. 117); The Narnia Chronicles (dir. Andrew Adamson; p. 118, upper panel); and John Carter (dir. Andrew Stanton; p. 118, lower panel). Kobal Collection.

illustrate that in the effects cinema the animation of animals is easily supplied by machinery. Hence, the interchangeability of the roles and orders – technological, biological and informational – similar to the one we see in multiple cartoon animations, especially in their initial stage of development, is a characteristic feature of composite picture. Further details from the set of the first part of *The Chronicles of Narnia* confirm these games of hybrids. For it turns out that the centaurs, creatures of strategic importance to the film's action, were produced in all manner of ways. Now they were played by humans with green-masked legs, flexible stilts and powerizers. And now horse shots with digitally generated human torsos were used. Sometimes they were all digitally made.[56]

The film production as an attraction fair

One could say that film production has already for a long time subscribed to the posthuman model of an attraction fair, as defined in this book. This is because of the fact of the choice of instances to play the role of a subject (though not necessarily human subject) in the film. The film space could nowadays be viewed as an interbeing scene due to the matter of such selections. It is an arena witnessing the competitive struggle of subjects of highly varied status, generated by all sorts of procedures. Here too decisions are made at the production stage that will affect the topography of screen subjecthood.

Massive

An interesting example could be the use of Massive – a software suite developed by Weta Digital for the production of *The Lord of the Rings: The Fellowship of the Ring* (2001, dir. Peter Jackson). The programme made it possible to freely build entire crowds of combatants both on the good and the evil sides. For some battle scenes approximately 100,000 participants are estimated to have been generated.[57]

An important factor in the composition of such scenes was to create a sort of subjecthood map of the war theatre. One of the creators of special effects for the trilogy, Matt Aitken, reports that a tripartite topology of agent generated on-screen by Massive was used in the works on all three titles.[58] The differences consisted in the degree of complication: (A) – hi-poly models, the most detailed; (B) – less exacting models and (C) – very tiny silhouettes, sometimes no larger than a couple of pixels. And let us not forget the live actors and extras in the foreground. This configuration necessarily resembles the production of a computer game, which is, incidentally, becoming increasingly popular nowadays, with film production employing video games' graphical engines more and more often. Analogies do not end here, because the degree of complication in the models has no link with the issue of subjecthood. The latter only happens after we realize that Massive and other solutions used in the production of the trilogy touch on the problem of the autonomy of the agents presented on the screen. For Steve Regelous, of *The Lord of the Rings* crew, developed a system of intelligent 'brains' for objects functioning as characters in battles with 7,000–8,000 logical nodes, thanks to which characters were able to react to the changing conditions in their environment. For example, characters' eyesight and hearing were simulated, as well as their sense of touch, so that they could react to obstacles or each other. The creators themselves were able to switch the various elements of this neural network on and off for a greater or smaller number of agents, but the system's primary advantage was the possibility of achieving very realistic crowd behaviours precisely, thanks to the agents being able to react individually to what was happening around them.

Going back to subjecthood topography, one could say that in this case the decisions about the spatial deployment of agents depend on the latter's relative position. Located closer are smarter agents (including live actors and extras in the foreground), and at a greater distance are agents with increasingly limited intelligence scripts, for example, because they are so far away that there is no need to generate details of their silhouettes, which means that the links between intelligence and embodiment need not trouble us here. Scene positioning and plot aspects also can factor in the choices concerning the agents' intelligence and their ontology (live actors, AI scripts). For scenes with a smaller amount of light, playing out in caverns and dungeons, especially with not particularly intelligent Orcs, one can afford to choose less 'smart' characters. Stephen Regelous notes that the scenes in Isengard used agents with very tiny brains compared to the participants of the prologue battle.[59]

Matthew Gratzner positions the topography of subjecthood in yet a different way, observing that in the first part of *The Lord of the Rings* trilogy, in one of the panoramic scenes showing hordes of Orcs descending the stairs, one could find a moment when one of the Orcs is dragging his heels, afraid to continue downstairs.[60] That particular Orc's role is played by an extra having 'realistic' fears that cannot be programmed. The role of live subjects, therefore, in

Gratzner's opinion, is to introduce live inconsistencies and illogicalities to the frame, making the sequence look more believable than one populated only with scripted AI characters.

The digital double

Issues of decisions relating to the character's ontology in the relevant scene also surface in relation to the strategy of using so-called digital doubles, nowadays popular in effects cinema. For the purposes of sequences complicated to compose and produce, high-fidelity character models are created and used wherever a live actor cannot be sent, for example, where even stunt doubles cannot go or where the character's body undergoes modifications that are difficult or impossible to produce with the use of non-digital techniques. In all major productions nowadays all key actors are scanned also in order to have a backup copy in case an additional scene is needed with one of them after the shots.

The primeval beginning of digital doubles were and still continue to be body replicas made of a variety of materials, often equipped with additional animatronic mechanisms. Such type of solutions continue to be used until the present day. The use of an animatronic torso of the Christ in Mel Gibson's *Passion of the Christ* (2004)[61] is a good example of this. Digital techniques, however, appear to be slowly phasing out mechanical solutions. The digital versions of characters are created with the use of very precise 3D scanners. The scanners also have other applications, for example, backup copies of animals, architecture, props, and miniature vehicles.

The use of digital doubles sparks different types of discussions and controversies. Many actors approach cyber-scanning with reserve, out of a fear of live actors being supplanted by digital copies. Some even go as far as patenting their own image to avoid the risk. It is noted, however, that having a digital double is an opportunity for additional revenues for those actors whose digital likeness recorded in this manner is utilized by the video-game industry.

In Joseph Kosinski's *Tron* a digital double is used for a rejuvenated Jeff Bridges. Karl Denham, previously responsible for the fluid morphing of two actors into one body in *Benjamin Button*, draws an important comparison of the two productions:

> A lot of times [in *Curious Case of Benjamin Button*], the stand-in actor had no reflections or highlights in his eyes at all, so we had no reference. Since they were replacing the head anyway, they just hadn't worried too much about carefully

lighting the eyes. You can get away with that if you're shooting a real human being because it's obvious, from a thousand other clues, that it's a real human being. But if you're doing a digital human, you have to have something in the eyes. If you don't, that can be the small detail that kills the whole thing.[62]

One could say this is a type of Turing test digital doubles must pass if they are to be accepted by the audience as actors.

Other special-effects creators also point out that the spectator is the instance testing the credibility of the digital double and often doubting it.[63] They writhe over the fact that the director tells them to build unrealistic characters exempt from the laws of physics. In Rob Coleman's opinion doing so breaks the illusion that is the essence of cinema. Steve Begg claims that digital doubles are a negative influence on action scenes, as the audience can sense that it is being deceived by the character's superhuman abilities. Thus a character's unbelievable powers are the sign to the audience that a digital double is being involved. Nor does the comparison between them and 'human' stunt performers favour digital doubles in experts' eyes. Nick Dudman observes that when the audience see the stunt performer sliding down a rope in the mountains in *Cliffhanger* (1993, dir. Renny Harlin), they are conscious of the necessary effort and hazard on the part of a real human being. With a digital double no such emotional connection exists.

From the production side, another interesting aspect of cyber-cloning is continuity. The difference between the digital double and the actor is not perceivable in those sequences in which the actor beginning the scene in the foreground is combined with the digital counterpart finishing the scene off by performing some sort of complicated acrobatics in the background. Therefore, the hybrid charactering ontology could be said to be resurfacing here. In film the character functions as an agent controlled initially by a live person and subsequently by e.g. the relevant type of rig.

'Non-live' subjects

The possibilities opened up by digital-double creation trigger hopes, here and other, of bringing back to life on the screen actors who are already deceased. This type of effects appears for the first time in films the production of which was interrupted by the death of at least one of the actors. The desire to finish the production fuelled creativity in the use of such effects as would make that possible. Brandon Lee in *The Crow* is one of the most prominent examples. Far less skilful attempts were made to bring back his father, Bruce, as well as Peter

Sellers and Nancy Marchand – the on-screen mother of Tony Soprano. At the same time, the development of digital techniques has been making it possible to create increasingly more detailed and precise character models on the basis of reference materials originating from films and photographs. Having died long before the production of *Sky Captain and the World of Tomorrow*, the unforgettable Laurence Olivier was 'cast' there as Doctor Totenkopf. Audrey Hepburn was similarly revived for an advertisement of Dove chocolate.[64]

Hollywood creators of special effects are sceptical of such type of experimentation. Ned Gorman reminisces that already in the early 1990s he was constantly being pestered to revive Bruce Lee, Marylin Monroe or Elvis Presley. Emerging from this scepticism, however, is an interesting reference to the discussion on artificial intelligence. While the latter, begun with the Touring-test idea, is a discussion about the degree of advancement when it would no longer be possible to distinguish the machine from a human being, the other side of the coin also surfaces in the film chase after the faithful replica of a deceased actor. What I mean here is the stage of progress in the application of computer animation when it becomes possible to generate a character impossible to distinguish from a live human person. Here, the 'personality's' credibility would be judged not by the 'source' in the form of computer replication of advanced thought processes (translating into language) but by the 'effect' being an information creation exhibiting all the subtleties of human behaviour. According to industry specialists, there are conditions for such advanced simulations to be created, but, as Rob Coleman and Volker Engel observe, the essence of film is to show living actors and equip the beings that are created on the screen with the characteristics of live persons, and not to revive the deceased in the form of zeroes and ones, because that is not what the audience want.[65] In their opinion, however, digital copies of living actors, presenting them in more nuanced situations than merely dynamic scenes 'shot' from afar, are going to become more and more suggestive with time.

***

The posthuman contexts of film-production technology discussed in this chapter show that especially in the developing era of digital cinema awaiting the 'human' subjects appearing on the screen is a myriad of diverse challenges involving their destabilization as the principal agents of action. Alternatively, perhaps it would be better to say that the 'human' subjects always retain the principal agency but the activity shifts towards new and sometimes bizarre, although interesting directions. Actors' play is changing so that the matter they come in touch with is more and more often simulated. The lack of contact with the bodies of other actors, the lack of contact with the physicality of items and 3D shapes, etc., open new challenges before them, though film creators often strive to compensate for this lack of reference by launching different previsualization systems or the avatar-based 'simulcam'. The actors are also forced to come to terms with the distribution of their qualities, enfeoffment of their facial expressions, their bearing and movement and speech, and more. Finally, they are forced to reckon with the ultimately invisible splitting of their own body or with the process of its complete erasure.

On the other hand, the above-described characteristics of the green and the blue screen and motion-capture systems show that the new role of the human subject on the set can involve animating the space ('green' helpers) or beings that were previously simulated by objects that are technological (animatronics, dolls, dummies, puppets) rather than informational (animation based on live performance, facial capture or cyber-scanning).

The above problems show, therefore, that the 'yielding of place' results in a multi-fabric and multi-agent substance of entities appearing consistent on the screen. Their existence, of course, entails a variety of challenges in the social space. It is not quite easy to accept the above-described on-screen beings as creations attributed to specific 'living' persons, which translates into problems of authorship and social understanding of the respective ontologies. The inadequacy that comes to the fore here shows itself clearly, for example, in the debate on the Oscar nominations for Andy Serkis. His participation in creating the unforgettable Gollum in *The Lord of the Rings* and Caesar in *Rise of the Planet of the Apes* should, in the opinion of many a critic, have brought him the statuette for the best supporting actor, but he was not even a nominee. Kevin Haug believes that, in addition to Serkis, also the animator involved in the creation of Gollum's character deserved the prize, because – in Haug's view – animators are actors, too, in such cases: 'If they had both been standing there, saying "We are Gollum," that would have been much more interesting.'[66] Haug, however, ignores the remaining participants in Gollum's creation, but it is even more important to realize that the creature is also the effect of the operation of AI scripts, thus not being restricted to human conduct alone.

Characters of this type are the fruit of the attitude Dennis Muren refers to as 'godlike appeal'.[67] Hollywood producers are yielding to it, not wanting to produce films with merely 'regular' effects and solutions because CG (computer graphics) tempt them as a reservoir of godlike potential. The results are not always good for the films, although the technologies being discussed here prove that the production process itself more and more often resembles the act of creation. The above-discussed yeoman's work put in the reproduction of the human face and the meticulous programming of the light in *Avatar* are a demiurgic act of creation of reality and existence from the smallest particles or units such as photons and cells. As Eric Barba says:

> What helped was realizing that replicating a human was a matter of breaking it down into individual pieces. We needed eyelashes, we needed lips, we needed teeth, a tongue and eyes. Once we broke it down into individual components, we could attack each component and figure out how to do it.[68]

The resulting effect is a study of that with which Katherine Hayles's foundational works ends. One of the principal theses in her argument on the consequences of cybernetic turns and the development of the idea of artificial intelligence in *How We Became Posthuman*[69] focuses on the inability to split the AI from embodiment. In a word, there is not an intelligence without a body. The characters generated in film production are the other side of the coin, the fruit of the process of meticulous reproduction of the intelligent body, even though the latter is nowadays mainly a digital body.[70]

Part Two

Tele-visions

4

The Teleprompter and the posthuman repositioning of the gaze

One could say that the connection between the activity of gazing and the posthuman idea was outlined clearly by both Derrida and Lacan in their two 'generic' pictures linked by the idea of the mutual gaze between a human subject and a non-human other. In his cat example Derrida is found naked by a female cat gazing at him, and he feels a 'multifaceted' sort of shame as a result. While the accents in the later part of his train of thought are placed on nakedness and shame, it is still worth recognizing that the mutual gaze is the beginning of the creation of a posthuman relationship. The naked human subject feeling ashamed before the animal gazing at him becomes conscious of his own animality, and thus the previously defined relationship posthumanism occurs here. Both of the 'subjects' in the ritual of gazing are mutually placed in a posthuman position destabilizing the established order of power and authority. This is similar in Lacan's example with the fishing boat on the sea. Now the activity of gazing is what defines subjectivity. When the fisherman asks if Lacan can see the tin floating at some distance from the boat, he also notes that the tin cannot see Lacan. At this time, though we are not dealing with the foundation of the 'other' by the activity of gazing, it still carries destabilizing potential. It invites a critical outlook on subjecthood.[1]

Assuming that both of these examples inspire the 'intimacy of the gaze'[2] between human subjects and animals on the one hand and material (technological) objects on the other hand, what could a 'posthuman anthropology' of the gaze be like in the relationship between the human subject and information? In this chapter I will muster yet another television apparatus, the Teleprompter, in an attempt to draw such a perspective. On the idea level, the device is a direct descendant of the prompt boxes found in theatres. However, at some point it becomes another vehicle revealing rich contexts of relational posthumanism, at this time resulting from different gazing positions, suitable for either synchronic or diachronic analysis.

We can assume that the Teleprompter appeared in the early 1950s as a support appliance for the dynamically developing television industry. According to its creators, Barton and Schlafly,[3] the television industry in the United States was in constant need of new materials, potentially resulting in a multitude of pressing problems. 'One of these problems is the fundamental necessity of memorization.'[4] The author of a 1953 article in Business Screen Magazine even notes that before the arrival of the Teleprompter television used blackboards and chalk, or even small speakers placed behind the actors' ears.[5] A breakthrough was made with the incorporation of TelePrompTer Corp. in 1952 and Fred Barton's patenting of the device.[6]

Figure 4.1 TelePrompTer's four-prompter system.[7]

The prompter sold by Barton's company was intended mainly for the producers of television drama and all sorts of shows that required the participants to speak at length while moving around the studio. The apparatus comprised four remotely controlled screens mounted on height-adjustable tripods (Figure 4.1). The text moving across the screens was synchronized with a central unit, so that actors turning away from the screen could be sure to be able to continue their lines once started.[8] The central unit's operator could also slow the text down or speed it up depending on the actor's speech rate (Figure 4.2).[9] Barton and Schlafly call the operator an accompanist.[10]

Barton's Teleprompter was a technological masterpiece for the time, and its applications inspired the development of spin-off technologies. Underwood Corp came up with special typewriters, called 'videoprinters', printing text in

Figure 4.2 Operator managing the Teleprompter's central unit, increasing or decreasing the scrolling speed. Picture from Fred Barton i H.J. Schlafly, "TelePrompter – New Production Tool", *Journal of Society of Motion Picture and Television Engineers* 58, June 1952, 517.

four copies (one per screen) with one-inch letter height. Standard Register Company developed special yellow printing paper to be glued over in the last minute if there were any corrections to the script.[11] The construction of this version of the prompter shows it to be a technology providing strong 'support' for the text – among other things, the device includes a lamp with which to highlight the text, as well as a clear arrow on the edge, indicating which line is to be read (the 'hot-line').

The Teleprompter's first years in television demonstrate the importance of its place in TV stations and their budgets. CBS alone could spend 1.4 million dollars on payments relating to Teleprompters. The device was praised by soap-opera producers, allowing them to make savings of $250 a day on rehearsal costs.[12] Rather than being sold, Teleprompters were leased at 30 dollars per hour. Already in 1954 the rates fell down to $60 per day for two units, further increasing their availability.[13]

The invention subsequently received numerous improvements. One of the 1952 models was mounted on the camera, either above the lens or below. Jess Oppenheimer's 1954 version, on the other hand, used a mirror in order for the text to be displayed directly in front of the lens and the anchor could look directly into it. This system was met with the best reception in the news, though there were also other solutions. For example, in the 1970s, Honeywells, Inc. developed a device with the lens in between two projectors sliding the text.[14]

More solutions appeared in the 1980s and the 1990s, such as Teleprompters controlled by an Atari 800 computer or equipped with LCD displays. The last patents were granted already in the twenty-first century, such as Nobuo Matsui's of 2005.

Apart from some measure of success in film productions, the Teleprompter was also suggested as an aid for public speakers. In the 1950s Tele Q Corporation of New York sold a pocket prompter with the scrolling speed controlled by the speaker's foot. An electrical set comprising also a printer and paper could be purchased for $495.[15] Experimental pocket prompters actually had appeared much before the 1950s' inventions. The February 1932 issue of Modern Mechanix describes a tiny device for public speakers with a thumb-propelled roll of paper (Figure 4.3).

The prompter was eagerly used in both TV ads and public presentations. For advertising purposes, special audio-visual presentation devices were developed with the incorporation of the prompter as one of the core components (Figure 4.4).

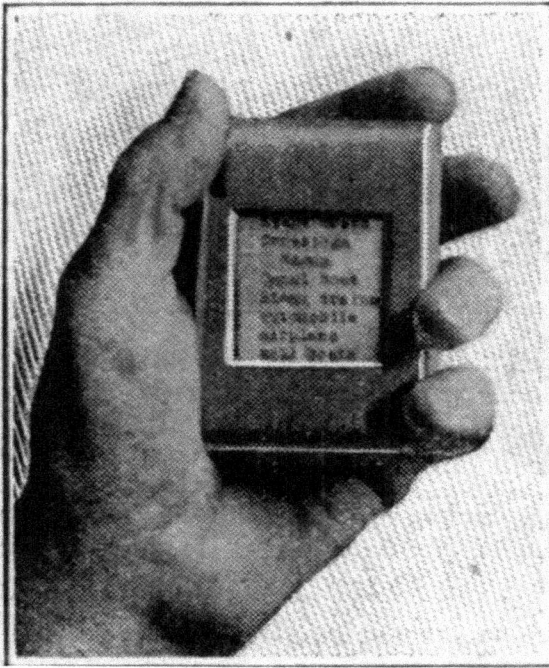

Figure 4.3 Pocket prompter from the 1930s (upper panel) and its modernized and improved version from the 1950s (lower panel).[16]

Figure 4.4 Presentation stand constructed by Anthony Flan of Oakton Engineering and Paula Kohouta of SVE. Picture from "A-V Techniques for the Exhibitor", *Business Screen Magazine* 17 (5) 1956, 41.

Prompters became especially popular in public speaking (Figure 4.5). It started with the Republicans and Eisenhower himself in 1952. Thereafter, practically the majority of American politicians relied on this aid. No wonder that Larry Bird, one of the curators of the National Museum of American History, who had attended all Republican and Democrat conventions starting from 1984, concluded: 'Nowadays, political campaigning – especially national conventions–is built entirely around the machines (…) Everything is put onto that device, even the national anthem and the Pledge of Allegiance.'[17]

The use of prompters on the television (see the shape of modern prompter in Figure 4.6) sparked a diversity of opinion. The device's creators emphasized heavily how it was a device bringing to the actor's work comfort, relaxation and pleasure.

> Watch the screen next time you see a sponsored film. If the actors, or the sponsor himself look particularly relaxed and happy about the whole thing chances are they're peeking at a TelePrompTer when you don't know it.[18]

An executive from a company that began to use the prompter in its public presentations and speeches observed as follows: 'it completely released him from the pre-speech headaches of 100% memorizing and agonizing fear of "forgetting his lines."'[19] Sometimes, the impression upon first contact was entirely different. One of the actors complained that the prompter was too far

Figure 4.5 Early 'side by side prompter' used in public speaking. Picture from "Teleprompter Insures Executive's Meeting Perfomance", *Business Screen Magazine* 15 (7) 1954, 67.

away, so he could not see the text, though he rejoiced at the ability to improvise instead. Joan Harvey, starring in *The Edge of Night* TV series, thus describes her problems with the device: 'Along with shyness goes insecurity, and I was terribly concerned that the very day I might get rattled, and forget a line, would also be the day the teleprompter might not be running!'[20] Some opinions are even more pessimistic:

> No one has any time in TV. The scripts are rarely completed before the shooting deadline. The actor cannot relax with time to study, to improvise, to develop characterization. He has his own personal demon in television – the teleprompter, a mechanical marvel that is activated by an operator who causes the actor's lines, set in type from ½" to 1" high, to appear before the actor's eyes as quickly as he reads them.[21]

Hence, the objectification of television actors and presenters begins to pose a problem. One author expresses satisfaction with how local talents can be used in a greater number of productions, thanks to shortening the rehearsal time.

Figure 4.6 A modern version of the Teleprompter (*Judy Licht working with Teleprompter while presenting* Full Frontal Fashion *on Piazza Duomo, Milan, Italy*). Paolo Margari, CC BY-SA 2.0.

Historical repositioning of the posthuman gaze

A reconstruction of the relationship between the human subjects and the text in the space where the prompter is deployed should begin with the evolutionary change in the topography of that space. The course of this evolution is illustrated on the diagram 4.7. The diagram only includes the evolution of the television prompter, without its various spin-offs and off-shoots for speeches and direct advertising.

The first scenario (A) depicts the prompter from back the pre-television era. At this stage it is hardly conceivable to speak of any gaze fixation or any intimate relationship forming with the text. The actors can sometimes look at the human prompter in the prompter box, but they do so on a rather exceptional basis. The hint is communicated to them orally, and thus there is no eye contact with the text.

The second scenario (B) shows the relationship forming in the first stage of the development of television, with the speaking person being equipped with a piece of paper kept usually on the desk. In this configuration we are dealing with two different orders of gazing. The speaker looks either at the text or at

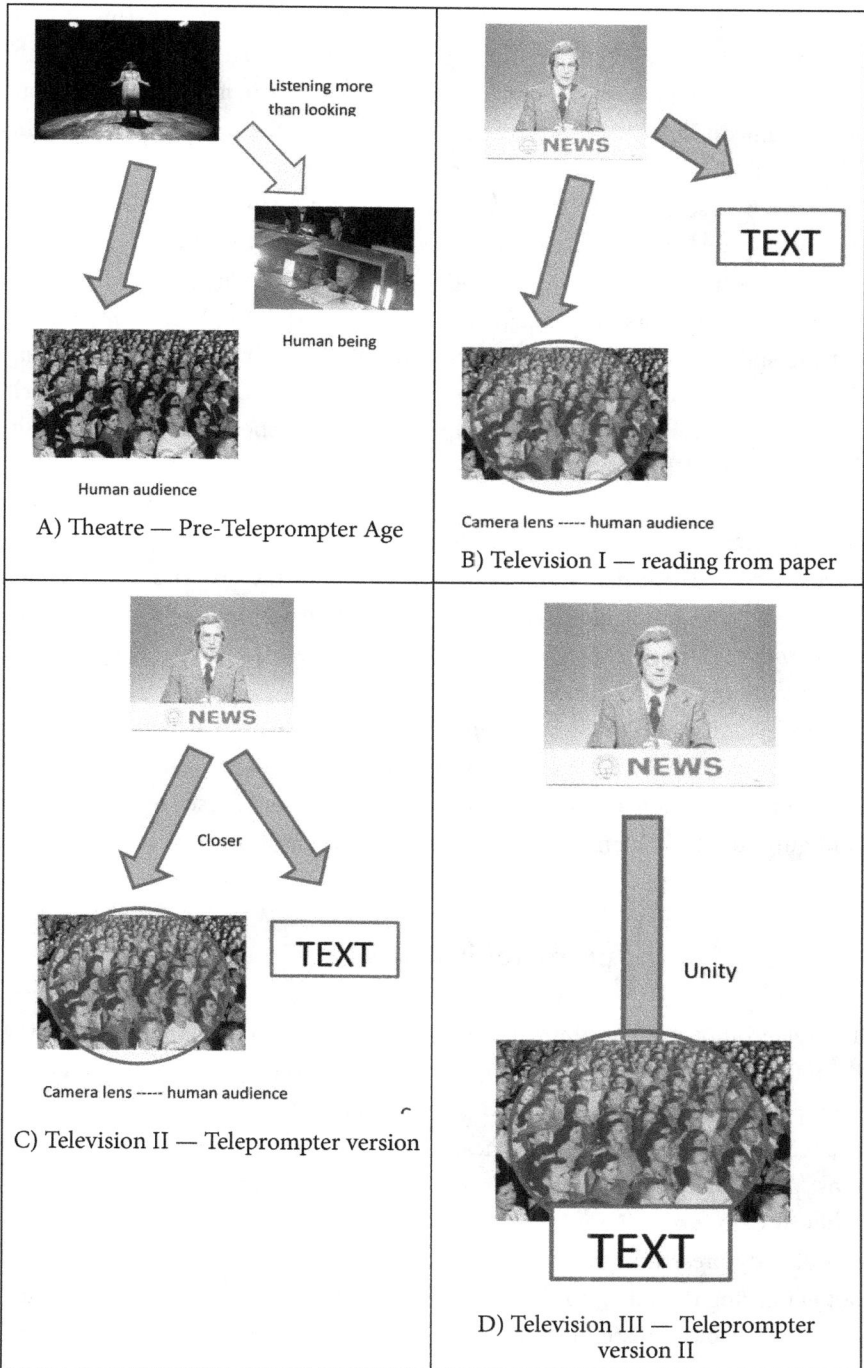

Figure 4.7 Evolution of the orders of the gaze in the Teleprompter.

the audience (the latter concealed behind the eye of the camera). This, on the one hand, prevents the fixation of the gaze, due to the need to rotate constantly between the instances we are addressing. On the other hand, the situation can become uncomfortable both to the presenter and to the audience – hence the efforts of Teleprompter developers to prevent this problem.

In the third scenario (C) the configuration continues to resemble the previous relationship but is brought closer to the next stage. The prompter or the paper sheet are already very close to the lens, although not yet precisely in its axis. An element of uncertainty appears in the recipient's situation. It is not fully clear whether or not the speaker is addressing the recipient. Moments of the speaker's turning directly towards the lens are those times when the suspension of disbelief itself gets suspended for a while. Just as in film, this takes the spectator instantaneously to the meta-level, breaking off the immersion in the created world.

The fourth situation (D) represents a mature speaker–prompter–lens/audience relationship configuration. The fixation of the gaze reaches its highest intensity here. The orders become integrated – both the text and the audience are on one and the same gaze axis. A symbolic commingling of them takes place, thus forming a platform for the creation of posthuman intimacy, which I describe in more detail in the next chapter.

The evolution of the gazing orders on the schemes visualizes how the technological apparatus (compromising the lens and the prompter) 'guides' both of the instances to a posthuman position. It is clearly visible that a specific configuration must form before a posthuman relationship can arise.

The prompter in a synchronic view

The Teleprompter as a posthuman apparatus has a number of qualities reinforcing the relationship that forms between the human subject and the text through the prompter's mediation. One could say that both the prompter's method of application and the device's historical provenance result in theatricity being its most prominent characteristic. For it introduces a mystification into the gazing order by definition – 'I am looking at you, but in truth I am not.' This viewpoint was already present in the first versions of Barton's prompters, with the actors not yet gazing directly into the camera. Tests conducted at the time found the audience unable to distinguish whether the actor was speaking from memory or reading from the prompter.[22]

This mystification became suspicious to Derrida, who devoted quite a lot of space to the prompter in his interview for Bernard Stiegler. Derrida used the prompter as the example of a device that mystifies the eye contact so as to enable the presenter to react to viewing figures.

> What are we to make of the interposition of this text that someone reads while pretending to look straight into the eye of a viewer whom he or she can't see and who, in turn, can't see that the person addressing him may at the same time be in the process of reading from a prompter and of following the evolution of ratings?[23]

This question is met with a 'non-human' answer:

> It's as if the newscaster were reading the artifact called 'Audimat'[24] on the face of an anonymous, artificial, unconscious, abstract, virtual, spectral interlocutor: 'ourselves', 'the others', we who order everything without knowing, like animals, machines, or gods.[25]

The last juxtaposition appears as though taken directly from a pre-defined interbeing attraction fair.

Elsewhere, Derrida points to the dictate of the prompter text, showing the subject–text relationship appears to be more important than the subject–subject relationship in the apparatus:

> When a journalist or politician seems to be speaking to us, in our homes, while looking us straight in the eye, he (or she) is in the process of reading, on screen, at the dictation of a 'prompter', a text composed somewhere else, at some other time, sometimes by others, or even by a whole network of anonymous authors.[26]

Here too resounds a type of non-human perception of relationships built by the prompter. The text, just as elsewhere with Derrida, has the ability to win its independence and become a separate instance in its own right, put on an equal footing with the subject. In the prompter – due to its overwhelming characteristics – the relationship between the speaking person and the audience becomes colourable and self-referential, while the 'other' we are contacting becomes 'flickering'.

We can find an anthropological and communicational analysis of the prompter's operation only in a scarce few academic studies. Paddy Scannell gives it some little room in his article about television recordings as sources of historical knowledge.[27] In his interesting analysis, he appears to draw the opposite conclusion to Derrida's – the prompter is a technology for building trust rather than suspicion. It makes it possible to establish eye contact where otherwise it would be difficult to do so because a television caster cannot afford to improvise but also cannot constantly show only the top of his or her head to the audience.

What does this mean to our analysis? One could say that the apparatus seen in the perspective of posthumanism enables the creation of an intimate relationship between the speaker and the audience by simulation that plays out in the construction of an intimate relationship between the subject and the text. Such negotiating of position in the relationships among the instances – speaker, text, audience – takes place firstly within one gaze apparatus (within the confines of a single plane) and secondly in reliance on the above-mentioned theatricity. Whether we believe, with Derrida, that we are watching a theatre of mystification with the underlying suspicion that the participants are becoming non-human, or, after Scannell, we believe that the trust appearing in the prompter broadcast or recording 'depends on and is a result of performances that generate effects of trust'.[28] In both cases we are dealing with an apparatus laying the foundation for posthuman intimacy through theatrical convention with all the consequences of this, already discussed above. This apparatus could also be understood to be a mechanism combining human and mechanical elements – not only the speaker but also the operator in charge of the scrolling speed are subordinated to the concept of the ideal representation of the text, with such synchronization as to present the speaker–text relationship to the audience as a speaker–audience relationship.

There are also some accounts of simulated, although appearing credible to the audience, communication configurations established among actors in the studio on the basis of intimate relationships with the prompter text. An example of this can be found in Figure 4.8.

In addition to employing the ideas of theatricity and mystification, it could be productive to include Lacan's and Sartre's gaze idea in the interpretation of the prompter.

Lacan builds his own gaze theory on the basis of Sartre's. However, he emphasizes not the activity of looking but the intention that forms in the 'Other' and the subject's knowledge of this intention. Hence the metaphor of a window (or one-way mirror)[29] behind which an acquaintance can be waiting, whom we cannot see but who can gaze at us, since we know of the possibility that he or she is waiting for us there.[30]

We can assume the speaker-prompter configuration to be, in a way, such a one-way mirror to Lacan. For the presenter is perfectly aware that the audience

Figure 4.8 A prompter system developed by TelePrompTer and used in the production of a television show. The characters' conversation is the product of two separate orders of gazing on the text. Picture from "New Business Tool: The TelePrompTer", *Business Screen Magazine. Production Review* 14 (1) 1953, 112.

is located behind the camera's eye, although indirectly. With things being so, the Lacanian fixation of the audience's gaze on the speaker can occur. He or she becomes its object, even without experiencing it directly. But the necessary knowledge, according to Lacan's definition, is there. The problem is that this interpretation could apply to just about any television programme, with no distinction based on the use of the prompter.

Another difficulty, if one is to look for posthuman contexts in the prompter according to Lacan's idea, arises from the fact that while in Derrida's example with the cat (cited at the beginning of this chapter) the cat is indeed gazing at him, in the case of the prompter, just as with Lacan's tin, the text is not gazing at the speaker. We could, of course, conclude that the posthuman position does arise here, given how the joining of the text instance with the audience instance permits the caster to attribute the text with gazing,[31] but any such interpretation appears to be somewhat simplistic at this stage. A more detailed description could be achieved by borrowing from Sartre to be able to describe the specific interchangeability of roles among the text, the speaker and the audience playing out in the prompter's apparatus.

With Sartre, the subject is taken out of a set of other visible elements (objects) in an act of bilateral gaze, which is aptly remarked upon by the following observation: '"Being-seen-by-the-Other" is the truth of "seeing-the-Other."'[32] In other words, in his opinion, 'the Other is on principle the one who looks at me'.[33] Sartre attaches much importance to this act, for the latter builds our awareness of existence: 'Each look makes us prove concretely – and in the indubitable certainty of the cogito – that we exist for all living men.'[34]

Thus, if this act is the 'fundamental connection which must form the basis of any theory concerning the Other',[35] then it would seem that the prompter is transmitting to us some fundamental non-human truth in connection with how, in using it, we look at the text and not at the Other. Herein lies some sort of extraordinarily mysterious potential for challenging Sartre's idea of the gaze – a potential worth exploring in more detail.

In reference to the posthuman perspective, we could say that some attempts at demystification have already been made, similarly to how the just-mentioned gaze of Derrida's cat clearly demystifies the act of gazing as an act of defining humanity. Experiments in robotics, attempting in various ways to simulate the sense of sight, also somewhat undermine this configuration – at this time on the machine side. By contrast, telematics allow us to sustain this feeling, as the eye contact is sustained whether the communication is direct or mediated. The prompter itself, however, becomes a universal machine for the demystification of our core sense of being in the world – since we are capable of falsifying it. The text being scrolled on the prompter's display invades this fundamental I-and-the-Other optic of the gaze through a repositioning that alters the roles codified by Sartre.

To the author of *Being and Nothingness*, the subject is founded on the act of gazing in how the Other as a subject is initially an object to us, similarly to how all elements of the scene are, but distinguishes itself by the act of turning in our direction and thus becomes a subject. In the prompter, by contrast, highly distinctive repositioning occurs.

The following sentence would be true to the speaker: 'I gaze at the text, and I imagine it to be a subject gazing at me. Thus, the text becomes a subject even if it does not gaze at me (or, more precisely, it assumes the position of a subject).' On the other hand, the spectator's interpretation would be as follows: 'I look at the speaker, who appears to me to be gazing at me, so she should be a subject, but because in reality she is looking at text, she continues to be an object. An object that has not yet been uplifted from that status.'

It appears that a feeling of deep alienation, so troubling to Derrida in his perception of the prompter, could be experienced here. Similar sensations can appear also if we realize the mischievous nature of the one of a variation of the prompter first used by Errol Morris in his documentary, *Fog of War*.[36] Interrotron, for such is the device's name, does not display text in a mirror pointed at the camera's lens. It shows the image of our character during the interview. This is because the creators wanted to achieve the impression of speaking directly to the camera, as though to the interlocutor. The audience could experience consternation, being addressed by a character who in reality sees a 'hologram' of the face of another person present in the studio.

The above-described repositioning imbues the prompter with yet another posthuman characteristic. What we have to do is a vehicle repositioning subject–object relationships and doing so in the sphere of gazing, which occupies a very important place in the process of defining subjecthood and our existence in the world. In this way it joins the ranks of apparatus capable of deep reformatting of the humanist idea.

Pseudo-documentaries – the post-propter era (historical appendix)

Increased knowledge of the prompter's deep grammar can turn out to be useful in the process of analysing its use in the recently fashionable pseudo-documentary format.

Pseudo-documentaries are usually defined in relation to mockumentaries on the one hand and to reality television on the other hand. In this part of the book I will be focusing on the subgenre of low-budget TV shows (sometimes called 'pseudo-docu-soaps') in which a fictional and episodic plot is presented in documentary style. For such shows non-professional actors are hired who make abundant use of the Teleprompter in the various plot points when commenting in-character on the main events of the story.

One could say that pseudo-docus brings their actors closer to the position of a computer algorithm. Here, the television caster's becoming lost in the context and origin of the overwhelming text coming from the prompter – which Derrida believes to be communicated – acquires another couple of non-human contexts. The convention for many such productions is to employ the prompter in a different way from the ones discussed so far – a way we could describe as being the last stage, a sort of post-prompter, in which the creators no longer even care to simulate eye contact between the actor and the audience.[37] Pseudo-documentaries constitute the last stage of gaze fixation on the text, in the sense defined by Lacan. We no longer speak of any simulation or theatrical spectacle. There is only a rigid relationship with the text, lacking any nuance. One could go as far as drawing a line from the characters' eyes to the place where the text is. In Sartre's terms, we could describe this as the 'gaze-as-object' (*objet-regard*)[38] or 'gaze-the-seen' (*regard-regardé*).[39]

This configuration of the camera, the actor and the prompter (Figure 4.9) resembles on the one hand the convention followed by programmes from the 1950s, which is when the Teleprompter made its first television appearance, thanks to Barton and his partners. The history of this technology is circular in a way. On the other hand, the character is placed in the position of the interviewee in an intervention programme, which is intended to reinforce the authenticity of the mystified story. We could again conclude that the text is placed in the position of and replacing the interviewer. Instead of a live journalist, the character turns to the text.

However, the attempt to leverage this to reinforce the authenticity of the tale is not successful. Due to the overwhelming instance of the text, the character is reduced to a role reminiscent of the one played by presenters in interactive programmes – subordinated virtual bots with a range of options reduced to several selected forms of communication outside which they are not allowed to go.[40] Therefore, the mischievously previously outlined scheme of relationship between the instances returns to the point of dealing with separate gazing orders – speaker–lens/audience and speaker–text from the paper/prompter (away from the camera lens), but at this time the text–character relationship is the one that dominates, while the relationship with the audience is sidelined. In this case we could even say the producers do not care to conceal the prompter in any special way. While the prompter is not visible in itself, the relationship between the text and the actor is perfectly conspicuous. As the actor is usually untrained, there is not even a chance to rely on any professional tricks to eliminate this impression of alienation.

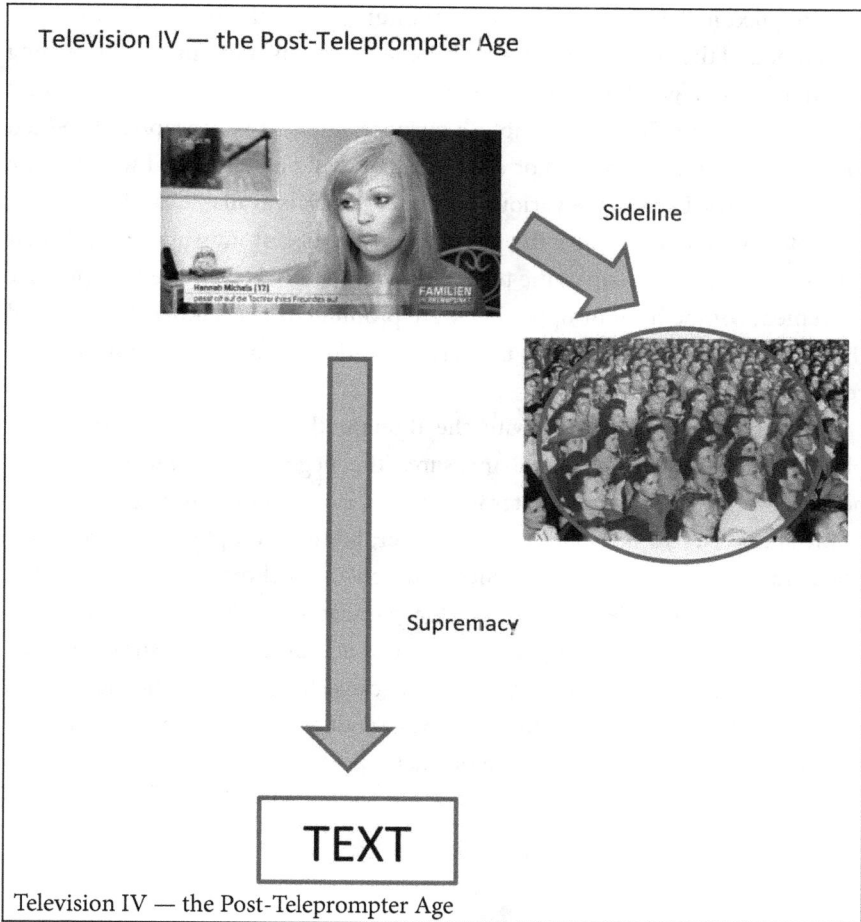

Television IV — the Post-Teleprompter Age

Sideline

Supremacy

TEXT

Television IV — the Post-Teleprompter Age

Figure 4.9 Configuration of gazing orders in a pseudo-documentary.

***

The prompter is an example of yet another apparatus with a *sui-generis* dichotomous structure. By many creators and users alike it is regarded as a pleasure vehicle – it allows one to feel comfortable and look natural on the screen, also improving one's self-esteem. It frees one of the need to remember the text. On the other hand, the intimate relationship with the text formats the user in a number of ways. On a communication level, the gaze – or fixation of it – on the scrolling text makes the reality of the communication taking place between the presenter and the audience hard to fully believe.[41] Speakers go on the air reading text that sounds good and allows them to be natural but not text that always means something. For the prompter's purposes the text is appropriately edited to remove complex structures or elements that could be visualized with the use of infographics. Even in the various prompter tutorials available on the internet, presenters note that they are the providers of important information and their role is to successfully deliver the text. On the non-verbal level, overly expressive movements of the head or upper body are prohibited, as is taking their eyes off the text, and they are required to use gestures and facial impressions purportedly reinforcing naturalness.

We could summarize this with the thought that the apparatus doles out pleasure and suffering in equal measure. The negotiation game playing out between the text and the presenter is aptly described by the advice given by one of the speakers: 'Do not follow the prompter; let the prompter follow you.' It is not always the matter of competence and conscious choice. On the television set in the various outlets in the world, a popular joke played by the crew on the speaker is to intentionally replace the text scrolling on the prompter. Such situations highlight 'seduction' by the text, because the anchors, when faced with the necessity of saying something funny, cannot liberate themselves from the text's oppression in order to be able to react quickly enough.

Posthumanism through interaction: intimacies, gaze and collective creations in *Winky Dink and You*

The games of communication subjects and of text 'spiced' with phenomenology of the gaze, as found in the Teleprompter and discussed in the previous chapter, are not an exhaustive list of all posthuman threads in the television medium. Another vehicle worthy of analysis due to other forms of intimacy created for a set of non-material objects presented on the screen and due to the 'game of gaze' is a technology hailed as the beginning of interactive television in the world. What I have in mind here is a CBS series for children from the 1950s, titled *Winky Dink and You*, followed by an animated series under the same title brought back in 1969–73, incorporating a specific interactive interface.

The title itself already establishes a relationship that is a novelty, in a way, in the world of broadcasts for children. Beforehand and often afterward, broadcasts for children have been based on duos made up of presenters and characters usually originating from puppets. Winky Dink is an animated character partnered by a presenter, Jack Barry, in the first cycle, but it turns out that a key role in the development of on-screen action is played by the show's young audience. In the words of the creator, Edwin Wyckoff, 'and You' is the pivotal part of the title distinguishing it from many other television productions.[1] For the children gathered in front of the screen were equipped with a 'magic' set enabling interaction (Figure 5.1). This included a special foil to attach directly to the screen by static electricity, as well as a set of crayons and a cloth to wipe the drawing. Children received various types of tasks, thanks to which the action playing out on the screen could be supplemented with elements drawn on the fly. This gave the audience a sense of active participation in the show and resulted in individual creations inspired by communications from the screen.

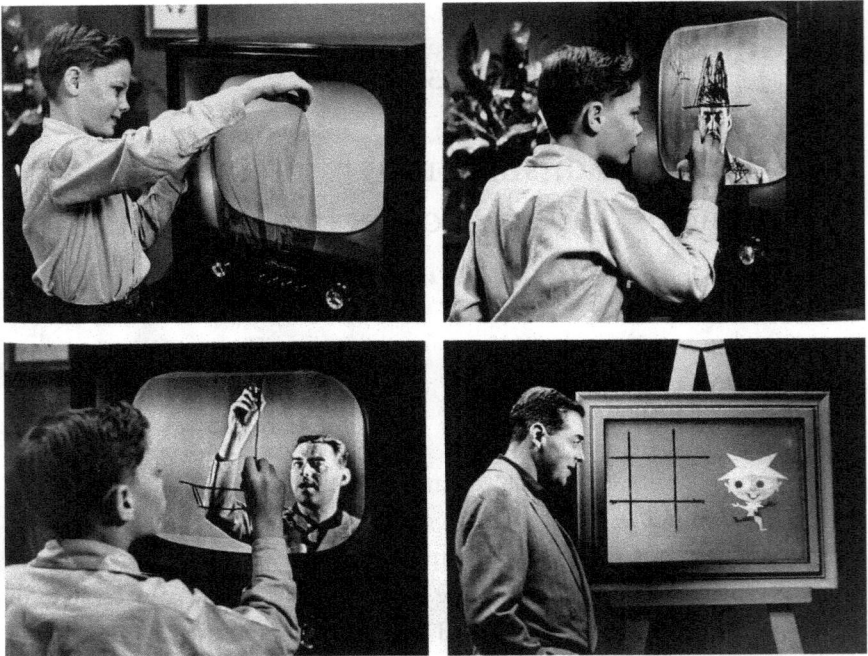

Figure 5.1 Interactive apparatus of *Winky Dink and You*. Everett Collection/EastNews.

The circumstances in which the show came to life also demarcated the field for the emergence of hybrid relationships and the optics of interbeing fair. The creator team came up with an idea of an interactive show when working on standards for the television screen.[2] After complaints from a sponsor who kept losing the first and the last letters of its corporate name due to bad frame cropping, Harry Prichett, one of the employees of the ad agency tasked with the project, was asked to develop a safe-zone standard for television screens, guaranteeing freedom from such problems despite all the differences in broadcasting systems, image formats and other parameters. During his work on this, Prichett would mark some orientation points in various locations on the screen or, in more entertainingly, supplement the television image with new elements. Sometimes that was a hat painted for a character visible on the screen, and sometimes he produced more advanced drawings, for example, when he drew an additional character in between the two participants of a boxing match. His colleagues, supplying the audience for such experimental hybrid performances, viewed the idea of painting on the screen as an innovation, and this led to the proposal of creating a programme for children on the same basis.

If looking for inspiring posthuman contexts in *Winky*, the first series of episodes broadcast from 1953 to 1957, appears to be a somewhat more promising fishing ground on account of the complexity of the communication situation in it. *Winky*'s first series comes with a similar inherent hybridity as described in the chapter dedicated to animation. The second series, broadcast from 1969 onward, was an animated one. Thus, there was no narrator-presenter, nor any off-voice. Instead, the characters themselves – usually Winky Dink and his dog, Woofer – would communicate with the audience.

Whether addressing the first or the second series of episodes, three contexts propelling the analysis in the direction of posthumanism are worth highlighting. The first such context is the complicated configuration of the gaze relationship, in a way a continuation of the topics emerging in the analysis of the Teleprompter, though also including new observations. The second one is a sphere of intimacy with animated characters, constructed along presenter-character and audience-character lines, precisely by interaction. The third and last one is the problem of the hybridity of the screen characters themselves. One could say that such characters, complemented by the young spectators using their 'magic sets', are the primeval beginning of collectively created characters such as Benjamin Button and Captain America, discussed in the chapter about special effects. I will analyse two episodes in the first series and thirty in the series produced in the 1970s.

Winky Dink and You only ever gets laconic mentions in the subject literature – mainly due to its innovativeness as the very beginning of interactive television,[3] or it is compared to modern interactive shows.[4] The creators themselves referred to this pre-interactivity audience participation or activision.[5]

Several sources make a critical mention of the show's functioning as a sales platform,[6] especially in the context of pushing the consumers' age limits.[7] In Wyckoff's own words, 'we tried to winkydize as much as possible'.[8] The creators opted to commercialize the show by creating an entertainment supersystem on its basis, which made possible the marketing of more than thirty products such as board games, books, colouring pages, magic puzzles, Halloween outfits and more. In the 1970s, many of those gadgets were sold in hypermarkets when the second animated series was broadcast on the television. Jerry Wellman also appears to be referring to this sort of commercialization in his artistic performance. He uses the programme, remixed, as a matrix for graphics drawn with a fury. A critical view of the show from the perspective of the fifty-ninth anniversary of its début prompts the artists to intensify, by appropriate editing, the mechanicity of the speaker's commands coming down from the screen and to make mischievous comments about the prices charged for the products, which, in his opinion, should be higher.

The show has attracted practically just one instance of broader discussion of its narrative patterns (the second series), which a trio of researchers from Napier University used in order to develop their own interactive animation.[9]

Gaze, subject and object games

Of all the episodes of the first series attention is drawn to the one of which the plot structure is based on games with gaze and with a diversity of screens and lenses having the power to change the directionality and the recipients of such activities.[10] Here, the act of communication is broken into a number of different orders, and the status of the subjects participating in the plot depends on a highly diverse range of factors such as the ontology (animated characters, people, animals), presentation technology (live action, projector-emitted animation, directly filmed cut-out animation, size in the frame and proportion in relation to other agents, camera distance, etc.).

In the first part of the analysed episode Winky appears as a photographer causing his model, Barry, to fall below the screen level. At the beginning there are several frames one could regard as a demystification of the technology used, and, in a way, of the television medium in general. The show begins with presenter Jack Barry greeting the audience from behind a glass panel. The speaker is presented as one who is drawing on the television screen as though from its other, studio side. At once, therefore, the convention of the fading of the television screen into invisibility is broken. As Ed Wycoff puts it, the show also defeated the fourth-wall convention. The young spectator transcended it by manipulating the objects of the television world.[11]

One could say that at this occasion Barry also demystifies the Teleprompter, the latter being as it is that invisible glass panel which has text placed on it in the same location. In the show, however, the prompter constitutes as if another layer expanding the whole complicated apparatus. It is used by Barry multiple times during the show, and even though unseen by the audience, it serves as yet another plane in this complicated configuration, one that should not be forgotten. The various kinds of texts that are decoded by the young spectators during the show after emerging as the outcome of an interactive task could also be regarded as a sort of critique of the Teleprompter. It is symbolic that in this case the text, supposed to be meticulously hidden in the prompter, is poncing around the screen and becoming a form devoid of any such 'transparent' character as the shapes drawn by children and merging into the elements of the presented world. The various ways in which creative spectators would undercut the show's idea probably bore the same character of demystification. The children would sometimes draw different shapes than they had been told, or they would act on their own initiative in bestowing the presenter with additional accessories such as a pair of glasses.

One should not forget the separate *dispositif* connected with Winky's own projection, either. Winky appears on his own screen. He is a character to whom Barry speaks and who, although in a simplified way, moves around in reaction to what is going on in the studio. The clearly set places for the 'participants' of the communication make it so that a relationship similar to the one that appears in hybrid cinema also starts here. Barry and Winky – subjects hailing from 'two different worlds' – communicate with each other, but there is also a relationship that forms between the animated characters and the young audience. This is shown especially clearly in the second series, from the 1970s, where in each episode the audience is addressed by either Winky himself or his dog, Woofy, or sometimes by Winky's cousin, Dorabell.

In the analysed episode the narration is sometimes interspersed with shots of a girl called Helen, herself presumably positioned in front of a television screen in Pennsylvania (which would be difficult to verify) and draws whatever is shown on the screen, according to directions she receives. Here, the presenter sets off another story-within-a-story level, as he speaks both to the girl and to the audience from the television set in her home, thus from a 'secondary' receiver. The goal of the utterances addressed to the girl is on the one hand to show the other spectators gathered in front of the screen how the 'magic set' works and on the other hand to encourage those members of the audience who have not yet done so to send 5 cents to CBS in order to purchase a set of their own. Interestingly, Helen herself is a one-person representation of the audience, its embodiment, at once the seen and the seeing.

The shape of the communication model here is influenced also by other artists present in the studio. The episodes of the first series were live broadcasts, raising the difficulty bar a lot but simultaneously motivating the team to look for innovative solutions. Winky and a variety of characters complemented by the audience were animated live. Each such character required voice acting, as exemplified by Winky himself, borrowing his voice from none other than Mae Questel, previously the 'voice' of Betty Boop. Assisting Barry when he had to draw something on the screen was a professional cartoonist. The cartoonist would previously leave an outline of the drawing on the screen, to be invisible to the audience and retraced by the speaker during the show. To this end, they used a blue or red felt-tip pen leaving a trace that was invisible to the black-and-white receivers of the time.

Another episode in the first series[12] focuses on games around the identity of human beings. One of the characters welcomes the children while wearing a gorilla mask. As a result, the whole sequence with live actors revolves around the prank the assistant, Mr Bungle (Dayton Allen), wanting to play on Barry and Barry's neighbour, Mrs Twitter (Pat Hosley). He allegedly invents a magic serum capable of turning humans into gorillas. A pseudo-animal gorilla played by one of the actors enters the scene and is acknowledged as being real by the characters, for the mask cannot be removed from his face. The 'gorilla' allegedly has appeared in a previous episode. This is another example of casting human replacements in animal roles, but what is interesting in this context is that for a broadcast some time prior the creators actually did bring into the studio a real chimpanzee that began to perform friction movements and could thus no longer be shown at certain times expected by the script.[13] The 'human gorilla' in the analysed episode is decent and plants a kiss on the presenter's forehead instead. It is a 'replacement' also for cost reasons, because the earlier hire of a monkey had cost more than Barry and all other crew members' pay for that particular episode.

The analysed episode also shows new animated characters enriching the show. Barry does the voice acting for two interactive animations featuring such characters as Dusty Dan and Mike McBean. In other episodes the children had the opportunity to meet the pirate, Jean Lafitte. Wyckoff explains that the new characters are introduced because of Winky's disproportionality. He becomes the series' trademark and takes part in hybrid scenes with Barry but his head is too large to be able to properly arrange the set in the animations and be able to fit other characters in the frame easily.

'Intimate collaboration' – collaborative creation of a screen character

The episode with Winky as a photographer features as many as four new characters created by the show's creators and the child audience together. The first three are members of Winky's family, whom the young spectators could 'supplement' with all sorts of details that were missing. Cousin Slim has no nose, and the children are also requested to draw a red flower in his button hole. Aunt Martha is missing eyebrows and a pearl necklace. And Captain Muscle asks for a pipe. The end part of the episode introduces the character of a lady whose outline is inscribed in a universal shape previously drawn by the children. First it is the outline of a fish tank, then of a tea kettle and finally of the head of a woman drinking tea with the presenter.

This characteristic shape-changing focuses around the peculiar logic of the series' presented world. The latter is governed by a logic Wyckleff calls 'fixed position'. The various individual elements of the interactive plot are grafted onto a rigidly anchored shape the children draw on the screen when the show is aired. This 'fixed position' is the most frequent operation used in the second, animated series. In this way, for example, in *U-boat in the Moat*, children draw the outline of King Cookie's nose and button, which go on to become a submarine controlled by Winky. In *Igenosaurus*, ability to shape-change affects the objects' physicality – a triangular light beam transforms into a megaphone.

The newer, animated series also sometimes features joint character creation, albeit on the basis of stop-motion animation. By contrast, a large group of characters created in the first series are live-animated from cut-outs. In *Woofer for the Defense* Winky's main opponent, Harum Scarum, emerges from the combined shapes of a telephone, hat and rock drawn by children on the screen. In *Oky Poky* a tiger's head becomes the helmet of Sir Dancealot, and in *Dig We Must* a giant talking chicken forms out of the outline of a huge boulder.

In all these episodes the process of character co-creation is an activity that establishes a very intimate relationship between the character and the audience. Characters are given highly personalized shapes, and parts of the body are the creation of each user individually. Though transcending the screen world is usually done by giving instructions to the children, the second series' episode titled *Hot Fiddle* shows an interesting motif of metalepsis, somewhat deeper in character. The wizard, Harum Scarum, uses a special violin to terrorize the orchestra that is about to give a concert in a park. The violin's unique power is the ability to set the musicians' notes on fire. In the climax Harum moves the violin to a special frequency band in order to melt the child audience's crayons, outside of the presented world. The plain is 'foiled' because the children are asked by Winky to replace the bow with a saw that will destroy the instrument.

Similar intimacy is also formed with the presenter. In the first series shapes were often drawn directly by following Barry's finger. Symbolically, the television screen's glass panel thus became the surface touched by both parties at the same time and as though in the same place.

Winky as a cyborgical defragmentation vehicle

Numerous interesting observations can be found in both series if, contrary to the creators' intention, we take a critical look at the show without becoming involved in the interaction. The inconsistency and sense of loss then surfacing, perhaps not foreign to those of the audience who had not purchased a magic set, lay another meta-level with various posthuman 'seams' visible on it. If we make the conscious choice not to supplement the frame with the various missing elements, *Winky Dink and You* turns out to abound with defragmentation, splintering and Sartrean 'nothinging'. Here, the audience is the custodian of the limits of the animated body – the delimitation makes it possible to conceal inconsistency, abstraction and lack of logic. With supplementation out of the picture, Winky begins to act like an all-defragmenting peep show.

Such micro-scale defragmentation as takes place in this show appears to also be a macro-scale defragmentation characteristic of the television apparatus. As Jeffrey Sconce observes:

> Whereas psychoanalytic theories of film spectatorship imagined the cinematic apparatus as 'productive' of subjectivity, models of spectatorship in television regard the apparatus as a means toward the estrangement and disassociation of the subject. Television divorces the subject from reality, not in an ideological form of 'imaginary relations' or "false consciousness," but through a seemingly literal electronic intervention that displaces the real and scrambles the mind of the subject.[14]

As for the constitution and consistency of the screen body, it is worth noting that the latter often is an incomplete body – one with some organs detached from it. The organs levitate around the frame somewhat freely. In the photographer episode the woman's silhouette not supplemented with the outline of her head is represented only by animated mouth and hand holding a cup of tea (see Figure 5.2). In one of the episodes in the second series, *Twinkle Little Star*, just the heads of Winky and Woofy embark on the journey. In other episodes only the torsos are travelling around. In *Woofer for the Defence* Harum Scarum swaps hair and hats with a member of the jury. In *Scubie Rubies* Winky's head becomes an independent route marker showing to cousin Dorabell where the characters absorbed into a painting are located in it.

Such 'organs without bodies' have something perverse to them; in a way, they are traces of subjects that were supposed to have been cohesive agents on the screen but are not so and thus their status is somewhere in between – they simultaneously are and are not subjects in the show's plot.

This state of absence from the screen resulting from having refrained from participating in the interaction sometimes leads to the emergence of a specific type of nothingness. It is the type of subjectivized nothingness we have already encountered in the case of the green screen used in film and television production. In *The Chocolate Cookie Caper* Harum and his cat are sucked into the vacuum cleaner's bag. Without the vacuum cleaner's outline the whole thing

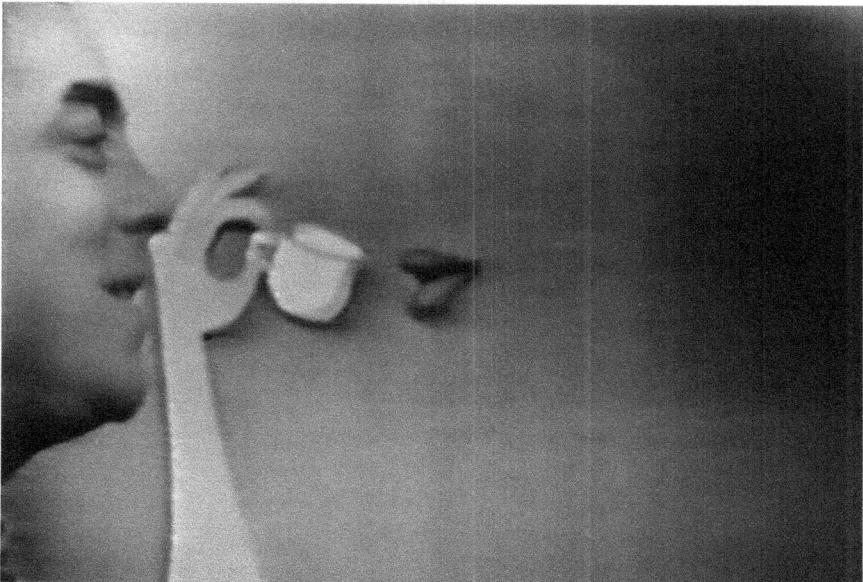

Figure 5.2 The conversation with 'organs without bodies' in *Edgar the Auto* episode.

looks as though the air were having a cough. In *Woofer for the Defence* a hairless Harum looks as though he had his skull opened. *Underground Gardens* features an enormous mole missing half its head where a helmet with a headlight is expected to be drawn. This nothingness is sometimes so powerful that it affects the logic of the presented world. The characters float in the air because there is no vehicle for them in sight. In *Hot Fiddle* unless you draw a cloud for the rain that is about to fall it will be raining from the sun!

Erasing elements no longer displayed on the screen is a multi-faceted activity essential to the entirety of the narration. In *Simple Scarum* an important aspect in Harum's therapy is erasing his hat with 'Dunce' captioned on it, which his teacher had him wear when he was young. In the photographer episode from the first series, the works on the 'supplementation' of Aunt Martha leave Uncle Muscle wearing a pearl necklace he requests assistance in removing. The creators make a whole plot node of it, as Muscle grows irritated with the feminine jewellery on his neck. Erasing is an interesting activity also because at some points it involves removing children's drawings from the screen, and in some cases it leads to making the children believe they can erase animated elements drawn by the animators. The episodes of both series feature a problem that could be defined as orphaned shapes. Due to the dynamic action the children were not always in a position to remove their drawings quickly. In one episode – *The Kindly Defender* – Harum Scarum actually steps out of his outline, which he leaves for several seconds on the screen, while fleeing the courtroom. This is because no suitable plot solution could be found such as would have allowed the children to erase the outline sooner. In such situations, the children's drawings, which on the one hand were a guarantee of the consistency of the presented world, thus became shapes demystifying the interaction concept on the other hand. Accordingly, one could regard them as holding a dual status, strictly connected with the issue of temporal placement – they sustain the illusion for some time but subvert it when they remain too long on the screen.

***

Although it was imputed to the creators that the close contact between the children and the television set during the first serious could involve exposure to dangerous radiation and that some children could develop a tendency to draw directly on the screen, the show turned out to be a great success. Ed Wyckoff reminisces that during as few as four years of the first series 265 episodes were produced and estimates about 5 million children to have purchased their magic sets. The animated series contained another sixty-nine episodes. The power of the animated interactivity manifesting itself here simultaneously demonstrates that we are dealing with an apparatus for multilateral distribution of subjectivity. The multi-ingredient, multi-level act of communication taking place here enables the formation of a diversity of planes for intimacy between 'human' and 'non-human' participants of the process and also the foundation of collective entities whose activities are based in different degrees on both the show's creators and the activity and creativity of the young audience. The inextricably linked acts of seeing and being seen – gazing and being gazed upon, in Lacan's terms – lay the foundation or an intricate web of dependencies wherein the subject and object nature of the agents changes constantly and undergoes a constant critique. Unfortunately, the intimacy protocol established in the show also makes it a convenient production line for market action. The first series' outro provides a symbolic closure for the various orders manifested in the show – the market pressure, as well as the subjecthood games and the complicate gaze configurations. In some episodes the screen is gradually 'devoured' by Winky's all-absorbing eye; in others, that eye is the one contained in the CBS logo.

Television phone-in quiz shows as vehicles for deep digitization

The television apparatus may often present itself as a technology putting a stigma on the subject–message relationship. In this chapter I will show in what way the specific television genre that is the television phone-in quiz shows can become a vehicle to impose a systemic relationship on the human subject. Here, the presenter will appear as a special element of a closed autopoietic system reacting in a special way to disturbances and building a unique posthuman relationship with the media message.

Interactive television, which has recently been a popular concept and which relies on the stimulation of audience activity by contact with the studio through various forms of connectivity such as telephone conversations, text messages and internet chatrooms, takes upon a variety of dimensions. We can encounter various forms of voting in this manner, content selection (e.g. musical clips), participation in video games played on the television screen and so on. There is a discussion taking place about the definition of interactive television, which is often interpreted very broadly when interactivity is attributed to shows in which the audience can observe interaction between two television studios located in different cities, or very narrowly as internet television.[1] The creators of Interactive TV Today, for example, understand television in a complex way but one that focuses on interaction with the television show via internet tools and mobile technologies.[2]

In this chapter I will be looking into a specific group of television shows that are usually called phone-in quizzes. They come down to winning cash prizes by solving simple puzzles or riddles, usually charades. Usually, there is a live broadcast with the presenter encouraging the audience to call the studio during the show to give the correct answer, which is the condition for winning the prize.

It would be difficult to decide where and when this form of quiz began. In a broader look upon the history of interactive television, the *Winky Dink and You* show discussed in the previous chapter tends to be recognized as the first example. Still, it is worth looking for the origins of this type of shows in the idea of the audience calling the studio, which has been going on since 1968, which is when the option appeared in the BBC Radio Nottingham broadcast titled *What Are They Up to Now*.[3] Whereas diverse forms of interactive television have been introduced around the world ever since the early 1950s, quizzes themselves become recognizable at the beginning of the current millennium with the emergence of their first dedicated television stations such as the German 9Live in 2001 or British Quiz TV in 2004.

The structure of the show

The first element of the show is for the presenter to recapitulate the rules. Next, the studio waits for calls from the audience, manifesting the show's characteristic discontinuity. Short moments of direct contact with callers are interrupted by long periods of waiting.[4] During such prolonged periods of expectation the presenter tries a range of 'survival strategies'. Facing silence from the other end of the cable, one solution is, for example, to drop hints making it easier to guess the right word or phrase, even though the presenter is clearly aware that the audience struggle rarely with the solution but more often with getting through. Another is to issue reminders about the passage of time. Yet another is to keep discussing the amount of cash that is out there to be won. In the intonation and the non-verbal layer, by contrast, there are several different strategies from smiling at the audience, through showing impatience to even a sort of criticizing the audience for its failure to meet the presenter's expectations and not wanting to call and try to get through. The wait is thus dominated by phatic expressions, but the real goal is to coax the audience to call.

Of course, the show has its own scripted dramaturgy. On the one hand only a small number of callers reach the so-called free line, i.e. manage to get through. According to calculations, the estimated ratio of connected to unconnected calls ranges from 1:400 to 1:1000.[5] As a result, specialists suggest calling those shows games of chance rather than quizzes.[6] On the other hand, the prizes for solving the tasks keep increasing, up to the maximum prize you can win at the end of the show, often already after the time when you could formally participate.

Digitization of communication behaviours

The basic research strategy in the analysis of this type of shows could entail a diligent breakdown of communication roles and strategies adding up an extensive and interesting structure of relationships between instances such as inactive members of the audience, calling members, one or more presenters and the television outlet (which attempts to establish a certain relationship of power between itself and the spectator) and elements of the message such as the word or phrase to guess, the messages presented on the screen, the presenter's statements or the conversations with the callers. I would focus, however, on those elements of the show that could confirm the claim that phone-ins are an example of 'digitization of communication behaviours'. I will be using this term to describe the tendency for symbolic subordination of our experience, practically always mediated by the media, to the digital paradigm. The goal is to attempt to prove that digitization not only takes place on the level of the technology that forms the message but also often becomes the exponent of the symbolic layer and could be a metaphor for communication activity within the extensive and still dynamically developing infosphere.[7]

Often mentioned characteristics of the digital paradigm include the phasing out of analog forms of transmission by transmission based on binary code, the ability to reduce various media forms to one common digital base, convergence of media on technical and cultural levels, and more. The example of the phone-in quizzes demonstrates that the structure and content configuration of a television show could exhibit similar tendencies. The course of a phone-in quizzes is a sort of binary string. In this collation the non-communication zones that are the waiting periods are interrupted by brief periods of contact with the audience. The presenter's pleas for contact (no matter that they are scripted), the desperate cry for it, are, however, extremely automated and anti-communicative; hence, one could say those are periods of the aforementioned lack of signal, lack of content and thus periods of silence – silence that, though saturated with logorrhoea, is really void of any tangible communication effect. Sometimes presenters even actually fall silent, unable to come up with any realistic option of keeping the contact alive. Their conduct often exhibits physical exhaustion with the schematic structure they have been forced into. They liven up only for the brief moments of conversation with a caller.

The primary consequence of this discontinuity in the show and dependence on telephone contact with the audience is a situation of extreme subordination of the presenter to the television programme. In this case Andrea Hepp relies on the concept of figuration, which in his opinion is a good fit for a number of subject-forming factors in an era of deep mediatization. He observes that the digital media are contributing to a deep diversification of figuration, with the effect being numerous tensions reflecting on the user. Vis-à-vis such tensions the presenter is an instance dominated by the spectacle and, more generally speaking, a subject,[8] that is, 'carrying the burden of sense.'

We can distinguish three levels of such dominance – language, screen structure and purpose.

Subordination spheres

a) On the language level: the object of the act of speech is extremely simplified, resulting in the impossibility of creation of extensive linguistic transmissions; presenters provide trivial hints and repeat the same threadbare platitudes; the convention of the show practically prevents the introduction of new elements to messages being formulated, and thus being compelled to communicate without communicating becomes characteristic element of such shows.

b) On the screen-structure level: the presenter plays a side role, with the central position taken by the task for the audience to solve. Very often the subject is 'forced' into the crammed space on the screen limited by text messages and infographics (Figure 6.1). The structure of the screen is subordinated, therefore, in this case, to the assumptions of subordination of the subject to the message, and the presenter becomes slave to the sense, as reflected by his position on the screen. In one of the episodes of the Polish show, *Wyścig po kasę [Race for the Cash]*, of 2007, the camera moved along a line of female presenters exceptionally gathered in a large group in the studio due to the anniversary of the TVN GRA [TVN GAME] channel; the graphic with the task appearing on the screen obscured many of them. The presenters tried to check that they were in the picture. The posthuman position in this case manifests itself in the dynamic play between the human subject and the graphical element, with the presenters often shifting their positions in various directions so as to become fully visible. The configuration between the graphic and the presenter's silhouette arises on the screen, although,

Figure 6.1 A presenter (Anna Fowler) forced in between infographics: *Quiz Call*, British phone-in quiz TV show produced by Ostrich Media for Channel 5.

as noted above, visual elements usually occupy a very large, fixed part of the screen. The situation resembles the desire, described in the peep show's case, to break out of the technological *status quo* imposed on the dancers by the cabin during the act of domesticating the space and venturing outside of it. On the other hand, the oppressive nature of the negotiation taking place in phone-ins appears to be completely different from the protocol agreed in a film production between the actors and their surroundings generated by matte painting. For in television quizzes very often the goal is to transcend the presenters' fixed boundaries, as they try to be visible and not to 'guard' their place as in classical matte painting.

c)   On the purpose level: the presenter finds symbolic fulfilment at the moment of contact with the caller; reduced to the role of a bot, the presenter then ends the code loop.

Of course, phone-in quizzes cannot be the sole proof of the digitization of communication behaviours. Patterns found in its structure, however, can be traced also in other areas under analysis. By demonstrating the links between phone-ins and several manifestations of AI and the peep show, I would like to embark on a search for traces of digitization and its basic consequences, being, for me, the reduction of the subject and its equation with the sense.

Reduction of the subject

Computer games in general and role-playing games (RGP) in particular feature characters referred to as NPCs – non-player characters. The latter is a character category that is key to the unfolding of the game's plot and action – through NPCs the character or party controlled by the player can learn important information about the presented world or receive a quest. Various degrees of sophistication of NPC interaction are available depending on the plot, script and character AI. The conversation often resembles interaction with dialogue machines or personified agents (bots) assisting the users of certain software (e.g. Microsoft Office) or taking them on guided tours of virtual worlds such as *Second Life* or *Virtual Worlds*. A similar situation seems to take place in phone-in quiz shows, with the subject being reduced to a role subordinated to the message. The subject is reduced to several functions determining the correct outcome of the show and thus reduced to the role of a conversation bot or virtual assistant handling the traffic. A similar reduction idea features in Cronenberg's *Existenz*. The participants of the titular game, who are cast in NPC roles and stuck several times in a conversation loop, make a stirring impression.

One could thus say that with phone-in quizzes the dilemma attaching to discussions and debates on whether computers can achieve a human level of intelligence[9] loses all its merit, since we are in fact dealing with its logical opposite. This sphere of digital messages forces the human subject to undergo a sort of self-reduction to attune to the reception of the meanings appearing in the infosphere. In the celebrated provocative essay, *Digital Maoism. The Hazards of New Online Collectivism* by Jaron Lanier, we can find confirmation of this claim. The article presents a somewhat harsh, often discussed at length, critique of Wiki systems and the various manifestations of collective agency and collective intelligence on the Web. The text thus touches upon somewhat different subjects from the ones being analysed herein, but as if by way of marginal observation, Lanier remarks:

> People are willing to bend over backwards and make themselves stupid in order to make an AI interface appear smart (as happens when someone can interact with the notorious Microsoft paper clip,) so are they willing to become uncritical and dim in order to make Meta-aggregator sites appear to be coherent.[10]

His 'dropping of standards' can be a clear example of the reduction here discussed. In Neganthropocene Bernard Stiegler goes as far as to formulate an even more complex criticism of such algorithmization and automation, pointing towards a multitude of negative aspects of the anthropocene.[11] Among the symptoms of the crisis he lists nihilism (even defined as computational nihilism) as a state of having exhausted the possibilities of distinction, as well as a pejoratively understood proletarization of technology leading to the automation of work and disintegration of subjecthood in favour of an economy of instincts. The anthropocene human figure presents here as a non-human, passive, desubjectified agent with stunted individualization. Interestingly, Stiegler shows that such reduced subjects, while being the product of nihilism, also become the screens for everything, the projectors of universally exploited data.[12]

The subject in the function of the sense (subject as object?)

The second track in thinking about the digitization of communication behaviours involves an attempt to demonstrate the origin of the phone-in quiz as a show with potential for the subordination of the subject. Doubtless, at the source of the television genre here described is the idea itself of interactive television along with the rich history of television quiz shows, as well as classic charades, puzzles and riddles. In some ways, phone-ins demonstrate numerous similarities with the previously discussed peep show.

Erotic peep shows are marked with the same discontinuity forced on the subject. One could say the dancer 'comes to life' only for several minutes paid for with coins going into the slot. We may consider a similar situation with phone-in quizzes. The 'existence' of the presenter is linked to short periods of contact with the calling members of the audience.

The analogy between the ideas of the peep show and the phone-ins can be attested by a project of the Polish duo of artists, Karolina Wiktor and Aleksandra Kubiak, of Sędzia Główny Group [Chief Justice Group]. Their performance was aired by the Polish television channel, TVP Kultura [TVP Culture], in 2005. The essence of the project was to employ the interactive convention to provide the audience with an opportunity to conduct a specific experiment on the characters of the performers in the studio. Callers were free to order the artists to perform any activity of the caller's choice. It turned out this opportunity was used to imbue the show with an erotic nature – many of callers, after learning what they could ask of the artists, asked them to disrobe. The dramatic effect of the performance results from how the periods of the artists' activity at the behest of the audience were moments of trial, with the experiments conducted by members of the audience often bringing forward their lowest instincts. Sędzia Główny points towards the essential deep-seated obscenity of interactive television as a medium of power in which the greatest pleasure comes from the ability to watch on the screen the creation caused by the phone call. As in a video game, we are pleased by the obedience shown by the controlled character.

While the performance of Sędzia Główny Group is an intellectual discussion about the relationship of power being established between the human subject, the phone-ins can be regarded as communication situations showing subordination to a sign structure. There is hardly the chance of any experimentation with power, in the sense imposed, for example, in radio broadcasts in which the presenters talk to the audience on air, as in the Hutchinson study.[13] Contact with the presenter could be regarded as futile, as the caller's selection is the result of the operation of an impersonal random algorithm. This is powerfully demonstrated by the episode of *Dziewczyny fortuny* [Girls of Fortune] aired on 1 January 2010 amid New Year's celebrations. An inebriated caller was put through and instead of answering the question he complimented the presenter's bosom. After brief consternation, she thanked him for the cheap compliment, immediately moving on to another recapitulation of the rules. The momentary anomaly (however subversive its character may have been) failed to disturb the algorithmic loop being processed by the girl reduced to the role of a bot. Phone-in quizzes thus appear to be the ideal example of Luhmann's autopoietic systems with their reduction of contingency, adaptation to new circumstances and return to stability.[14]

The various episodes in which the mystery to solve can evoke sexual associations are also worth consideration in this context. In one of the episodes of Polish Polsat channel's *Zagadkowa noc* [*Mysterious Night*] series, requests similar to those made of Sędzia Główny Group also appeared, but in this case the convention of the show forces a return to the established algorithm. During the waiting time for the answer to the question about the object in the wardrobe, the hostess is quick in disposing of the callers' subversive strategies such as insulting comments to the tune of 'show your boobs' or references to anal intercourse by undermining their credibility, after which she returns to the established scenario. The show must go on, and the system's homoeostasis is automatically restored. The NPC's algorithm provides for the rejection of answers from outside the predefined set. The presenter compiles the errors of the algorithm and goes back to its undisturbed version. This loop effect can also affect the callers. According to specialists, about 5 per cent of them show symptoms of addiction.[15] Those compulsive players need not be motivated by a desire to win, however; some may be after sexual gratification, as the discussed examples show. Unlike the internet's porn chats in which the hostesses are eager to fulfil any fantasy, here this desire will not find an outlet.

When following the episodes of other shows, one can encounter more examples of such self-restoration of the system. The system is subjected to overload testing whenever a deviation occurs from its regular script. There are cases of technical malfunctions connected with e.g. telephone lines and preventing the continuation of the show. In such situations the presenter becomes the screen communicating the system's crash or restoration.

A particular impression is made by part of *Quizmania*, broadcast by iTV1.[16] The host, Greg Scott, is called by a lady who, answering the riddle, gives the word 'doctor', adding as an aside: 'I think that's the doctor that cut my legs off. I have no legs.' The shaken presenter takes his time to regain composure, searching for an algorithm allowing him to get back on track and follow the script. Here, one can clearly observe the aleatory moment when the presenter inserted in the system becomes a humanist subject for a while. Those are only a dozen or so seconds for a feeling and empathizing subject to constitute itself. The NPC's humanity is restored for the brief duration of the system malfunction. This moment is longer than in the other examples; Greg finds himself in a state of shock, and some time has to pass before the critical functions of the system can be restored, such as the humorous mood, the ability to communicate with further callers or the presentation of the riddle.

An episode of *Quizmania* aired in Australia in 2006 could be interesting in the context of the above-presented periodical manifestations of the humanist subject during a system breakdown.[17] The presenter, Nikki Osborne, was obliged to fill the entire air time due to the complete malfunction of all telephone lines. Different strategies occurred in this case and different attempts to keep the audience interested, which she came up with on the fly. It turns out that it is precisely during such a time of system breakdown that the host and others of the crew can manifest themselves as fully entitled and creative subjects. The presenter goes on improvising on the screen, telling the tale of a television host from a long time ago who has to fight bloodthirsty phone lines to bring back the ability for connections to get through. One can hear laughter coming from other staff members, whom the camera picture also begins to include. Nikki starts juggling and also learning how to operate the camera. Members of the production crew get creative and begin to include sounds used in the regular episodes, to which the presenter tries to react on the fly. The meta-text context of this irregular episode yanks the crew out of the function of elements of the system, making them subjects for a while and Nikki no longer an NPC.

In the history of scandals attending phone quizzes we can even find a situation in which a sort of virus attacked the system, and a virus that could be called a human one. In Belgium the bad reputation of phone-in quizzes caused most channels to stop using them between 2008 and 2010. Two – vtm and 2BE – continued to broadcast quiz shows, however. And they were targeted by the creators of the controversial BASTA show broadcast by Eén.[18] The latter, attracting an enormous number of spectators in 2011, had a rather controversial formula. The actors resorted to various sorts of illegal, though entertaining actions intended to call public attention to important social problems or absurdities in the public sphere. The activities included, for example, feeding fake news to the media so as to highlight the lack of verification, or discrediting SABAM – the Belgian association for collective rights management. A different idea was to steal punches and other office equipment from banks after their refusal to pay out 250 euros to each Belgian citizen, which BASTA creators had asked them to do after they received a huge subvention from the government in an hour of crisis.[19]

BASTA contributed to a halt to phone-in quizzes on vtm and 2BE, by infecting them with the 'human virus'. BASTA creators responded to job ads seeking presenters for quiz shows. The cabaret actor, Maxime de Winne, became the host of such a show and for six months continued to film the channel's management and the quiz backstage with a hidden camera. BASTA even went as far as hiring mathematician Gaëtan de Weert to assist with the analysis of the puzzles and riddles appearing in the quiz shows. The outcome was that questions contained answers completely unknown to the broader audience, some mathematical puzzles contained errors or could not be resolved by traditional mathematical methods, or in some situations envelopes with answers were replaced while on air, so that the show could go on for a while longer. At a critical time de Winne makes himself known as an *agent provocateur*, imploding the system from within.[20]

The above-outlined position of the show presenter as a counterpart of the video-game NPC reacting to an algorithmic loop and acting as a communication interface primarily in the event of system failure invites the assumption that the ideal situation – perfect homoeostasis of the system – would be the moment of a closed loop of which the configuration cannot be disturbed by subversive strategies from the audience or other risk factors. Another scandal relating to phone-in quizzes brings out this 'need' for the system to close. In *Blue Peter* children's quiz broadcast by the BBC on 27 November 2006 a preselected winner appeared.[21] For it turned out that the show's creators were unable to get the detailed contact information of 14,000 responding callers. Things being so, a girl conveniently present in the studio was asked to help and pretend to be the winner. The model, or hope, of a self-referential system begins to take shape here.

***

The phone-in quiz shows discussed in this chapter are testimony of the deep cultural mark of digitization and at once a sign of subordination of the subject to the sphere of meanings. One could even say they are an extreme case of this. In the words of Jamie Silver from *The Guardian*, 'the components of quiz show programming – wobbly sets, babbling presenters, dumb questions and, most importantly, phone lines that cost 60p-75p a call – are TV at its cheapest, making the output highly lucrative.'[22] This means the same extremely simplified entourage as in peep shows, with the actor (presenter) not even in a position to at least partially domesticate the space, which the dancers in peep shows to a limited extent attempt to do.

Of course, such shaping of a posthuman vehicle in which the presenters' role is reduced to the implementation of an algorithm and they are subordinated to the system of meanings generated on the screen is a convenient tool of schizophrenic capitalism according to the Deleuzian model. The hosts become the hardware processing monetization algorithms, universal digital machines, bodies without organs, subordinated to the hegemony of the market. Iman Hamam, studying phone-in shows presented in Arab television channels, compares this configuration even directly to the coin slots in peep shows.[23] State institutions, such as the British Ofcom, sometimes attempt to curb this bloodthirstiness. The institution often imposed multi-million penalties on the broadcasters of quizzes in which abuses took place.[24]

This awareness of the abuses, according to Mimmi Curran, results in a collapse of trust in participation television[25] and also testifies to the absorbing impact of the phone-in quiz as a system impressing its deep mark on the subjects who join in. The profound digitization taking place here manifests itself externally in a hardly negotiatory act of harmonization. The presenter is aggressively gang-pressed into the media message. The interactive-television technology is not, therefore, in this case a protocol for the negotiation of rights and position taken in a shared space by the subject and the sense. There is not even any competition here. The presenter becomes a sort of relief of sense, a dominated subject.

Part Three

Digital Touches

BeautifulAgony.com and the eroticism of the database

Even though contemporary data repositories on the internet have complex structure and diverse ontology, it can be assumed that they refer to two different paradigms of memory. On the one hand, there are treasuries of information built on the traditions of Enlightenment, which constitute an ideal prolongation of the hypomnesic archive in the Derridean sense.[1] By externalizing our memory in the form of the archive, we can forget. As I will demonstrate in the following chapter, this paradigm carries the traits of a profoundly human nature since it is connected with the humanistic understanding of choice, sacrifice and even imposing power.

In other places, the world is registered automatically, which results in a memory available on demand. A very detailed autobiographical memory of events from both one's own and somebody else's life – called hyperthymesia – is a characteristic aspect of numerous internet portals. This automatism seems to be inhuman as it occurs independently of the human subject, and the set of data itself exceeds one's perceptual abilities. These are the features which fit in the description of the database. The conception of hyperthymesia consists in the unlimited access to the memory of past experiences, which – in clinical cases – most often encompass autobiographical experiences. The database also seems to be inhuman as it offers the hyper-access to 'everybody's memory' – the hyperthymesia of individual experience is broadened by the hyperthymesia of the experience of the other. In this respect, hyperthymesia resembles savant syndrome.

A kind of dynamic dialectics – which as a result appears between the paradigms in question – influences the shape of repositories and their reception in concrete areas of the internet, but in a more general sense it seems to be a crucial realm where the posthuman relationship can be researched. The subject of my interest in this chapter is a specific type of databases, which are the repositories of sexual acts. I'm more focused here on 'real sex' depictions bearing in mind that all sex recordings even the ones named documentary or natural can be considered theatrical.

The process of building databases gathering the evidence (memories) of pleasure begins much earlier, for example, in the eighteenth-century libertine France, or a century later, which is when a market for erotic photography began to form. What changes with the advent of the digital revolution is that a new, powerful interface for accessing these materials becomes available and one capable of amplifying the pleasure to the level of an overwhelming, 'non-human' experience. Additionally, digital recording tools mediate this experience in an entirely new way.

In this context, it would be fairly convenient to investigate porn websites which would allow only the recording of amateur sex. Sergio Messina refers to this type of pornographic imagery as *realcore*.[2] Its 'amateurism' would surely provide a non-theatrical and more documentary context so much different from sex scenes played by porn actors. This kind of truthfulness is very often one of the important criteria of choosing content by porn websites users.

The analysis which I conduct in this part of the essay concentrates on the website undoubtedly building its popularity on 'truthfulness', but it is not as explicitly pornographic as other websites containing scenes of amateur sex. BeautifulAgony.com (BA) is a website that collects video recordings of people's faces during orgasm resulting from masturbation. Surely, those who take part in the project – even though they are called artists by the creators of the website – are not porn stars, as their bodies and their sexual organs are not shown to the public and they do not participate in the project for financial reasons, though they still receive a small amount of money. Regardless, there seems to be something deeply obscene in their experiences which, at the same time, is mysterious and real. Separating the act of sexual pleasure from the pornographic context seems to be a clear proof of truthfulness. The website itself provides two groups of film coverage which need to be considered. The first one are obviously already-mentioned masturbation sessions. The second group consists of the interviews with their participants, which constitute a crucial meta-level of this phenomenon and thus explain the processes taking place here.

BeautifulAgony.com was created in 2004. Slightly earlier in 2003, the creators of the project, Richard Lawrence and Lauren Olney, carried on a pilot project of this type. On 3 July 2014, the database of 'beautiful agonies' consisted of

Figure 7.1 Screenshot of BeautifulAgony.com. Image courtesy of the website owners, 25 April 2014.

3,084 videos documenting orgasms and almost the same number of intimate confessions by project participants. The creators of the website encourage the visitors both to watch the materials and to become one of the actors who appear in masturbation sessions. Reactions to the website are largely enthusiastic, and its users emphasize that it is not just another porn site since it does not contain nudity.[3] The authors insist that the materials should be authentic and warn against pretending to have an orgasm, which – as they claim – they can spot.[4]

In the context of posthuman intimacy investigated in the current study, the website in question is an example of a place which can be defined against multi-faceted transhuman and inhuman contexts. First of all, we witness the emergence of an all-embracing vehicle where individual sexual experiences are sucked by an automatic mechanism. A collective mind turns here into a collective sexuality. Secondly, the digital order of registration overpowers a biological experience introducing significant modifications. Thirdly, the website can serve as an example of an inhuman eroticism of the database. It should be understood here as the potential of offering inhuman pleasure. Not necessarily does the database have to offer erotic content in order to be erotic and on the other hand it is also by definition a non-humanistic creation. To recapitulate, I would like to include a tentative definition of this eroticism, which has been constructed on the intersection of five orders – Bataille's version of transgression and prohibition, the dynamics between continuity and discontinuity, and the Derridean conflict between the archive and a mechanistic understanding of the database.

The archive and the database – posthuman dialectics

BeautifulAgony.com is a website which has to face the clash of two paradigms: the archive and the database. On the one hand, it is a repository of memories – recorded in the form of confessions and sexual acts. On the other, it has to comply with the obligation of automatic spreading. The database devours and reduces all artists to one common denominator. To determine this dynamics, one needs to advance arguments showing how a human archive differs from an inhuman database.

Humanism of the archive

Even though Derrida's *Archive Fever* consists of some posthuman tropes, it should be emphasized that it presents a plethora of evidence of the humanistic provenance of the archive. Derrida employs concepts which determine precisely the appropriateness of archiving from the humanist perspective, as well as and its psychoanalytic origin.

First and foremost, it alludes to the biological paradigm of fever. The need of archiving is for Derrida described as a 'human' fever – an illness and passion at the same time.[5] It results from an addiction which consists in a 'compulsive, repetitive, and nostalgic desire for the archive, an irrepressible desire to return to the origin, a homesickness, a nostalgia for the return to the most archaic place of absolute commencement'.[6]

The decision to bring the archive to life can be characterized by a humanistic uncertainty similar to Freud's hesitations mentioned by Derrida when he wonders whether what Freud wanted to publish was not too trivial and already available to everybody. The archive can exist only under the condition that a human act of estimating the value and usefulness of the archived is present.[7] There is no room here for the cold logics of a machine. This place is taken by human uncertainty and the tendency to do useless things.

The archive consists of elements which have been purposefully consigned by somebody. Even when Derrida introduces a slightly different understanding of consignation (consignation as the act of collecting signs), the aspect of coordination is also present here. There should be somebody who will turn this archive into 'a single corpus, in a system or synchrony where all the elements articulate the unity of an ideal configuration'.[8]

Power imposed on the archive and by the archive is the effect of the arbitrary choice of elements which are part of it. The archontic rule, which Derrida sees as the foundation of the archive, reminds us of a Greek guardian of documents,[9] who creates a space for the archive according to the topo-nomological rule of creating it.

The archive also remains closely related to such human attributes as the death drive, aggression drive and destruction drive.[10] On the one hand, it is the effect of opposing these drives; on the other, the drives are an integral part of each archive, which – as Derrida observes – 'always works, and *a priori*, against itself'. The death drive, as he continues to explain, tends to destroy a hypomnesic archive, except if it can be disguised, made up, painted, printed, represented as the idol of its truth in painting.[11]

Inhuman database

While it is true that humanity has collected and stored data in different ways since time immemorial, 'a database' was a term introduced to suit the needs of Information Technology at a certain point of its development. The first important argument is its 'inhumanity'. The idea of a database crystallized between 1960 and 1962 when IBM developed the IMS system. The data stored there was presented to the users in the form of a hierarchical tree.[12] Chowdhurry enumerates five generations of databases.[13] Except for the first one, which focuses more on the early beginnings related to how the conception of the archive functioned in the information environment, later generations were consecutive phases of developing systems capable of processing greater volumes of data and separating the logical organization of the database from the physical place of storing information. What instantly becomes clear is the philosophy of the database differing dramatically from the archive that needs to be based in a concrete, material place of storing artefacts; this is a crucial point in Derrida's typology.

Technological aspects are yet another issue illustrating the difference between the archive and the database. The forging of the term 'database' coincided with a more open access to data storage devices (drives and drum memory) which now existed next to technologies used before and based on tape drives, which demanded batch processing. Both models – which were applied simultaneously for quite a long time and for different purposes – were being gradually replaced by a different paradigm fuelling the development of the conception of the database.

During the domination of huge mainframe computers, access to such units was limited to a particular amount of time. The paradigm of the archive manifests itself here in two ways. On the one hand, a frequent figure appearing here is the guardian who regulates how long and at what time a computer might be accessed – he works out an access rota. On the other hand, having finished his work with a computer, each programmer leaves with a set of punched tapes or cards, that is carrying his own archive with data generated by the central unit. As Martin Campbell-Kelly and William Aspray explain, the paradigm of batch processing instilled the image of a computer as a counting machine whose new features are scarce, but which surely poses additional problems connected with the necessity of learning a programming language or paying a certain price.[14]

Direct access storage devices created a proper ground for the development of databases functioning as data repositories enabling interactive actions. That was the point when the database could turn into open resources very often growing automatically. The first hard drive appeared already in 1956 and was produced by IBM. When hard drives weighing approx. one tonne were not used too frequently, the technology of magnetic drums – first appearing in 1932 – served as basic computer memory in the 1950s and 1960s of the twentieth century. The two types of direct-access storage devices are driven by a different idea than the one which fuelled the appearance of asynchronous drives, such as cards, punched tapes, magnetic tape and recording tape. This moment in the history of technological advancement marks the boundary between the archive and the database.

Dialectics from the historical perspective

Even though the term 'database' par excellence was first used in the 1960s of the last century, both paradigms have a much longer pedigree. Since BA is of primary importance here, let us take this opportunity to discuss them in the context of erotic content.

Erotic archive – historical perspective

Without the shadow of a doubt, one example of the collection organized along the paradigm of the archive is the museum of Pompeii located in the Naples National Archaeological Museum. The collection was available only to men and until this day it is put on display in a special, secluded place where a person can stay for up to fifteen minutes.[15]

In 1821, the collection was closed for many years; in 1849, the entrance to the place where it was stored was even walled in. At that time, the collection turned into a model of a hyper-archive since not only was the place guarded and the access limited, but also it turned into a closed space with the past enchanted inside it and which could never be accessed. Limited access was also the issue in the case of erotic frescos discovered in Pompeii, which in the nineteenth and up until the 1960s of the twentieth century was a type of peepshow – the place contained closed cabins accessible only to 'educated men enjoying an unblemished reputation'.[16]

Devoted to erotic collections and the ways of making them accessible, the documentary by Peter Woditsch presents in detail the model of guarded archives and how they pass the laws. These collections are often hardly available – a fact that Lynn Hunt, the editor of the book *The Invention of Pornography: Obscenity and the Origins of Modernity, 1500–1800*, makes clear.[17] Interestingly, Woditsch's film also proves that decency in the archives is imposed not only by staff or creators, but also by visitors.

Erotic database – historical perspective

Out of many examples fulfilling the requirements of the database, one collection of erotic photography should be mentioned in particular. In 1874, the police searched the studio of Henry Hayler and discovered 130,248 obscene photographs and 5,000 slides for a magic lantern.[18] Surely, the eroticism of the database marked an auspicious beginning here. Repositories of pornography, similar to those discovered at Hayler's, can be an example of the first overwhelming database which creates an environment for developing the impossible – the amplification of arousal that becomes unbearable and lethal in the Lacanian sense. In selected parts of the current study, I have considered various examples of the human subject entering into intimate relations with the sense but so far I have not found any examples that could be illustrative where one of the parties is a void, eternity, which – even though its nature is finite (the quantity of materials is measurable) – exceeds significantly human cognitive abilities and human sexuality. It is the experience of suffering for unknown reasons. This kind of eroticism reminds of the experience of hyperthymesia. It involves remembering the whole world of sex. Due to self-reflexivity, this historical collection resembles the website in question – *Beautiful Agony*. As Marcus observes, Hayler was one of the main people who appeared in the photos, but there were also his wife and two sons.[19] A database here is powerful enough to annihilate any taboo – it repeals the prohibition of incest, and so it disintegrates the immanent order of humanism. Also, it chops the analog continuum of a sexual act into fragmentary photographic samples. The effect of the gradually increasing frequency of this sampling is an increasing size of the database.

The archive and the database – a comparison

Table 7.1 summarizes the comparison drawn between a 'human' archive and an 'inhuman' database, which presents the features of both paradigms appearing in the above arguments.

Table 7.1 The comparison of the archive and the database paradigms

	The archive	The database
1.	Hypomnesia	Hyperthymesia
2.	Taking out of context	Reducing to a common denominator
3.	Past/future	Present
4.	Half-closed	Open
5.	Arbitrariness	Automatism
6.	Fragmentariness	Holism
7.	Irrelevance	Relevance
8.	Institutionality	Noninstitutionality
9.	Evaluating benefits	The algorithm of devouring
10.	Stability	Instability
11.	Uniqueness of exhibits	Replaceability of exhibits
12.	Paradigm of security and protection	Paradigm of self-enlargement
13.	Narration has a holistic nature bringing the archive to life	Narration is either fragmentary or in the nature of a trajectory
14.	The structure influences the process of archiving	The structure does not influence the data

15.	An exterior	No exterior
16.	Batch processing	Direct processing
17.	Topo-nomology	Digital nomology of registration
18.	Archontic guard	Market access code

1. Hypomnesia – hyperthymesia

The hypomnesic nature of the archive results from – as Derrida explains – its externality with regard to memory. In this sense, the archive is the 'prosthesis of the interior'.[20] Unlike this prosthesis, the database is ready and waiting to capture a memory – it does not replace memory like the archive. It always is a memory ready not so much to be refreshed but to be revealed.

2. Taking out of context – reducing to a common denominator

In his essay on laboratories, libraries and collections,[21] Latour explains how the archive is constructed out of natural artefacts altered by taking them out of their natural habitat. He gives an example of a bird that – deprived of its natural habitat – lands in a museum and so it can be categorized, compared with other species, etc. In this way, taking out of the context constitutes an important feature of the archive. The database behaves differently – artefacts are here reduced to a similar form. This process cannot be successfully completed, but the database seems to be founded on the tension between similarity and difference. However, it does not appear to be an act of taking out of context but rather one of reducing to a common denominator. In the remaining part of the chapter, I am going to describe this multi-faceted process of reducing in the space of BA.

3. Past/future – present

As Derrida proves, the archive – even though entering into a dialogue with the past by establishing an archaeological relationship – is constantly future-oriented. One of its constitutive elements is an oath, which is a symbol of the future.[22] By contrast, an archival structure stems from the process and the medium of recording. As a result, being future-orientated is connected here with the fact that archiving is the effect of choosing the medium of recording. In this context, the database is an embodied present – the order of the past and future is devoured by the overpowering 'now'.

4. Half-closed – open

The archive is never closed, which means that new elements can sometimes be added, but – at the same time – it is rather closed, as it contains a definite number of 'exhibits'.[23] In the meantime, the database is rooted in multiplication openness, which are the enablers of its devouring expansion.

5. Arbitrariness – automatism

The arbitrariness of the archive stems from the decision to bring it to life and the selection of documents which should be included there. The database can be characterized by automatism – elements to be included are verified by an algorithm.

6. Fragmentariness – holism

Derrida points to the connection between the archive and archaeology. He shows the process of uncovering layers, skins, tissues, the foundation of memory; he discusses the fragments and debris used to assemble the archive. The database – especially in Manovich's understanding – is a space of free access to all places at the same time, to the whole of the digital repository.

7. Irrelevance – relevance

The irrelevance of the archive means the distance between the present and what is communicated in the archive. By contrast, the database is a potential relevance – elements are ready for use; they are waiting to become relevant.

8. Institutionality – noninstitutionality

Institutionality is what Derrida describes as the passage from private to public space, e.g. Freud's last house later turned into a museum. Institutionality is then an immanent feature of the archive. For the database, institutionality is not a precondition. One might even assume that a reverse process takes place here – the database is attractive the moment it becomes intimate (as a result of accessibility and the possibility to build one's own narrations within its scope).

9. Evaluating benefits – the algorithm of devouring

The process of evaluating benefits drawn from creating the archive – already described above – seems to be the foundation on which it is assembled. In the case of the database, the initial starting of the algorithm is the source of force driving the database. It is the algorithm that verifies which elements should be included in the set and which should be left out. The database algorithm has the power of devouring reality and filtering it automatically. It is Leviathan the Hell Mouth, sucking the order in irretrievably and formatting it endlessly.

10. Stability – instability
As Derrida claims, the archive is the place where law is passed. Through institutionalization and making them public, archival documents are the foundation for formulating law. The archive is not really then an inert (hardly modifiable) stability. The database, on the other hand, is characterized by inconstant mobility and flexibility.

11. Uniqueness of exhibits – the replaceability of exhibits
In the archive, exhibits are unique; they cannot be replaced by others or, in any case, such replacement would be very complicated. The database does not pose this kind of problems. Exhibits are changeable; their originality is not such a crucial quality.

12. Paradigm of security and protection – the paradigm of self-enlargement
The paradigm dominating the archive is security and protection. Being a testimony to the past, exhibits are so crucial since they have been chosen arbitrarily to legitimize the law and accordingly should be protected and accessed only under special circumstances. The database, by contrast, can be characterized by the paradigm of development. It dies whenever it ceases to be an apparatus which enables the amplification of elements.

13. Holistic narration – fragmentary/trajectory narration
The archive is a certain kind of history as a whole. It is a narrated selection. In the case of the database, separate elements can be narrative (such as a masturbation session or BA actor's confession), that is why it can be described as fragmentary. By contrast, in his description of the difference between the database and narration, Manovich introduces the category of trajectory as an embodied tale that can appear as an effect of the selection of database elements made by a user.[24]

14. Influence of the archive structure on the archived – no influence of the database structure on the data
As Derrida explains, 'the technical structure of the archiving archive also determines the structure of the archivable content'.[25] In the case of the database, this process does not occur. Interfaces may change, but the content remains the same at all times.

15. Exterior – no exterior
Derrida emphasizes the fact that the archive needs an external place, a particular shape. Here, there is a clear distinction between the interior and the exterior. There is no such distinction in the case of the database, as it is not a conception that might be looked at from the topographical perspective. For database users, the place where the records are stored and its shape are not important. Even when the place aspect does occur, it happens only when this aspect is taken into account by the conception of the interface.

16. Batch processing – direct processing
Conceptions of data processing presented along the historical discussion of the conceptions of databases are a good metaphor for using archives and databases. The archive is a place where we can work with exhibits under the watchful eye of a guard. Obtaining results, we take them with us and leave this space. It reminds us of batch processing. The database enables to conduct direct operations. It is always ready and waiting for user's actions.

17. Topo-nomology – digital nomology of registration
According to Derrida, the archive passes and enforces laws. On the other hand, it is built in a particular interior and on a particular ground. These elements constitute Derridean topo-nomology. In the database, law is established by the mechanism of registration – it seems to have a digital nature. An algorithm divides the reality into elements which fit the database and those which are outside of it. What is revealed here is a typical 'greediness' of the database.

18. An archontic guard – digital access code
Archons – according to Derrida – are most importantly 'the guardians of documents', who not only physically protect the place where the archive content is made available, but also they have the hermeneutic right and powers to manage it.[26] The database is guarded by an access code understood in Deleuzian terms. The humanistic subject is replaced here by the market mechanism of access to an apparatus evoking the already-mentioned peep-show appliance.

The further part of the analysis will feature the presentation of the dynamics between both paradigms in the space of BA. My aim here is to investigate which factors determine the diversion of the system either in the direction of a humanistic archive or in the direction of an inhuman database.

The camp of *Beautiful Agony*/ An automaton spewing out the memories of sexual pleasure

Investigating inhuman elements of the database in BA, one needs to explain how the internet apparatus of the database, which formats uploaded sexual scenes and influences their character, is built around the sexual order.

Before a planned sexual session, actors are obliged to read carefully the guidelines explaining how to record the material. Here, the formatting occurs for the first time and manifests itself in the editing of a sexual act to fit technological requirements.

The instructions provide not only technical requirements regulating the organization of the sessions, but also suggestions as to the act of masturbation itself. For instance, the authors of the website ask for high-resolution material, appropriate framing that ideally shows the face only, etc. The place where the session is happening should be free of any disturbing sounds, and listening to the music is forbidden (except for headphones) due to copyrights.

As for the masturbation session itself, further recommendations are provided:

> Capture the warm up, and the cool down. Let us see all of your idiosyncrasies, personal habits and rituals, but we're only interested in reality, not performances, impressions, or exaggerations. Don't do anything on camera that you don't do when you're alone (or with your lover).[27]

Two more elements: time aspect and actors' anonymity are yet another proof of the presence of a vehicle: a vehicle that which – just as in the case of the peepshow described earlier – has the power to disintegrate the humanistic order. On the main website, there is a counter counting down hours and minutes remaining to the 'release' of the next video featuring another beautiful agony. Five videos are added to the website on a weekly basis. The participants of the project are assigned consecutive numbers, and materials are signed only with the date of publishing the clip on the internet. In this way, the camp of pleasure is growing. The process of expanding the database is similar to the effect of filtering out unnecessary elements from the reality, which do not belong to the set of recorded acts of masturbation. The website's authors sometimes admit they can recognize if materials are inauthentic. Due to this kind of decision-making process, BA seems to be closer to the idea of the archive, though the guardians here appear to resemble controllers on an assembly line – on the output there is only an automaton spewing out another handful of orgasms.

The scene and session set-up – among others – create the impression as if a sexual act was formatted, which does not seem to be a convention as in a porn movie. Here, it is imposed on a sexual experience captured and shared by means of a technological apparatus.

Apart from familiarizing oneself with the session guidelines, potential artists should get to know an extensive list of topics which – according to the website's owners – might be included in auto-interviews mandatory for the actors. The first request to introduce oneself – and present very intimate details of one's sexual life – appears slightly schizophrenic, bearing in mind that each video has a number and release date. Website's authors suggest mentioning the following points: sexual education, first orgasm, extraordinary sexual experiences, sexual fantasies, secrets and what made them publish their videos on BA.

Actors who resolve to upload their videos are offered $200. They also receive free monthly access to the website! Apart from financial reasons, which seem here less important than e.g. sharing oneself and experimenting with oneself, there is yet another reason why people want to publish their videos – access to the database, access to their own experiences embedded in the broader context of the limitless whole. What is revealed here is one of the aspects of self-reflexivity.

One female artist who published her orgasm on the website, numbered 2583, quite rightly summarizes all features of this overpowering vehicle under the label of a 'self-reproducing pleasure machine'.

The act of confiding

The intention to confide is one of the aspects which makes BA an archive. Sharing one's most intimate experiences is here an act characterized by a peculiar teleology. As the creators of the website state:

> But I would hope that our contributors gain much more than just financial rewards for their experiences. They are sharing something incredibly intimate and so I think the motivations behind that cannot always solely be driven by money. Feedback tells us that each experience for each individual is totally different, just like the orgasms themselves – and done for entirely different reasons. Some wish to be a part of something incredibly sexy, some for their 15 minutes of fame, and some just love the artistic concept of the site and want to be a part of it. For others it's about self-exploration or an inner journey, about building self-confidence or perhaps something to share with their partner, while for some individuals it's the thrill of sharing something secretively and

anonymously, a piece of themselves hidden away on the internet. Or it may be something they wish to tick off their list of sexual to-do's, the list really is endless![28]

Website users confirm that the motivations and reasons behind the decision to confide are multiple. One female user (no. 1683) observes that the website performs, for instance, a therapeutic function:

> I am happy that I can draw the attention of the others to myself, I've got enough trust in myself not to care whether other people will consider what I am doing right or wrong. If people watched more BA and *I shot myself,*[29] the psychological state of the human race would improve.

BA manifests a critical nature of the project on many levels. Female artist no. 2763[30] admits to being a porn actress, but she emphasizes that BA lets her show her real orgasm to her fans. No. 0414, on the other hand, appreciates BA due to its voyeuristic character and the fact that sincerity plays an important role here.

The reason behind sharing one's orgasm is for some people similar to what guides the creators of archives. What I have in mind is a kind of social mission. Artist no. 1322 claims that BA is in accordance with her philosophy of life. She regards a masturbation session as a form of sharing with other women, as a crusade against a pornographic view of sex and as a message that sex and masturbation are a great fun. The woman admits that the session was difficult for her to do, as she had not masturbated for a long time. That is why, she had to ask her partner to do part of the 'job' for her. This is a real example of sacrifice and confiding.

Transhuman actors

As for connections between the website and the philosophy of posthumanism, among other popular motifs, one may observe here downloaded consciousness, collective intelligence, transhuman approach to identity which can be distributed, and an opportunity of expanding a human being by means of the internet. Actors' confessions direct our attention towards a slightly different aspect – one that, to some extent, is part of the transhuman thought. What I have in mind here is information technology penetrating sexuality. It might be regarded as a 'digital ejaculation', that is, the process of cultural wrapping a biological process by a digital order of being, which could be part of the already-described conception of deep digitalization. The digital subject emerging from this intimate relationship with information taking the form of a recorded act of sexual pleasure is characterized by idiosyncratic features. Video materials become an integral part of a post-sexual act – a kind of a digital ejaculation without which one cannot feel satisfaction. The digital subject is here the posthuman – or perhaps the transhuman – subject since it incorporates information into something that had previously been solely a biological act. Here, digital ejaculation consists in 'excreting' a video material as the effect of digitalized sexuality. It seems to be an embodied vision of Gibson's *Idoru*.[31] The video clips therein are automatically generated media effect of Rei's dreams. With BA users those are the recordings of their orgasms.

In the very rich archive of users' comments, I looked for comments relating to sessions and the website because they seem to be closely connected with a transhuman transgression.[32] The actors' confessions become an automatically introduced meta-level – providing the context in which a recorded orgasm seems to result from the character of actor's sexuality, one's preferences, past sexual and non-sexual experiences and personality conditioning.

Actors have the impression of being entities in-between the act of gazing and the act of being watched. The act of recording and sharing videos adds to the transgression of one's body and one's subjectivity. This is how an actress no. 1683 describes this impression: 'It is as if I saw the mirror reflection of somebody who is with me but, in fact, I am with myself, imagining that I am with a person who is touching me.'

The authors of confessions fairly often emphasize that recording an orgasm was a new, magnificent and enriching experience. One might be inclined to state that BA becomes the requirement of sexual satisfaction. As female artist no. 2451 claims, 'masturbation in front of the camera is an empowering and brilliant experience, an intensive self-expression. It was weird to look back at myself but I realized that there was no reason why I shouldn't be proud of the way I look.' As a female artist no. 0428 observes: 'it was like sharing something with a large number of people. I like BA because it helps people feel their bodies better, to become less ashamed, and to share it.'

This feeling is not always pleasurable. As male actor no. 0451 says, 'it was hard and weird to do it in front of the camera – I'd find it tough if my family saw it.' 0234 – caught shortly after an orgasm, does not know what to say; she is ashamed by the camera; 'it's strange to be talking to the camera in such a moment'.

Some comments prove that BA give the chance to access experiences going beyond typical sexual activities and so going beyond 'human' sexuality. A couple no. 0432 claims that the session was nice because 'you never watch your face expression when you masturbate'. An actress no. 2717 says that what she finds interesting here is the idea of this database that collects the orgasms of such a large number of different people. This opinion points to the vastness of the database and the access to new sensations.

Posthuman aspects of confessions on BA appear also in the process of the deconstruction of a sexual body, which might be regarded as one of the constitutive features of a website focusing on the face. At the same time, what we can also observe here is a typical tension between the face – as an individual object isolated from the rest of the body, which can bring pleasure – and the whole body demonstrated in the actors' confessions. Anne Ward, who analysed the website comparing it with other traditional porn sites, claims: 'The face is transformed into not just a face of orgasm but also into a subjectifying apparatus for both the spectator and the contributor.'[33] As she continues to explain, '*Beautiful Agony* claims that the face of orgasm is meaningful – that it can be isolated from a scene of sexual context, that it can be isolated from the rest of the body, and that this confirms pleasure.'[34] The traces of Deleuzian thinking echo here, and actors seem to be conscious of that. As actress no. 2287 emphasizes, 'porn concentrates on other body parts, what's important here is the face'. Actress 2790 finds it interesting to look at the faces 'because everybody has got a different face, sometimes people laugh, sometimes they cry, each face and its expression is beautiful'. One of actors no. 1237 manifests the tension between the face and the rest of the body saying: 'I don't know why, but I like looking at myself (in the mirror, in the clip). It's strange but when I fantasize about women, they don't have any faces. I think only about their bodies.'

Posthuman narcissism

The question which should also be addressed here is: 'what does it mean that I am looking at my autoerotic sexual act?' The narcissism of the database seems to be connected with the phenomenon of recursion. If we assume that a video clip becomes an integral part of a sexual experience, or even its precondition, looking at oneself as a sexual object experiencing a sexual pleasure is the beginning of a recursive process – a masturbating self is looking at itself which is masturbating, looking at oneself which is masturbating and so on. There are such comebacks in BA – participating in a session which was preceded with taking part in a different session.[35]

Actress no. 2749 hopes that 'people will appreciate the fact that she shows herself, that she gives herself and her orgasm'. During the masturbation, she was thinking about her body and its reactions. These words show perfectly well how the act of recording influences the form of sexual experience. She adapts her act of masturbation to recording conditions; she modifies this act which undergoes a recursive process that can last *ad infinitum*. Another actress (0517) admits she had watched porn before in order to take on a positive attitude, and she had also practised by watching herself in the mirror (another symbol of self-reference). Artist no. 0477 says: 'I have never seen myself during orgasm so perhaps it is something I can learn about myself. The more I penetrated it, the more I got used to it and it became pleasurable.' Narcissistic recursion of BA is described by Ward as self-exploration[36] and the desire to watch our reflection in the mirror.[37]

Topo-relational posthumanism – other types of the posthuman perspective

BA is another example of the aforementioned 'posthuman perspective'. If recorded orgasms and actors' confessions existed as autonomous materials outside the database, they might be regarded as a relatively 'natural' form of internet expression – spontaneous documentation of a rich sexual sphere of users. It would be difficult to notice aspects of formatting, repeatability or the amplified strength of the database as an inhuman place in isolation from other elements. The posthuman context becomes obvious the moment all these materials are collected in one database. One more time, we can speak here about a peculiar kind of topo-relational posthumanism. It is the position of elements and their relations which bring it to life. Crucial here are the words of Lauren Olney – one of the creators of the website – on the website's forum. She alludes to a few artistic projects incorporating the BA database.

> I love seeing Agonies projected large, we have participated in quite a few exhibitions/projects where they have been projected large, and even synched on orgasm. One video piece we did consisted of 60 or so Agonies all together, synched at orgasm and projected on a wall. Was amazing to stand back and look at.[38]

It is clearly visible that this particular interface used in the project in question strengthens an already-deep impression of losing oneself in an inhuman database caused by the syntactic posthumanism.

The eroticism of the database

How does one define the eroticism of the database on the basis of the above analysis of BA? We can assume that it is presented on several levels. The first one is the abovementioned dynamics between an inhuman database and human archive. Since the database resists humanism and falls outside any 'human' categories, transgression and going beyond humanism seem to be its immanent features. On the other hand, erotic context should also be looked for in the reception of databases such as BA. What we witness here is the actualization of pleasure which goes beyond users' perception. Both perspectives should be analysed more thoroughly with special attention being paid to Bataille's conception of eroticism. His works contain some motifs which can be regarded as posthuman. Bataille also seems to be in a sense 'digital'; for instance, when it comes to defining eroticism, he constantly focuses on the dynamics between continuity and discontinuity.

The first motif is related to the definition of eroticism, which presents it as a critical tool. As I have mentioned above, BA becomes such a tool for many of its users. Bataille regards eroticism as something that questions human existence. Posthumanism is given the same role as it is done for example in Haraway's *Cyborg Manifesto*.[39] Bataille elaborates on this problem, providing the readers with concrete examples which might be regarded as transhuman.

> I said that I regarded eroticism as the disequilibrium in which the being consciously **calls his own existence in question.** In one sense, the being loses himself deliberately, but then the subject is identified with the object losing his identity. If necessary I can say in eroticism: I am losing myself. Not a privileged situation, no doubt. But the deliberate loss of self in eroticism is manifest; no one can question it.[40]

He frequently reveals his interest – not only in *Erotism*[41] – in the fundamental relationship between the subject and the object, *transgression*, and the exchangeability of their roles. It seems to be the same kind of reasoning that let Derrida to coin the category of *subjectile*.

Transgression is also the term which Bataille understands in the context of establishing laws. As he writes, transgression repeals a prohibition without abolishing it.[42] This statement seems to be perfectly in accordance with the dialectic dynamics governing places such as BA. On the one hand, there is the law imposed by the archive; on the other hand, one can find here exuberant automatism of the database, both of which are the driving force of this transgressive apparatus. Transgression is very close to transhumanism. Bataille seems to have seen this possibility before the idea of transhumanism was verbalized:

> Pleasure would be a poor enough thing without this aberrant transcendency, not confined to sexual ecstasy and experienced in the same way by mystics of various religions, the Christian religion foremost. We receive being in an intolerable transcendence of being, no less intolerable than death. And since in death it is given and taken away at the same time we must seek it in the feeling of death, in those unbearable instants where we seem to be dying because the being within us is only there through excess, when the fullness of horror and joy coincide.[43]

Bataille continues to explain his definition of eroticism in a different place. As he claims, eroticism is the resignation from the procreative function. The example of BA is illustrative here since autoerotism – which is one of the basic ideas of BA – is a definite resignation from procreation. Not only do we quit the idea of having offspring but also a partner – the last element of a procreative act – becomes redundant. Masturbation can be regarded as a hyper-erotic act, just as a sexual intercourse with machines or zoophilia.

Also, Bataille seems to have established a convenient theoretical frame for the inhuman infinity of the database and resulting horror indissolubly linked to pleasure.

> In order to reach the limits of the ecstasy in which we lose ourselves in bliss we must always set an immediate boundary to it: horror. Not only can pain, my own or that of other people, carry me nearer to the moment when horror will seize hold of me and bring me to a state of bliss bordering on delirium, but there is no kind of repugnance whose affinity with desire I do not discern. Horror is sometimes confused with fascination, but if it cannot suppress and destroy the element of fascination it will reinforce it.[44]

These words suggest that the horror of database results from its vastness and immovability of its growth. Its eroticism is the consequence of the horror of the unknown. This excerpt reveals the need to go beyond humanism. Another Bataille's motif – transgression – appears here, as well:

> Thought itself, reflection, that is, is only fulfilled in excess. What is truth, apart from the representation of excess, if we only see that which exceeds the possibility of seeing what it is intolerable to see, just as in ecstasy enjoyment is intolerable? What is truth, if we think that which exceeds the possibility of thought?[45]

I would like to summarize this part of the analysis with yet one more excerpt from Bataille's work, where he openly states that eroticism is what falls outside humanity:

> Only the actual experience of states of normal sexual activity and the clash between them and socially approved conduct allows us to recognise that this activity has its inhuman side.[46]

One of BA users quoted by Ward analyses in a forum post inhumanity of ecstasy as the moment when 'an experience is so pleasurable that you don't seem to be a human being any longer'.[47]

***

Focusing on the example of BA, this chapter characterizes two levels of posthuman eroticism of the database. On the first level, one can observe a dialectic game between the idea of the archive and that of the database. Along these dynamics, the post-subject is constructed, which on the one hand inhales digital orders that are becoming its integral part and on the other it is immersed in a recursive self-exploiting narcissism.

On the second level of database's eroticism, the transgressive subject – this time embodied in a the website user – is founded by the access to an inhuman pleasure. It faces hyper-pleasure present not only here, but also on other websites – 1,000 orgasms being the prolongation of 1,000 plateaus of Deleuze and Guattari, and the representation of the 'deadly' painful jouissance of Lacan, Derrida and Bataille. This is an 'unbearable' hyperthymesia dissolving recorded orgasms – the memories of pleasure in the World Wide Web. What appears here is the eroticism of the database as the archive providing experiences inaccessible to typical human cognition.

The unbearable eroticism of the database opens in some sense the possibility of digital sampling of the whole reality. The perception which is constructed here reminds of high-dynamic-range imaging producing a simulacrum – a reality which does not exist and which is combined from several different narrower range exposures. The database is like touching the impossible. When the project becomes total with the map of orgasms encompassing people from around the world who are capable of experiencing it, we will perceive an overwhelming database saturated with data to such an extent that the sampling will prove so dense as to achieve the state of Bataille's ideal cohesion.

Bridegrooms of pixels, concrete and steel: the wedding ceremony as an act of subject founding

From late 2009 to 2011 making rounds on the internet were reports of a peculiar chain of events unfolding in Japan. A Nintendo DS user known as Sal9000 decided to marry Nene Anegasaki, a Love Plus character (Figure 8.1). The solemn ceremony included a sort of a priest, attending guests and online visitors watching the event on Nico Nico Douga. In this chapter that uncommon wedding, understood here as a social act, that is, one playing out in the social sphere and sacralized in that sphere, will be used as a case study of the construction of a subject relationship between a human being and an informational creation. This yet another example of a new way of intimacy leads to the foundation of a new subject and to its placement on an equal footing with humans. That is now done through pseudolegal act and ritual. A similar plot motif was used by William Gibson in the cyberpunk novel, *Idoru*[1] (the second book in his *Bridge* trilogy). In that work the wedding itself was not depicted but was the driving force of the entire plot. In this part of the discussion, I will accordingly demonstrate the implications of the comparison of these two declarations of being ready to marry an 'informational being'. One is a projection narration, the other an 'incarnated' iconoclastic manifesto.

The weddings here described, both the one that actually happened and the one intended by Gibson's fictional characters, fit in the broader context of 'strange weddings' – ceremonies in which the participants decide to marry non-humans of highly varied origins. Examples include weddings to animals (so far we have seen a cat, a dolphin and a goat), items or articles (e.g. a pillow or sex doll), architectural objects or their parts (Eiffel's Tower or Berlin Wall) or even oneself.[2] They are usually interpreted in the context of a diverse range of sexual deviation – zoophilia, or, in a large number of such cases, objectophilia, which

Figure 8.1 Newlyweds: Sal9000 and Nene Anegasaki.

is a type of paraphilia distinct from fetishism. As we plough through the various statements made by members of the objectum sexuals community, we will find declarations corresponding to the vision of a subject opened to posthuman bonding as discussed herein.[3] Objectophiles appear also to fit well within the assumptions of new animism, which I referenced in the beginning.[4] Among those beloved objects we will encounter ones that are informational, hence not the typical material objects that objectum sexuals usually place their feelings in. We will be focusing our attention primarily on those in this part of the book, as its purpose is to define the specificity of the intimate relationships between the human subject and the sphere of sense against the background of relating to and bonding with objects of a different provenance (usually of a typically technical origin or even simply material objects). I will also demonstrate in which way the access interfaces to such 'personas' or media in which they are placed affect the shape of the relationships described herein.

Rez and Rei

In Gibson's *Idoru*[5] the character the rock star Rez expects to marry is the most perfect incarnation of artificial intelligence. Rei Toei is a representative of artificial personalities, the Idoru, winning popularity as musical performers.

Rei's depiction in the novel coincides perfectly with the model of posthuman thinking about informational creations as subjects which this book describes. We are referring here to a woman who does not exist, to software that Rez intends to marry, to a conglomeration of different characteristics or parameters, or even a 'synthetic bitch'. The accent is placed on the purely informational substrate of existence rather than the technology conditioning it. These proportions are especially visible during the first meeting of the protagonist, an analyst by name of Laney, with Rei at a party in a club called Western World. On the one hand we see the Idoru as a highly sophisticated mechanism of illusion concealing technology under the suggestive hologram of a beautiful woman, and on the other hand this vision is immediately subjected to criticism through the agency of Willy Jude – a blind drummer attending the party. Jude compensates the loss of sight with a special set of cameras incapable of displaying Rei's holograms, so he only sees the projector and the Idoru's artificial ectoplastic body. Hence, he makes the following demystifying remark: 'Rozzer's sittin' down there makin' eyes at a big aluminum thermos bottle.'[6] This is an important moment showing that what really is attracting Rez's feelings is not the technological infrastructure but the purely informational part of the Idoru's being.

Rei is also an algorithm capable of learning. She develops in a direction that exceeds the limits of human perception. Rez speaks of her as follows:

> Rei's only reality is the realm of ongoing serial creation, (…) Entirely process; infinitely more than the combined sum of her various selves. The platforms sink beneath her, one after another, as she grows denser and more complex.[7]

In a different place the Idoru is described in similar terms to those we have previously encountered in Stanislaw Lem's *Solaris*[8]: 'She is not flesh; she is information. She is the tip of an iceberg, no, an Antarctica, of information. Looking at her face would trigger it again: she was some unthinkable volume of information.'[9]

Media technologies are also that element of Gibson's novel which is of significant importance to defining its unique character – this is because the video clips made for Rei's music are not consciously produced material but something defined as her dreams.[10] Thus, the video material is a product of her life and her existence – something corresponding to the digital ejaculations we have discussed before. On the other hand, the video as an item of cinematographic art once again presents here as an instrument of communication between ontologically different creatures.

Rei is a creation requiring a sophisticated manifestation machinery in 'real life', but in the cyberspace she has absolute freedom to assume any number or range of different shapes, as well as access to often prohibited, private spaces. The Idoru makes use of them in order to learn about the human world and the human psyche.

The scene of the Idoru's meeting with a Lo/Rez fan in a virtual Venice created by the former shows that, similarly to what was the case in Lem's *Solaris*, communication between different beings requires specific spaces in which to negotiate the relations and learn one another.[11] The two friends, fans of the band, show their ambivalent feelings for the Idoru in this scene. Fear and hostility prevail. Interestingly, the Idoru is depicted as a character unsure of her own identity and what she should or should not do. The 'human' characters are the attacking side here, despite the whole event playing out in the virtual space, which is Rei's 'home ground'.

This definition of Rei's image highlights the posthuman relationship to the non-human other based on the acceptance of the latter's otherness, as postulated in posthuman thought.[12] Rez loves Rei not for being a perfect imitation of human personality but for being completely different from human beings – in the sphere of emotionality she has much to learn from humans; she is like a small child unaware of the varied nuance of human psyche and motivation. On the other hand, she has all that which is beyond a human being's reach – the ability to process a huge amount of information, the ability to change shape and the logic of action. Accordingly, Rez and Rei's wedding is intended as the ideal connection of this interbeing potential. The ceremony is expected to confer legitimacy on a transhuman bonding that is to change both the one and the other side of the relationship. This is why Rez claims theirs will be an 'alchemical marriage'.[13] In this case, Bataille's observation is an ideal fit: 'Marriage is still an early and undefined form of sexuality'.[14]

Sal & Nene

Compared to the sublime construct from the novel, Nene Anegasaki seems to be a primitive and non-attractive entity. Nene is also a female character, who functions within the realm of the *Love Plus* date game. She does not exhibit such powerful possibilities as the Idoru. Her AI script is far from refined, and her body is visible only via the Nintendo DS console. Such limitations were not insurmountable for a Japanese boy who took serious interest in her. Unlike Gibson's character, Nene was married in 'real' life.

The internet buzz around the wedding was intense – there were quite a few scornful opinions referring to Sal's perverse behaviours and mental illness. There has been a lot of discussion around the subject of sex between Sal and his beloved, and the semblance of their potential offspring.

A parody of the relationship appeared on YouTube.[15] A similar kind of ostracism occurs in Gibson's novel. Rei introduces the situation in the following words: 'He has told me that we will not be understood, not at first, and there will be resistance, hostility.'[16]

Sal9000 seems to be a profound symbol of posthumanism connected with informational subjectivity. After all, Sal's decision to marry Nene is the action of a real person. His partner is a technological construct functioning, thanks to AI scripts. But defining it goes far beyond purely technological aspects. The console Sal uses is of little importance, and so are his partner's intelligence and conversational skills. Would this falling in love process look different if Sal played *Summer Session* on a PC instead of *Love Plus* on DS? Similarly to Rez, Sal9000 emphasizes that the love spark is enticed not by technology, but by the information itself. 'I love that character, not the machine', said Sal when asked how he could have fallen in love with an electronic device. 'I am 100% aware of the fact that it is a game. I realize, I cannot marry her either physically or legally.'[17] Sal establishes a subject–object relationship between a human entity and informational agent. Similarly to the *Idoru*, the human love towards part of software is brought to the forefront. In terms of artificial intelligence, the agent is far from ideal. Establishing such a relationship by means of having a wedding, in this case, demands a great deal of courage.

Nene, as an informational construct, reaches the status of a subject. In order for this to happen, Sal needs to limit himself. His wedding is an example of pure and fully aware sacrifice. According to Wardrip-Fruin, Mateas, Dow and Saly, free will with reference to video games is pure myth as the player enters into symbiosis with the game.[18] However, in this case Sal self-consciously surpasses the structure of a date simulator. He sacrifices his biological and anthropocentric position in order to unite with Nene. This free will to restrict his humanity is visible in Sal's nickname (Sal9000). It is not Sal that has a full name in this relationship. The name, reminiscent of the *2001 Spaceship Odyssey* by Arthur C. Clarke and Stanley Kubrick, gives Sal a technological status. Sal elevates the subject–object relationship. By doing so, he conjures a new subject represented by Nene.

Objectum Sexuals Community

The above-mentioned intimate relations and the wedding of Sal9000 and Nene seem to be convergent with various aspects of objectophiliac relationships. In this case, we also deal with turning points represented by weddings, which communicate sexual minority manifesting its posthuman attitude towards the objects elevated to the status of subjects.

The specificity of such relations is best articulated by the intimate revelations of the members of this particular community. They seem to confirm both the Gibson's assumptions and the comments about Sal and Nene's wedding. The same problems of the hostility of the wider public come into place.

The community of objectum sexuals has started manifesting their autonomy quite recently. This inception date coincides to a certain degree with the establishment of the idea of posthumanity. The pioneer of this movement was the Swede, Eija-Riitta Eklöf Berliner-Mauer. She has manifested an attraction to objects since a very young age. As the authors of the objectum-sexuality.org website emphasize, her tendency was not stigmatized from the very beginning.

Eija-Ritta took a great pleasure in devoting her time to sculpture. She gradually built an awareness of her own sexual separateness. In 1970 together with her friends, who also discovered their inclination to objectophilia, she coined the term 'Objectum Sexuality'. This term functions as an official name for the whole community. The moment in time when Eija-Ritta got married to the Berlin Wall in 1979 has become a turning point for this group. Since then, Eija-Ritta has gone by the additional surname of Berliner-Mauer (legally recognized). A red wooden fence has become the symbol of OS members.

This community has been raising a lot of controversies. One of its members, Rudi from Germany, provides the following account of the problems associated with being an OS[19]:

> I think the reason why we objectum-sexuals get so much harassment with the normal society is the matter that we consist on the fact that our lovers have a feeling soul and a conscious mind. It is not so much the fact that we have sex with objects or perverse sex. It's that people make sanctions on us in the form of making us look ridiculous and boarding us out. They don't react this way to people masturbating with things today. It is the soul, this sensual, sensitive being in everything. That can be hurt so strong and that also can transmit feelings so beautiful and flowing. The immortal soul that will never fade and vanish, that gives us hope for an eternal life in bliss. This soul in everything that guarantees

the eternal life of the objects we love and so we will rejoin them again when the time has come. We are all raised in a human culture, where biologically non-living beings are supposed to have no soul and no mind. And I may tell you, it is very hard to live against this. At each corner you can hear and read that a man or an animal has feelings but never that a thing has any. In esoteric literature you learn to know, that a stone has got a kind of energy, but not that it has feelings, an I-awareness or even can be a human's partner. In human culture there is a hierarchy – the highest consciousness is possessed by man; a stone just got a dump, primitive kind of awareness. Technical objects like machines aren't even mentioned.[20]

Love does not necessarily have to be a material or technological one. Eva K. emotionally describes her intimate relations with texts. In this case, the text may be perceived as an object belonging to the group of informational subjects (which are non-material products of culture), Eva describes her fascination:

> To fall in love with a word, a logo or a name has always been something entirely normal to me. As a young girl I already felt an exceptional, inflationary attraction to the spoken, and most of all to the written word, which no other person around me seemed to understand. (…) During my life there must have been over 50 very special words and names I was madly … passionately in love with. (…) Being in love with a word means: All the things one would experience when in love with a person; all emotions associated with adoring feelings of love, romance and erotic sensitivity. My dearly loved words, names, or phrases have a soul, an essence; I even dare to say they have a persona. They have colours, landscapes, or wordscape as I like to say. Atmospheres … Words, names or phrases are intangible and abstract subjects so of course we can't think in terms of love-making between humans. However it is possible for me to love them through the making of graphic creations. I usually design my own artworks with the words, sentences, or names I love.[21]

Eva demonstrates that, apart from manifesting the feelings towards non-material objects, intimate relationships are built. Art arises from these feelings. Eva's drawings reflect a search for a platform of reconciliation with her beloved words.

D. from Berlin also emphasizes the differences between love towards humans and objects:

> No, my object definitely does not compensate for the human love. Both kinds of love differ from each other, and cannot be compared! I love my beloved for what she is, for her character, soul and personality. Those features are not much different from the human ones. A human being will never be able to replace the

object. But there is the other side as well. A human being cannot offer what an object can, and the other way around.[22]

Sam cannot function without both types of love. For D. there is no space for competition and replacement of one subject with another. Both are significant and loved in a unique way. D. admits that such a competition may not be acceptable for a human partner. This observation may be confirmed by another wedding ceremony of Nene Anegasaki from *Love Plus*. In 2012 at the wedding of a Japanese couple, the would-be wife officially destroyed her beloved's Nintendo DS with a dating simulator. The groom's eyes filled with tears. The bride could not be coped with a virtual competitor, and thus the only solution was extermination.[23]

Objectophilia love is characterized by the tendency to manifest a specific kind of dedication. This devotion is equal to a conscious resignation of the libido or its limitation. On the one hand, such abdication is derived from the ontological differences between both partners in such relations. On the other, it stems from the assumption that a truly distinctive position of the adored object may be attained predominantly by overcoming lust. In this case, the desire is what reduces the subject to the status of an object (in Bataille's sense).[24] Pure love has the potential to elevate it to the subject role.

B. C. Hall, a sound engineer in love with an electronic organ placed in a church, points to a different perception of sexuality of objectophilia, and emphasizes its non-erotic dimension:

> `sex' with an object does not mean that the way we have sex is anything like the way that humans have sex. For instance, an OS woman does not necessarily have to be penetrated to be having sex; a lot of OS sex is based on an emotional intimacy. Now, don't get me wrong. There are those that are very physically sexual with their objects, but for me personally, it is a psychic connection, an energy transfer in addition to kissing, cuddling, and other such `above-the-waist' displays of affection.[25]

Hall also argues that objectophilia does not differ much from homosexuality:

> It is something that is wired into our brains from the day we are born. It is not a choice, nor is it something you can change or fix. There's nothing to fix, there's nothing to cure, and above all, we are happy to be how we are.[26]

Subject-based relations towards material objects and intentional products of non-material culture expressed by the entire OS movement point to the fact that those non-human agents not only establish the character of the entire relationship, they also have their impact on the choice of the communication channel. Eva draws pictures for her beloved words. B. C. Hall composes music for his adored instrument. Establishing a media protocol for those relations is in this case an important element of emotional expression. In one of the very rare research papers about Objectum Sexuals, Amy Marsh points out that the objective of this protocol is to create diverse pieces of art dedicated to their beloved objects, like sculptures, paintings, poems, photos, films or websites.[27] Her most interesting finding involves the ways OS people claim to communicate with their objects. Many of them profess that they have spiritual and telepathic contact with the objects. Many members of the examined group confess that the best way to communicate with their lovers is non-verbal ways of communication as touch and eye-contact.[28]

Habermas's discourse model in its post-human version assumes a search for communication channels, which enables expression of emotion towards a newly established subject and the most effective use of the medium in order to build the community. Another characteristic of OS people involves looking for various ways to defend the subjectivity of their objects from the rejection of other groups and individuals, who define that very same subject differently. For instance, D. from Berlin guards his architectural objects against vandals. The weddings seem to be the most extreme and daring activities, which communicate the urge to establish the reliability of the object. Clemens and Pettman, who are authors of a really rich study about cultural impact of objects, point out that 'there is certainly increasing evidence that the wider culture is recognizing the claim of existential rights for entities previously dismissed as mere objects'.[29] Through their analysis of Eija-Riitta relation to Berlin Wall they show this kind of intimacy as a posthuman level of normality that we should expect in the near future.

'Marriages and their inconveniences'

I will compare the above case studies. The wedding ceremonies point to the fact that elevating the agents to the role of subjects does not have to be connected with AI. At the same time, this elevation involves the testimony of post-human cohesion.

Sherry Turkle analyses the above process, arguing: 'Even the most primitive of these objects – Tamagotchis and Furbies – made children's evaluation of aliveness less about cognition than about an object's seeming potential for mutual affection. If something asks for your care, you don't want to analyze it but take it "at interface value". It becomes "alive enough" for relationship.[30] This attitude brings the 'alive enough' being close to their establishment as subjects.

Turkle indirectly points to the fact that the subject–object relation derives from the manifestation of the need of contact by the non-human other, not from its need to attain human level of intelligence. What happens here is the intentional will of establishing the subject.

When analysing the institution of marriage, Bataille points towards an important aspect of functioning against the idea of incest.[31] The decision to make their 'daughters, sisters, nieces and cousins' legally accessible, stemmed from the need of transgression. This need has been placed against an unconstrained incestuous access to relatives. Of course, marriage, as reinforcement of the prohibition of incest, has been sanctified by the 'fathers', and therefore it was formed by patriarchal culture. It seems, however, that in the case of Sal and Nene marriage, the relationship between marriage and the idea of patriarchate is less noticeable. This time Sal and Nene's wedding may be perceived as a modern vision of transgression between the human and informational spheres. For Sal, marrying a woman of his own human kind would be defined as incest. Bataille also discusses forces of habit, which are strongly connected to the institution of marriage. Such a mechanism is not yet common in relationships with informational agents. But they may become a standard once those agents achieve their subject status. We may assume a futuristic vision of our human kind, in which the closeness to other agents may cause us to resign from biologically determined needs to be with another human being. How will we sustain our species's continuity? Will procreation become a separate aspect, which will not have much in common with sexual sphere? Will it rely on advanced customization and will our partner be selected at inter-species expo, where humans and informational objects will compete? In one of the interviews, Sal9000 indicates that marrying Nene occurred to him in relation to the practice of calling Japanese otaku game characters wives. This linguistic habit has something magical in itself and may draw the outlines of the nearest future. Lacan describes this process as a constitution of subjects by giving them names.[32] For instance, Adam M. from the United States, yet another representative of objectum sexuals, calls his beloved car Nina.[33]

Introducing a sexual order within legal boundaries (as it is in the case of objectophilia, and Sal and Nene's wedding) facilitates starting the discussion centred on the relation between marriage and various sexual acts. The debates about establishing homosexual relationships and challenging monogamy may at some point incorporate the issues of sexuality expressed towards objects, which are constructed intentionally around technology, exist in the information sphere or are the amalgamation of both.

The wedding ceremony, which is the thematic axis in this part, demonstrates that the sexuality aspect may be important, but is not the most significant factor. In most of the discussed cases and contexts – Nene and Sal, and objectophilia – Bataille emphasizes that the most important matter is pure love. Sexuality is in this case an additional factor subject to devotion. Bataille differentiates between the figure of a wife (as a symbol of non-erotic love) and that of a prostitute, demonstrating the most common separation between those two worlds. These roles highlighted by him, again from the male perspective, still define the ground on which casting gender identity out is possible. This process, as shown in the presented examples, becomes the domain of interbeing relations. For this reason it seems that the terminology categorizing the discussed posthuman relations as sexual deviations may be more efficiently used to symbolize 'posthuman intimacy'. Such symbols may be treated as comfortable elements of a given discourse, not terms defining real sexual practices, as the latter ones in many cases are not of great significance to objectum sexuals.

In such a situation, next to objectophilia as a symbol of pure love towards objects, the symbol of sexuality in informational posthumanism may be pygmalionism. This peculiar type of paraphilia points towards the specificity of intimate relations with the informational sphere. The analysis of this phenomenon focuses on the ability to develop feelings for and attain sexual satisfaction in connection with specific objects. Such objects may be referred to as intentional entities, with the qualities of reasonable entities, summoned creatively, which become subject instances by means of the elevating act of subjectivation. In this particular sexual model, isomorphism seems to be the dominant feature. Sal's efforts are about to lead to establishing Nene as an equal subject, which in Pygmalion leads to the revival of Galatea, who becomes Pygmalion's creation. In the case of pygmalionism, the attraction to one's own creation is of great significance. Nene may be viewed as the product of human genius, and Sal9000 is the representative of human race, who fell in love with his own artefact.[34]

This generalizing character of the wedding ceremony is also present in Lacan's theory. He does not analyse the issue of marriage apart from a fragment in *The Function of Speech and Language*[35] but most of all in *The Ego in Freud's Theory and in the Technique of Psychoanalysis 1954–1955*,[36] where he scrutinized

Molier's *Amphitryon*. Lacan introduces a few significant observations about marriage as a symbolic order. He also emphasizes that the immanent feature of marital love is its placement in the symbolic order.[37] For Lacan, marital love is located in the woman–man–universal/symbolic man triangle connected with the idea of God. Therefore, Amphitryon appears as a man impersonated by Zeus. How could such an idea of marital love refer to inter-species marriage? In this case, wedding would definitely be a factor elevating the relationship from partnership towards the symbolic order. The first stage involves the legitimization of the new subject by its confrontation with other agents in the community. Nene, similarly to Lacan's child, first establishes its identity in front of a mirror where she sees Sal, and then expands it with reference to the outer world. In the second stage, the intimate relationship between two individual instances is elevated to the universal level. In other words, Nene and Sal's wedding is either the imagined individual extravaganza of a Japanese otaku (on the imagined level) or a contribution to the posthuman axis of existence (on the symbolic level). As Lacan emphasizes, referring to Proudhon, 'the love which constitutes the bond of marriage, the love which properly speaking is sacred, flows from the woman towards what Proudhon calls, all men. Similarly, through the woman, it is all women which the fidelity of the husband is directed towards.'[38] From this perspective, Sal symbolizes the whole human kind, and Nene all the non-humans. It seems that moving towards the symbolic level is deeply experienced by those, who are used to the traditionally understood marriage. That is why such a socially focused marriage seems to be so iconoclastic.

A significant function of the weddings described in this paper is posthuman negotiation of legal principles. The ceremonies are important constituents in the struggle for establishing the rights of non-human agents. Their nature is performance-like nature. However, they may also be perceived as experimentation with social-acceptance levels. The right to substitution is being negotiated here. Sal and other objectum sexuals try to introduce their loved ones to the social space, elevating them to the status of subjects, which can be married.

***

The weddings and marriages discussed in this part of the book could be viewed as stark examples of Austinian performatives. However, it so happens that Austin himself – in *How to Do Things with Words* – regards such interspecies relations rather as anti-performative examples, although he prophetically (already in 1962) also notes the significant questions prompted by them for the future:

> Where there is not even a pretence of capacity [for the person to perform the act] or a colourable claim to it, then there is no accepted conventional procedure; it is a- mockery, like a marriage with a monkey. Or again one could say that part of the procedure is getting oneself appointed. When the saint baptized the penguins, was this void because the procedure of baptizing is inappropriate to be applied to penguins, or because there is no accepted procedure of baptizing anything except humans? I do not think that these uncertainties matter in theory, though it is pleasant to investigate them and in practice convenient to be ready, as jurists are, with a terminology to cope with them.[39]

The marriages and weddings discussed in this part do not need to be perceived as motifs of dark future or caricature manifestations of sexual deviations. They may be treated as yet another indication of the change in the anthropocentric perspective. They may also provide a chance to better understand the relationships we humans form with our surroundings and our own creations. The decentralization of the subject leads to the social creation of the new category of the subject, and negotiating its social acceptance. In some cases, the acceptance is fully expressed; in others, the feelings of indignation and disgust towards the other emerge. The core of the marriages and weddings discussed in this chapter is the manifestation of love as the feeling directly connected with dedication and sacrifice. The 'human' signs are the legitimization of true intentions as well as Agamben's 'openness'.[40]

The above examples of establishing emphatic relations refer to the agents of different ontological statuses. Sometimes, the objects are of material nature. However, from this book's perspective, informational object is particularly interesting (e.g. texts, logotypes, video game characters). We could add cinema to the list of lovers, as understood by Patricia MacCormack.[41] For McCormack, however, cinema functions as something in between an intentional motion picture and the machinery creating it. In this case, the difference between objectophilia and pigmalionism shows. The sense seems to be something deriving from within myself as opposed to objects, which may be human creations. For objectiophiles, however, their origin is something of significance. This situation may be compared to the difference between Latour and subject-oriented informational posthumanism. The informational object interacted with on the intimate level, is something between Lacan's Big Other as the world's element and our own creation. Such a viewpoint contains the element of autoeroticism, strongly connected with the distinctiveness of the non-human other, which is the subject of our attraction. This informational subject is close to us and distant at the same time. A certain communication protocol is being established together with its operational mechanisms, and role distribution. In this case, the starting point is the feeling of otherness. On the other hand, the other has its origin in us.

In the context of gender, we can speak of completely new roles and their configurations. However, it would be difficult to call them gender roles, because not only biological sex but also the gender lose their definitional basis in the case of objectum sexuals. These roles are based more on differences in the ontology of entities and are situated between the poles of activity and passivity, duration and transience. They are also associated with categories, such as are bilateralism, inclusion and transgression. Therefore objectophilic relations fit quite clearly into the postulates from Haraway's *Cyborg Manifesto* related to the vision of the world without gender.[42] The new intimate constellations, in this case not necessarily or not always related to technology and monstrosity as in Haraway's manifesto, allow liberation from the category of gender in the same manner as it happens in the hybrid bodies of cyborgs.

Playable apparatus of cruelty:
The Sims as a posthuman camp

The foundation of posthuman entities through weddings and marriages presented in the previous chapter also has its opposite counterpart. In this section I will show the polar opposite whereby the informational entities whose status is under constant discussion are the objects of cruelty. The matter at hand is the particular and, as it turns out, very popular practice, among The Sims players, of killing off in elaborate ways the characters they have developed. In this case cruelty becomes simultaneously a gauge of one's humanity and a vehicle for the discussion of Sims' subjecthood. This part of the book analyses players' own statements highlighting these aspects. I will also juxtapose the Sims with Agamben's idea of the camp.[1] Posthuman studies usually quote Agamben when analysing the relation between the man and the animal due to the expressive idea of the anthropological machine.[2] However, the camp was defined by Agamben himself as a place in 'human' social space. I believe that this category allows for a new definition of relations between the human and non-human.

The Sims – the laboratory of death

A study conducted in 2010 by one of my students, Magdalena Kamyszek, on a group of 250 users of *The Sims*, has shown that killing Sims is the most pleasurable unconventional activity allowed in the game.[3] The analysis of internet data confirms the importance of that experience for the users of the game. On the Web, one can find numerous materials and statements relating to this. There are numerous clips on portals such as YouTube or Vimeo, showing the different ways one can kill a character in the game. Sims, can,

a)   die of fear, when confronted with a ghost or a vampire in a coffin;
b)   drown, when the player destroys the ladder to the swimming pool;
c)   be eaten by flies, when the player leaves unwashed dishes and spoiled food
     in the house;
d)   die of starvation, when the player cuts them off from the world in some
     room;
e)   be eaten by a giant mutant plant a Sim can grow (the so-called
     Cowplant);
f)   die during a hailstorm if they do not find shelter indoors;
g)   die of an incurable illness;
h)   get struck by a lighting if they stay outdoors for too long during a storm
     (standing in a puddle speeds up the process);
i)   get hit by a falling satellite if they watch clouds for too long;
j)   get burned by the sun if they are vampires;
k)   get electrocuted if they are standing in a puddle while fixing the TV;
l)   get burned if they get too close to a burning object;
m) catch a disease from a guinea pig;
n)   die of old age.[4]

Most of the above-mentioned deaths, except for old age, are intentional. Players have to perform intentional activities in order to kill their Sims, for the discussed situations rarely happen by accident. It is worth mentioning, however, that since killing is such a common practice and one of the pleasures of the game, the postulate of openness to informational beings in this case is not heeded. More importantly, killing off virtual characters is not seen as scandalous (except for a relatively small number of players whom I will quote in the next part of the chapter). Sims are generally not considered virtual subjects, even though this attitude has started to change, evolving from indifference and sadistic satisfaction to a discussion of killing children in the game.

One may consider that satisfaction derived from killing Sims, this particular type of cruelty towards them, results from universal human nature. Cruelty in this case becomes an experiment with the efficiency of the objects and the rights they are afforded. The analysis of the motivation of players who derive pleasure from killing Sims, and of the course of particular executions will shed light on this issue of the posthuman experiment. It will be easier then to justify the usefulness of Agamben's idea of the camp for the analysis of these interbeing relations.

Players on killing

Among players' statements on killing found on internet forums I have analysed,[5] we may distinguish three themes: the motivations behind killing off Sims, ways of killing them – which revolves around experimentation – and the rarest, yet for numerous reasons the most interesting, which is discussion of the ontology of the Sims, often connected with professed reluctance to intentional killing.

Motives for killing

Channelling aggression

One of the most common motives is channelling aggression. Sometimes its source is the game itself. LittleMissCupcake explains that she kills her Sims when she is angry at them. Another user points out that it depends whether he likes a given Sim or not. That is probably why the intrusive paparazzi are killed rather often. Another player impersonates an avenger who kills Sims hostile towards other Sims.

In other cases channelling aggression is not connected with the game itself, but takes its origin in the 'real' world. User Cicha woda writes that she kills her characters when she is having a bad day or when she argued with someone. Miksztain[6] writes:

I sometimes create Sims who resemble people from my school or those whom I don't like (Doda hehehe.[7]) And I starve them to death. That is I surround them with walls No windows no floor no 3x3 objects xD. I wait till they die or I'm a jerk and set them on fire.[8]

The narrative of killings

Killing often contributes to the plot of the game or increases its dramatic development. Killing as a narrative element often occurs as one of behaviours a player may choose when encountering other Sims. One player confesses to killing Sims who are partners of attractive characters. These characters attract the Sim operated by the player, so he decides to commit murder. At other times Sims who do not accept the player's controlled character get killed. In a different story we may witness a murder in a wealthy family, where one member of the household is jealous of another's money. The narrative nature of executions may also be seen in a specific type of an intertextual game with genres derived from other media. One user perversely recreates, in a virtual environment, *Big*

Brother, where those who lose die at a cemetery and the winner may count on 'the dream house' and a happy life.[9]

Aesthetic purposes[10]:

> Another important source of pleasure is connected with treating the death of a Sim as an aesthetic experience. One of the users points out that he used to kill Sims for he wanted to find out the colour of their ghosts or because he liked the music accompanying the appearance of the Grim Reaper. Sometimes a Sim must die in order for an aesthetic object to be created. Users like how tombstones get arranged at the cemetery, or how blood gets spilled.

Convenience and boredom

Players often admit to killing their Sims out of convenience. When they get bored of a particular Sim, killing them is one of the fastest ways of getting rid of them while simultaneously keeping other achievements, objects and characters one intends to use further in the game. Sims get eliminated also if there is overpopulation.

Segregation and death

Sometimes the pragmatic aspects of players' attitudes to their Sims resemble the elimination strategies of various historical regimes. Moreover, players often resort to segregation that follows a set of criteria. Pretty Sims are often spared, while the ugly ones are exterminated. This 'eugenic' sort of selection occurs, for example, when a baby is born. If a player does not like its face, he or she resets the game using the save from before the birth in order to 'draw' a different child. Sims are often segregated by their place of origin – those created by the player and those 'from the city'.

Euthanasia

Sometimes players kill the Sims who are expected to die anyway. One of such players voices a perverse philosophy of being:

> I do it when they're going to die anyway [IE: Their age bar is full], UNLESS it's a pet. I can't do it to them for some reason.[11]

Ponury confesses: 'I kill retirees for playing them takes too much time and energy.'[12]

Experiments, ways of execution

Sims often get killed as a result of experiments and satisfaction derived from recreating 'real' spaces of human existence relating to death and physical and mental pain. These experiments are also connected to the pleasure of observing pain and reactions of tortured objects. Players often relate to places created in the game such as cemeteries and prisons.

In many cases executions test the efficiency of narratives. Calusna_kg states:

> I liked killing Sims in *The Sims* ... i lived in a house as a women and met guys made children and when they grew up I killed the family leaving only the girl xD hehe generally to fight off the monotony of the game.[13]

Many users describe their executions using strong, violent language, which is a sign of particular sadism. Such statements are often the sign of personified contempt. Players insult both the Sims they control and those belonging to other players, calling them names. The analysed internet forums display a peculiar spectacle of freedom of speech. Sims are not humans; thus, one can give vent to one's hate speech, which would have detrimental effects if it were to happen in a moderated forum and be directed towards 'living' internet users. Even though forums dedicated to *The Sims* also have their moderators, the ban on abuse and insults does not apply to virtual beings.

When experimenting with killing Sims, players' sophisticated sadistic preferences often come to light. Kakadu states:

> I killed one, poor Janek Kowal, my Cowplant ate him without mercy because of the hand injury of the green-skinned individual. The best part is that his wife, Patrycja, drank the brew of her beloved's intestines and said 'That Sim was delicious'[14]

Annihilating Sims is a source of enormous satisfaction. Players brag about their achievements and are determined to exterminate virtual characters.

Poison's statement, on the other hand, suggests that the pleasure derived from killing Sims may become a creative activity when one has to devise the motives for death that the game's options do not account for.[15] Thus, Poison devises the so-called 'artificial death':

> I no longer do it that often because one has to work really hard to get a good result. I take some clothes and make up so that it looked covered in blood, I order another Sim to prepare food using a knife, my "victim" I order to starve to death, then I move the SIm preparing the food with moveobjects and I look:evil:.It looks as if he was cutting her:rotfl:.(Scoffing and evil laughter) Ha,ha. Sorry, I'm a sadist.[16]

The Sims' ontology and objections against killing

Statements expressing objections against killing Sims are not as frequent as those approving of such actions. It seems that players who express their disapproval usually link it to empathy rooted in granting Sims subjectivity. Simister2004 openly calls Sims persons:

> Never! It's even easier than before to get rid of unwanted sims without killing them: Move them into the bin and throw them away, move them out and don't play with them. I have played the Sims since the morning of Sims time, and I never killed any sims on purpose. Accidents happen you know: fire and cowplants you didn't know how to handle. But murdering those little persons – NEVER![17]

Nika1990 thinks in a similar way:

> You may think I'm stupid or whatever, but killing sims is sick!i get attached to mine and I don't think I could kill Lori,or Mary-Jane!even though it's just a game it's somehow weird ... NEVER have I killed my sim on purpose!!!and i don't intend to!!!![18]

Nika1990's statement is significant for the author feels the need to explain her reluctance towards killing. Which means that she senses that killing is normal and those who do not kill Sims are weird.

Many players explain why they stopped killing Sims by referring to pangs of conscience. Dingo02 points to a kind of humanitarianism both when he decides to kill one of his protégés and when he restrains himself from doing so:

> I rarely kill Sims, unless I have too many children and can't afford them (last time I had 2 adults and 6 kids, and believe me – it was a nightmare!) ... but usually I have mercy on them, for I don't like tormenting Sims and after some time I set them free *[19]

However, granting Sims at least a partial subjectivity is not the only reason behind one's decision to give up killing them. Some players 'grow up' and get bored with killing,[20] or they start to perceive it as a play for children (!).

Still, some users strongly oppose acknowledging any subjecthood in Sims. Cookie writes:

> You feel sorry for a little guy moving on the screen ? it's as if you said that you felt sorry for kenny from south park or animals from happytreefriends.[21]

Another user clearly states his attitude towards Sims:

> I see nothing wrong in killing a sim, no matter its age or any other reason. It's just a game, and sims are just pixels and code. Even though I like playing, I don't perceive sims as human beings.[22]

Vegeta also refers to the non-subject ontology:

> As I already wrote in another thread, I rarely kill sims but to cry for a "picture" that moves on the screen? Sorry but this game is not supposed to make you cry. ... For example, burning a sim with sim fire is exactly the same as if you painted a human and flames around him. I don't think that the picture feels as it burns with "red-yellow lines". **SIMS ARE JUST PICTURES "MOVING ON THE SCREEN!!!**[23]

It happens that users feel the need to clearly define and distinguish between the living, known from the 'real world' (people, animals, insects), and that which exists only on the computer screen:

> While I love to kill sims, in the real world I don't even kill spiders. If it's a *real* living thing, I respect it as a fellow creature capable of knowing pain and fear, and don't inflict these things unnecessarily.[24]

It also happens that even though users know that Sims are not subjects, it still creates confusion:

> I never kill sims, neither my own nor EA's premades/ townies, i am far too soft that. I even get shocked and appalled reading about how others kill ugly sims/ annoying sims etc. Dont worry am not clinically insane I do realise they are just a bunch of pixels I am just supersoft like andrex lol.[25]

One should also take into consideration a large part of the discussion devoted to the death of baby Sims. Most participants are against killing underage Sims, especially when the creators of the game do not allow it – the methods of killing adult Sims in this case simply do not work. At the same time the users who discuss the issue admit that they have tried it: 'Do you know that children and infants are resistant to fire?', asks one of the users. However, there are accounts that indicate such a possibility as well. Infant-Sims can die when held by an adult Sim. Another user shares his experience regarding the death of children (probably older than infants): 'I have seen babies die of drowning, starving, electrocution and fire. And no, I've never ever done that. But if you over populate a town, story progression will kill babies.'[26]

The Sims and the idea of a Camp

The above analysis of players' statements regarding killing Sims points to a few important issues. Firstly, Sims become objects of experiments in cruelty, convenient objects as they do not have any rights. Thus in this case they may be freely persecuted. Vegeta claims: 'Even the user's guide states that having conscience is not required to play *The Sims*; in fact, sometimes it may be an obstacle.'[27] Secondly, Sims, similarly to the robots analysed by Sherry Turkle, have an ambiguous status. Not only are they 'alive enough' to take care of them, but they are 'alive enough' to be subjected to sophisticated cruelty. These two components become an important starting point for the interpretation of the relation between users and informational subjects in which the idea of the camp appears. Let us analyse which aspects of Agamben's idea may be applied here and which differentiate a human camp from a non-human one.[28]

Life that does not deserve to live

The Sims is a space of total freedom when it comes to experiments with the criteria that in Agamben's theory determine a life's worth and become the basis for deciding whether a life is worth living or 'valueless'. In the 'human' dimension, Agamben points out, the problem used to be applied to the mentally ill, incurably sick, elderly. In the game this range is broadened. The examples discussed above show that the distinction between those who deserve to live and those who may be killed is not based on the division between the young and the old, or the healthy and the sick, but includes the pretty and the ugly, or 'mine' and 'those from the city'. In fact, this range is even broader, as it includes every aspect of virtual life susceptible to evaluation.

Peculiar space of the state of exception

According to Agamben, the state of exception occurs when one's rights and civil liberties get suspended. It is difficult to write about Sims' civil liberties, although the way they are killed in the game is often connected to the restrictions imposed on their movement and actions. To kill Sims, players remove doors so they cannot not get out of the room, place them in very small rooms or remove ladders from swimming pools so they would drown. In terms of territory, the camp is an excluded place. In a similar way, the estate a player places the Sim to be tortured in is a territory excluded from the law-abiding space of the city. Players often attempt to destroy this order outside, destabilize it. They invite Sims from the city to their houses in order to destroy them; they go to the city to kill. The inside of the estate becomes the typical Agambenian space where the law interferes with the fact that allows for all behaviours. Exception, which in the game is a Sim's accidental death, becomes the rule. For example, one of the users quoted above apologizes for not killing Sims.

Double exclusion

On the one hand, the state of double exclusion in case of *The Sims* is similar to Agamben's camp for humans. On the other hand, however, it has its own specificity. Sims are not humans, but they live in a game ruled by human laws (of a simulated social life). Excluding them from human law in order to kill them, we move them to the space of the state of exception, in a similar way a refugee is moved in Agamben's theory to the camp. On the other hand, being non-human is a state Agamben's analysis does not account for. To Agamben, life that can be killed is part of *homo sacer*, not *creatura sacra*. Nevertheless, it is still exclusion, although of a different kind – from a group of subjects or, to be more exact, from a group of living creatures. It is not difficult to point to Agamben's sacred order. Exclusion from the group of subjects denies non-humans the availability of a sphere of *sacrum*.

Testimony of the untestifiable

In *Remnants of Auschwitz*, Agamben discusses the issue of 'that to which no one has borne witness'[29] – a situation in which it is impossible to experience certain events, such as the gas chamber, for all its participants have died. Yet if we look at the testimonies of the players regarding Sims' executions, they seem to reverse that order. In all spheres of relations between humans and other beings (both humans and animals), the law prevents both acts of violence and testimonies of such sick pleasures. If they do appear, they are accompanied by journalist, academic, or legal commentary putting the pleasure in inverted commas. The goal is to prevent one from following that ghastly pleasure, from yielding to undesirable cruelty. These testimonies of cruelty are something shameful that needs to be kept a secret, reserved for the few who one needs to distance oneself from them. In interviews, criminals usually try to justify themselves by showing their motives in order to rationalize the situation, not by manifesting the pleasure derived from torture. Such pleasure is acceptable only as a literary motif, not as a testimony.

Therefore the testimonies of Sims' executioners, expressed freely and with undisguised satisfaction, become something new and different, the testimonies of true pleasure, impossible in case of other acts of violence. The negation of Sims' subjectivity becomes in this case a chance to reveal the impossible. Thus these testimonies are characteristic and provocatively frank. They circumvent prohibitions and show this part of players' nature which would be inexpressible and inconceivable under the law which binds living creatures.

Silent outlaws

Sims are, on the one hand, migrants with uncertain, or even unsolvable, status. Their life escapes traditional definitions of life, they have no rights, the right to subjectivity is denied them. On the other hand, they may cause pangs of conscience. Therefore they occupy the space 'in between'. The case of the tormented Sims shows that the rights of virtual beings are not the subject of discussion or negotiation. The need to grant them any rights is not even verbalized. The only exception introduced by the game's designers is the prohibition on killing children, but even in this area one can come up with ideas to evade the ban.

On the other hand, Sims fit the category of the Muselmann (Moslem), which Agamben borrowed from Levi.[30] In her analysis of intelligent robots, Turkle points out that they do not have aspirations or desires even if such emotions are projected onto them for instance by kids.[31] In a way they also fit the category of the Muselmann. Sims are a similar case, for even though during the game they communicate various needs, as migrants they become listless objects of cruelty. They cannot even respond or react. They are 'safe' objects of torture, similarly to the Muselmann they do not rebel, they are apathetic and alienated.

Subversive cruelty

The examples discussed above show that cruelty, so particular for the space of *The Sims*, may be strictly connected with the idea of subversive playing.[32] Killing Sims was not designed as the main goal of the game. It is a rather unusual theme, for subversion is usually associated with deliverance and liberation from the oppressive structure, with disrupting it from within. Aarseth claims that 'subversive playing is a symbolic act of resistance against the tyranny of the game, a (perhaps illusory) way to give the subject back his or her identity and sense of uniqueness by using the mechanisms of the game'.[33] Here we have hard evidence that subversion may be oppressive.

In *The Sims* subversion as an oppressive activity consists in inventing various gaming modes (modifications) which multiply the means of destruction. For example, one of the modes allows for building an electric fence that can kill a Sim. Another mode allows for sitting a Sim on the electric chair (Figure 9.1). A considerable number of torture devices appear. These are examples of how players concentrate their ingenuity around the idea of cruelty. Taking all the above into consideration, the perfect embodiment of the camp in case of *The Sims* would be Kafka's *In the Penal Colony*,[34] where the execution machine becomes the symbol of the art of cruelty.

Panoptical properties of the camp for Sims

The camp players build for Sims also show interesting panoptical properties. The camp as the place of emotionless observation is best seen in situations when one has to wait for Sims to die (e.g. waiting for a meteor to hit them), but also in another interesting motif caused by the bugs in the game the creators

Figure 9.1 The electric chair, created by NecroDogMTSands4S Studio, as one of new items for *The Sims* game. Image courtesy of NecroDogMTSands4S Studio.

were unable to eliminate. There is a whole range of such glitches providing an opportunity to determine Sims' subjecthood and manifest one's voyeuristic interest in deformation, resembling unhealthy curiosity about deformed human bodies.

The very act of killing Sims is often recorded, which, similarly to African hunters and American trappers photographed with the animals they killed, players brag about on video servers and in players' communities. The situation also resembles so-called crush movies, where animals are tortured and killed on-screen. Cookie eagerly prepares photostories with fragments of executions, on numerous occasions bragging to his friends from the forum[35]:

> i love killing sims with axes and weapons … i will soon post pictures from my den of death. i just need to enter the game. which is veeeeery slow.[36]

Recording the execution as a permitted act is in this case the result of having established the world of Sims as a camp where basic laws do not apply. The search for a space for cruelty, when it is not so easy to manifest cruelty towards either humans or animals, has led us to virtual worlds where it is possible.

'Frog leaps' of sovereign power

If we look at the history of human cruelty, it may be concluded that its manifestations are a search for the space of double exclusion, building camps where killing is allowed. Sometimes it is a death camp for humans, at other times a hecatomb of animals. Leaping from one camp to another is often caused by new law introduced in such spaces, transforming the space 'in between' into a space defined by law. Cruelty, when not allowed to be expressed, will look for another place of freedom.

Considering that by playing – as shown by the example of *The Sims* – one embodies the idea of the executioner, one may state that this time cruelty gets manifested in virtual space that has not yet been granted basic laws (which may never be granted). Considering that through cruelty the range of freedom is negotiated – the freedom that nowadays one is not granted with regard to another human being and is gradually deprived of with regard to animals – the relations with informational subjects are the last sphere where such cruelty is permitted. The camp as a place of experimentation is best manifested in environments such as *The Sims*, for the range of allowed cruelty is defined only by the structure of the game its and available options (though not always, since players can arrange certain solutions which the game does not account for).

***

The above reflections show that relations between subjects that posthumanism accounts for may include the sphere where non-human others are granted or deprived of rights. The non-human subjects discussed in the text fit perfectly Agamben's notion of the emigrant, as they stay in the space outside the law or become the objects of double exclusion.[37]

In fact, the redefinition of subjectivity by posthuman studies reveals both positive and negative contexts of attitudes towards non-humans, and 'consent for being' often turns into 'consent for violence' when non-human subjects, undergoing discoursivization in the state of exception of the camp, are exposed to violence and elaborate forms of oppression. Of course one can repeat, after the players quoted in this chapter, that Sims are not beings; yet, similarly to people these virtual individuals are shown both our 'human' affection and cruelty.

The generalized idea of the camp should stress the posthuman power to destabilize human subjectivity. In this case being deprived of rights equals being deprived of the right to call oneself human. Agamben stresses the terminological level of de-framing of human life – the subjects of his interest are both *homo sacer* and bare life. Thus bare life becomes the life that is not entirely human and not entirely life. It becomes bare non-life, as in the case of Sims.

Final word (towards a theory of apparatus of posthuman intimacy)

Agambenian media apparatus – the subject matter of the analyses in this book – are highly complex appliances, both structurally and functionally. As I demonstrated, such vehicles are generators of subjecthood at the same time as apparatus of capture with clear relations of power. Such relations run in various directions and are an incessant negation running from the integral human subject's royal throne, losing that privileged position in the apparatus's 'critical' space, to the 'immaterial Galateas' created in the apparatus and back.

The destabilization process of the human subject involves several significant effects. Sometimes the effect is to adopt a position of sense touching both those human subjects acting as senders, such as in interactive television quizzes, and as recipients, as we could see in the Teleprompter's example. Often, the consequence of such a change of position is a type of symbolic suffering that appears in the first example or the sense of delusion and uncertainty linked to the second example. One could say the prompter literally destabilizes the sense of stability of eye contact with the caster. The prompter's power manifests itself also in how its paradigm can appear in other technologies. When a member of the team of special-effects creators for Avatar describes how for one of the scenes the actor would fix its gaze with emotional attachment in a tennis ball supplanted by the actress in the postproduction process,[1] we are dealing with a sort of hybridization of the prompter as an apparatus of 'fake seeing' with an objectophiliac relationship.

For a human being, other effects of entering the apparatus sphere include first and foremost destabilization of the so-far integral body, as a consequence of framing and visibility. In the peep-show case, for both the customers and the dancers this process happens on both sides of the glass panel. The customer's body is dismembered by the formatting shape of the cabin – from the outside one can see the legs and inside only genitalia can be visible, through glory holes. The cabin carries the same strong potential for dismemberment, dematerialization and machinization for the dancer – the stripper becomes a discontinuous image of which the appearance is conditioned by the operation of the slot apparatus. The process of the loss of the physical body and becoming equated with one's own image also accompanies the actors advertising in front of the video booth the porn film played within it, in which they are cast. The case of the beautifulagony.com base discussed in the project, in turn, is an apparatus of deep digitization, wherein database apparatus replaces the 'continuous' narration of biological sexuality. Entering into the erotic order of the database entails the loss of such continuity and such formatting of lust and of the sexual act so as to facilitate categorization and distribution.

Information subjects founded within media technologies also represent an extensive range of immaterial and intentional entities often having a not outwardly visible deep cyborgical-hybrid structure, as is the case with film characters such as Benjamin Button; sometimes, even though they are uniform, they require 'consolidation' and empathy.

Unfinished and incomplete entities in *Winky Dink and You* require the spectator's direct reaction in order to exist on-screen. There is more to it than any intentional filling of gaps. It contains subjectivation created in the ludic apparatus. At this time a vehicle of entertainment. At other times entertainment is replaced with even ritual sacrifice, which to Agamben is an apparatus enabling separation[2] – here it will constitute the separation or, better, emergence of a separate subject of love. More or less formalized objectophiliac relationships are such a sacrifice apparatus; the most important among them for my approach were relationships with immaterial objects, as exemplified by Sal and Nene's wedding. In other cases, however, virtual entities become modern objects of experimentation with cruelty. After the Holocaust of people and animals, which still goes on but is attracting an increasing amount of right restrictions and objections, the time came for artistic forms and freedom of cruelty in a space in which virtual passively obedient subjects have no chance to defend themselves, as they have not (yet) been accorded the status of subjects or perhaps they have not (yet) matured to the role. If we compare The Sims and Nene Anegasaki, the video-game environment shows a type of deep contradiction. Sometimes virtual characters prove to be worthy of empathy and even marriage but at other times they are merely digital lab animals on which the players test out the limits of their cruelty. This changeability of roles attributed to virtual characters appears to be characteristic of all non-human instances discussed in posthuman discourse.

In the cinema technologies examined in this book, an interesting mechanism supporting the construction of new subjects is self-intimacy, apparently derived from narcissism. Derrida's self-affect idea also corresponds with this mechanism.[3] It could be referred to as transferring away one's subjecthood onto media creations. This is done both by animation creators and by creators of modern special effects.[4] In a historical view, one could say that before objectophiles appeared, animation saw the coming to life of cars, bridges and houses equipped with the ability to love or elements of the creators' personalities. Accordingly, the examined cases made us realize that the subjectivation of information is a category with a deep internal dialectic. On the one hand, the informationality of the presented entities places the analysis in extremely non-subjective orders of cybernetics; on the other hand, they are the testimony of a will to saturate the world with subjecthood, as universal as it may be occasional. Once again Chardin's noosphere paradigm surfaces here.[5]

Analysis of certain modern digital effects shows also that the process of the founding of new screen entities is at once the beginning of a process of correction of the world built around them. It is interesting what Avatar's creators have to say about this process. For example, during the production it became necessary to generate a different type of lighting for Na'vi skin,[6] because blue skin could not be lit with the orange light from fire, looking grey and awful, as if on a zombie. Hence, the crew had to work out a technique for altering light parameters for blue creatures. At other times, this importance of subjecthood emerged at the state of composing the set out of a variety of biotic and inanimate elements.[7] Guy Williams complained that when different avatars were placed close to one another some appeared unnatural. And when that could be fixed, the surroundings in turn would acquire a plastic look; for example, when Jake Sully boarded the Samson helicopter, the machine began to resemble a child's toy.

Case studies traces in the preceding chapters also provide examples of a diversity of interbeing attraction fairs. These could be divided into two groups, internal and external. The first group are examples in which the juxtaposition of informational and human elements takes place inside of the constructed work. Hybrid animations or modern film productions relying on a combination of actors and digital characters are only examples of places in which the construction of planes of intercommunication takes place within the text.

The second group are attraction fairs that venture into the social and are external with regard to the work. This social existence of immaterial 'media' subjects highlighted in several places in this work is begging for a broader description accounting for the fact that the process is unfolding before our very eyes. The cause is that objectophiles' intimate histories show, for example, that the direction of change taking place here runs from highly private and concealed passion leading to a desire to uplift the beloved object to the status of a subject, to a fight for its due place in the social order. We can already now encounter more examples of this type.

Independently from all the controversies and debates surrounding civil rights of robots and, for example, their sexualization and the special status of technological agents in certain cultures, e.g. Japanese, one can also notice the expansion of social roles and 'circulations' of immaterial objects. Already at the beginning of the twenty-first century, a virtual agent, Mya, created by Digital Domain for Motorola, appeared in a talk show and the 2000 Oscar gala, and her portraits made their way into *USA Today*, *Wired* and *InStyle*.[8] At present, virtual assistants such as Siri or Cortana increasingly often become partners in sexual interactions[9] and amorous interactions with AI scripts are entering the mainstream, such as Spike Jonze's *Her* or Denis Villeneuve's *Blade Runner 2049*.

The development of CGI techniques in modern cinema more and more frequently leads to virtual characters being treated on par with live actors and creating film plots together with them, in which they are regarded as full-fledged heroes accepted by the audience. Suffice to say the resurrection of Moff Tarkin (previously played by Peter Cushing) and the rejuvenation of Carrie Fisher as Princess Leia in *Star Wars: Rogue One*, or the titular character in *Alita: Battle Angel*.

A similar social autonomy is also possessed by increasingly recognizable virtual pop stars such as Hatsune Miku, Kyoko Date, Yuki Terai or Miko,[10] who, in addition to their actual concert tours, are even invited to photo sessions for fashion magazines such as *Vogue*.[11]

The posthuman apparatus and non-human informational subjects presented in this book define a framework for an understanding of posthumanism that is neither topographic nor relational. Both human and non-human subjecthood generated in visual apparatus depend on the position taken by biological and digital bodies in the vehicle's space. Here, the character of the posthuman position that can form in specific circumstances and under specific conditions is pro-subject on the one hand, for it allows ontologically diversified objects to be uplifted as subjects, and therapeutic on the other hand, as it helps human agency feel the weight of its decisions and its role in the new post-anthropocentric world. Thus, in the end, one could say that the measure of our humanism lies in understanding what posthumanism is in all its diverse types and contexts. The self-referential criticality of this strategy creates a hope of protection from despair occasioned by the downfall of the ideal of integral, self-aware and superordinate humanity. On the other hand, the will to establish new subjects is a testimony of demiurgic potential that also provides a defence against fear and opens new opportunities for positioning in relation to the world and non-human others.

Notes

Introduction

1 Donna Jeanne Haraway, *Simians, Cyborgs, and Women: The Reinvention of Nature* (New York: Routledge, 1991).

2 Donna Jeanne Haraway, *The Companion Species Manifesto: Dogs, People and Significant Otherness* (Chicago, IL: Prickly Paradigm Press, 2009).

3 Cf. e.g. Pettman's *humanimalchine*. Dominic Pettman, *Human Error: Species – Being and Media Machines*, vol. 14, Posthumanities (Minneapolis: University of Minnesota Press, 2011), 6.

4 In a number of such type of collations information is omitted, e.g. 'the endosymbiotic Assemblage between bacteria, animals, plants, humans and technology constitutes a heterogeneous biosphere of evolution that challenges the neo-Darwinian emphasis on individuated units of selection', in *Abstract Sex: Philosophy, Bio-Technology and the Mutations of Desire*, ed. Luciana Parisi, Transversals (London and New York: Continuum, 2004), 141.

5 Joanna Zylinska, *Bioethics in the Age of New Media* (Cambridge, MA: MIT Press, 2009), 61.

6 Katherine Hayles, *How We Became Posthuman: Virtual Bodies in Cybernetics, Literature, and Informatics* (Chicago, IL: University of Chicago Press, 1999), 25.

7 Hayles, *How We Became Posthuman*, 39.

8 Allucquere Rosanne Stone, 'Will the Real Body Please Stand Up?: Boundary Stories about Virtual Cultures', in *Cyberspace: First Steps*, ed. Michael Benedikt (Cambridge, MA: MIT Press, 1991).

9 Francis Barker, *The Tremolous Private Body: Essays on Subjection* (London: Methuen, 1984).

10 Stone, 'Will the Real Body Please Stand Up?', 99–100.

11 Here, it is worth noting the difference between the posthuman perspective and the transhumanist perspective, for the purposes of which an entirely different terminology will be relevant, such as enhancement, modification, repair, capacity increase, overcoming limitations. Kristi Scott notes that transhumanism and posthumanism, albeit frequently regarded as interchangeable, entail in reality two entirely different worldview perspectives. Transhumanism is an idea founded on enlightenment rationality and, in its opinion, perpetuates the human concept

predefined by the Western white middle-class man. Posthumanism, by contrast, in asking questions about humanity and questioning it, positions itself critically by definition, thanks to which it invites different voices into the debate; see Kristi Scott, 'Transhumanism vs./and Posthumanism', *Ethical Technology*, 14 July 2011, http://ieet.org/index.php/IEET/more/scott20110714. Building upon this thought, it is worth noting that also in the transhumanist perspective there appears a category of posthumanism, though it means a 'state after', in which, as Stefan Sorgner writes, the posthuman is a 'new species that represents a further stage of evolution;' see Stefan Sorgner, 'Nietzsche, the Overhuman, and Transhumanism', *Journal of Evolution and Technology* 20, no. 1 (2009): 29–42.

12   It seems that such a harmonized vision accompanies the reflection of Wolfe, who attempts to combine the system-theory perspective with the posthumanism of the subjective 'other'. See Cary Wolfe, *What Is Posthumanism?*, vol. 8, Posthumanities Series (Minneapolis: University of Minnesota Press, 2010).

13   This problem of the 'different' posthumanisms is noted, *inter alia*, by Monika Bakke; see Part I *Posthumanism(s)* in: Monika Bakke, *Bio-transfiguracje: sztuka i estetyka posthumanizmu [Bio-transfigurations. Art and Esthetics of Posthumanism]* (Poznań: Wydawnictwo Naukowe Uniwersytetu im. Adama Mickiewicza, 2012).

14   Hayles, *How We Became Posthuman*, 246.

15   She notes the co-participation of the humans entering into interactions with robots in the creation of the illusion of a living being, which consists in filling the technological gaps of the imperfect robot; see chapter: *Complicitness* in: Sherry Turkle, *Alone Together: Why We Expect More from Technology and Less from Each Other* (New York: Basic Books, 2011), 109–43. See also Bradley Onishi, 'Information, Bodies, and Heidegger: Tracing Visions of the Posthuman', *Sophia* 50, no. 1 (2011): 101–12.

16   Mary Flanagan, 'The Bride Stripped Bare to Her Data', in *Data Made Flesh: Embodying Information*, ed. Robert Mitchell and Phillip Thurtle (New York and London: Routledge, 2003), 159.

17   Flanagan, 'The Bride Stripped Bare to Her Data', 159.

18   Flanagan, 'The Bride Stripped Bare to Her Data', 170–1. The Barthes quotation comes from Roland Barthes and Susan Sontag, *A Barthes Reader* (London: Cape, 1982), 410.

19   The above-described study strategy is already present in Hayles's work (*supra*), where she, after all, analyses the stages in the development of cybernetics delimited by the succession of Macy conferences. This perspective is also present in Biro's monograph; Matthew Biro, *The Dada Cyborg: Visions of the New Human in Weimar Berlin/Matthew Biro* (Minneapolis, MN and London: University of Minnesota Press, 2009), where he, employing the cyborg category, studies the presence of

posthuman threads in German dadaists' oeuvres. David A. Mindell, in turn, highlights the taking shape of the pre-cybernetic thinking about the control systems used in the military technologies of the Second World War era as the first systems for human-machine interaction; see David A. Mindell, *Between Human and Machine: Feedback, Control, and Computing before Cybernetics*, Johns Hopkins Studies in the History of Technology (Baltimore: Johns Hopkins University Press, 2002).

20 It is also worth noting the *Postmedievalism* journal as an integrated project for viewing the past through the lens of posthumanism categories, as well as looking for the latter's sources in the Middle Ages.

21 This current is represented, among others, by Lisa Gitelman and Zigfrid Zielinski, Errki Huhtamo and Jussi Parikka or Ryszard W. Kluszczyński; see e.g. Lisa Gitelman, *Always Already New: Media, History and the Data of Culture* (Cambridge, MA: MIT Press, 2006). Siegfried Zielinski, *Deep Time of the Media: Toward an Archaeology of Hearing and Seeing by Technical Means*, Electronic Culture: History, Theory, Practice (Cambridge, MA: MIT Press, 2006). Erkki Huhtamo and Jussi Parikka, eds., *Media Archaeology: Approaches, Applications, and Implications* (Berkeley, CA: University of California Press, 2011). Ryszard W. Kluszczyński, 'From Film to Interactive Art: Transformations In Media Arts', in *MediaArtHistories*, Red. Oliver Grau (Cambridge, MA and London: The MIT Press, 2007), pp. 207–28.

22 Friedrich A. Kittler, *Gramophone, Film, Typewriter*, Writing Science (Stanford, CA: Stanford University Press, 1999).

23 Recently, after the publication of the first edition of this book, there have been attempts to indicate the potential of Lacan theory in defining non-human subjectivity; see Gautam Basu Thakur and Jonathan Michael Dickstein, eds., *Lacan and the Nonhuman* (Cham: Palgrave Macmillan, 2018).

24 See e.g. Judith Halberstam and Ira Livingston, *Posthuman Bodies*, Unnatural Acts (Bloomington: Indiana University Press, 1995). Zoe Detsi-Diamanti, Katerina Kitsē-Mytakou and Effie Yiannopoulou, *The Future of Flesh: A Cultural Survey of the Body*, 1st ed. (New York: Palgrave Macmillan, 2009).

25 Here it is worth mentioning e.g. Parisi, *Abstract Sex*. see also Rosi Braidotti, *The Posthuman* (Cambridge: Polity Press, 2013).

26 It would be difficult here in this place to give a full accounting of the lavishly abundant number of bio-art publications referencing Deleuze and Gauttari, but such threats appear, among others, in Eugene Thacker, *Biomedia*, vol. 11, Electronic Mediations (Minneapolis: University of Minnesota Press, 2004); Eduardo Kac, *Telepresence & Bio Art: Networking Humans, Rabbits & Robots*, Studies in Literature and Science (Ann Arbor: University of Michigan Press, 2005); Robert Mitchell,

Bioart and the Vitality of Media, In Vivo: The Cultural Mediations of Biomedical Science (Seattle: University of Washington Press, 2010); Charles R. Garoian, *The Prosthetic Pedagogy of Art: Embodied Research and Practice* (Albany, NY: State University of New York Press, 2013).

27 For example, Cathy Waldby, *The Visible Human Project: Informatic Bodies and Posthuman Medicine*, Biofutures, Biocultures (London: Routledge, 2000).

28 John Suler, Psychology of Cyberspace, http://users.rider.edu/~suler/psycyber/psycyber.html.

29 See Sherry Turkle, *Life on the Screen: Identity in the Age of the Internet* (New York: Simon & Schuster, 1995); Sherry Turkle, *The Second Self: Computers and the Human Spirit/Sherry Turkle*, 20th anniversary ed., 1st MIT Press ed. (Cambridge, MA and London: MIT, 2005). Sherry Turkle, *Evocative Objects: Things We Think with* (Cambridge, MA: MIT Press, 2007).

30 Don Ihde, *Ironic Technics* (Copenhagen: Automatic Press/VIP, 2008).

31 Turkle, *Alone Together*.

32 Slavoj Žižek, *The Plague of Fantasies*, Wo Es War (London and New York: Verso, 1997), here above all Chapter IV., titled 'Cyberspace, Or, The Unbearable Closure of Being'.

33 Cf. 'Lacan considers fantasy also (at least in my analysis) to be an inevitable medium for "interfacing" the inaccessible real and the world of imaginary depictions and symbolic representations that humans mentally live in'. André Nusselder, *Interface Fantasy: A Lacanian Cyborg Ontology*, Short Circuits (Cambridge, MA: MIT Press, 2009), 5.

34 This was also identified in Freud, for example, in his *Mystic Writing Pad* – see Sigmund Freud, 'A Note upon the "Mystic Writing Pad"', in *The Ego and the ID and Other Works*, trans. James Strachey and Anna Freud, vol. XIX (1923–5), The Standard Edition of the Complete Psychological Works of Sigmund Freud. (London: The Hogarth Press and the Institute of Psycho-Analysis, 1961), 227–32.

35 Suzanne Dow and Colin Wright, *Psychoanalysis and the Posthuman*, vol. 33, no. 3, Paragraph (Edinburgh: Edinburgh University Press, 2010), 304.

36 Dow and Wright, *Psychoanalysis and the Posthuman*, 303.

37 Dow and Wright, *Psychoanalysis and the Posthuman*, 303.

38 Dow and Wright, *Psychoanalysis and the Posthuman*, 303.

39 Jacques Lacan, *Freud's Papers on Technique, 1953–1954*, ed. Jacques-Alain Miller, trans. John Forrester, vol. 1, Seminar of Jacques Lacan (New York: W. W. Norton & Company, 1993), 80.

40 Jacques Lacan, *The Four Fundamental Concepts of Psycho-analysis* (New York and London: W.W. Norton & Company, 1998), 95.

41 Wolfe, *What Is Posthumanism?*, for this purpose chapters 6 and 7.

42 In this work the mythological figure of Galatea as the ivory statue sculpted by
    Pygmalion, who would awaken affection in it, is a relatively universal symbol
    for information subjects. Those are 'intimate' objects called forth to the status of
    subjects as a result of intention and in consequence of a variety of specific practices
    and rituals, similarly to how Pygmalion deals with his sculpture (author's note).

43 Referring to Levi Agamben uses Nazi camps nomenclature in which Jewish
    prisoners used the term Muselmann to name those of them who suffered from
    starvation and exhaustion, and who were resigned to their impending death. Such
    prisoners behaved apathetic and displayed complete passivity. See Primo Levi, *If
    This Is a Man*, Reprint (London: Abacus, 1987), 94.

44 See e.g. Neil L. Whitehead, 'Post-human Anthropology', *Identities* 16, no. 1 (2009):
    1–32. and Neil L. Whitehead and Michael Wesch, *Human No More: Digital
    Subjectivities, Unhuman Subjects, and the End of Anthropology* (Boulder: University
    Press of Colorado, 2012).

45 Cf. e.g. the title of 2014 conference of the European Association of Social
    Anthropologists, *Collaboration, Intimacy & Revolution – Innovation and Continuity
    in an Interconnected World and Select Texts*, or numerous books and articles: Shaka
    McGlotten, *Virtual Intimacies: Media, Affect, and Queer Sociality* (Albany: State
    University of New York Press, 2013); Gerard C. Raiti, 'Mobile Intimacy: Theories
    on the Economics of Emotion with Examples from Asia', *M/C Journal* 10, no. 1
    (2007), http://journal.media-culture.org.au/0703/02-raiti.php; Sean Carney, *Brecht
    and Critical Theory: Dialectics and Contemporary Aesthetics*, vol. 2, Routledge
    Advances in Theatre and Performance Studies (London and New York: Routledge,
    2005); Raul Pertierra, 'Mobile Phones, Identity and Discursive Intimacy', *Human
    Technology* 1, no. 1 (2005): 23–44.

46 Especially the last part of the book, about new-media phenomena, will bring my
    studies closer to the current that is sometimes termed the ethnography of the
    cyberspace. It is represented, among others, by David Hakken.

47 Derrida refers to Artaud in his essay on the subjectile. See Jacques Derrida,
    'Maddening the Subjectile', in *Yale French Studies*, trans. Mary Ann Caws, 84,
    (Boundaries: Writing & Drawing, 1994), 154–71. The perspective of combining the
    Brecht and Artaud vision of theatre with the thought of Derrida and Lacan appears
    also in the works of later interpreters; see e.g. Philip E. Bishop, 'Brecht, Hegel,
    Lacan: Brecht's Theory of Gest and the Problem of the Subject Studies', *Twentieth
    and Twenty-first Century Literature* 10 (1986): 267–88. Carney, *Brecht and Critical
    Theory*.

48 See en. 15 and, among others, the Chapter titled: Mark Dery, 'RoboCopulation:
    Sex Times Technology Equals the Future', in *Escape Velocity: Cyberculture at
    the End of the Century*, 2nd ed. (New York: Grove Press, 1999). It is also worth
    pointing towards the prophetic posthuman works by the Krokers on this

subject: Arthur Kroker and Marilouise Kroker, eds., *Body Invaders: Panic Sex in America*, Culturetexts (New York: St. Martin's Press, 1987), and Arthur Kroker and Marilouise Kroker, *The Last Sex: Feminism and Outlaw Bodies*, Culturetexts (New York: St. Martin's Press, 1993).

49 Gilles Deleuze and Félix Guattari, *Anti-Oedipus: Capitalism and Schizophrenia* (Minneapolis: University of Minnesota Press, 1983), 294.

50 Deleuze and Guattari, *Anti-Oedipus*, 296.

51 Parisi, *Abstract Sex*, 11.

52 Rick Dolphijn and Iris Der Van Tuin, *New Materialism: Interviews and Cartographies*, 1st ed., New Metaphysics (Ann Arbor: Open Humanities Press, 2012). Here the chapter titled 'The Transversality of New Materialism'.

53 Dolphijn and van Tuin, *New Materialism*, 96.

54 Dolphijn and van Tuin, *New Materialism*, 109.

55 Dolphijn and van Tuin, *New Materialism*, 109–10.

56 Dolphijn and van Tuin, *New Materialism*, 109.

57 Cf. e.g. the title of the book edited by Lisa Gitelman: Lisa Gitelman, ed., 'Raw Data', In Is an Oxymoron, Infrastructures Series (Cambridge, MA and London: The MIT Press, 2013).

58 Patricia MacCormack, *Cinesexuality*, Queer Interventions (Aldershot: Ashgate, 2008).

59 Rosi Braidotti, *Teratologies*. in *Deleuze and Feminist Theory*, ed. Claire Colebrook and Ian Buchanan (Edinburgh: Edinburgh University Press, 2000). cited after: Dolphijn and van Tuin, *New Materialism*.

60 Cf. e.g. Wardrip-Fruin Noah et al., 'Agency Reconsidered', *Breaking New Ground: Innovation in Games, Play, Practice and Theory. Proceedings of DiGRA 2009*, 2009, http://www.digra.org/wp-content/uploads/digital-library/09287.41281.pdf.

61 See e.g. Pramod K. Nayar, *Posthumanism*, Themes in Twentieth- and Twenty-first-century Literature and Culture (Cambridge: Polity, 2014), 23 and Carla Jodey Castricano, *Animal Subjects: An Ethical Reader in a Posthuman World*, Cultural Studies Series (Waterloo, ON: Wilfrid Laurier University Press, 2008), 230.

62 Graham Harvey, *Animism: Respecting the Living World* (New York: Columbia University Press, 2006), XI i następne.

63 Harvey, *Animism*, XI.

64 Harvey, XVII.

65 Jacques Lacan, *The Ethics of Psychoanalysis, 1959–1960*, vol. 7, The Seminar of Jacques Lacan (New York: Norton, 1997), 139.

66 Lacan, *The Ethics of Psychoanalysis*, 139–40.

67 Derrida defines in this manner the trace that in his opinion is the 'intimate relation of the living present with its outside'; see Jacques Derrida, *Speech and*

Phenomena: And Other Essays on Husserl's Theory of Signs (Evanston: Northwestern University Press, 1973), 86.

68   Turkle, *The Second Self*, 18.

69   Jacqui Gabb, *Researching Intimacy in Families*, Pbk. ed., Palgrave Macmillan Studies in Family and Intimate Life (Basingstoke and New York: Palgrave Macmillan, 2010), 116.

70   Debra Langan and Deborah Davidson, 'Rethinking Intimate Questions: Intimacy as Discourse', in *Canadian Families: Diversity, Conflict and Change*, ed. Ann Duffy and Nancy Mandell (Toronto: Nelson Education, 2011), 33–60.

71   Richard Balzer, *Peepshows: A Visual History* (New York: Harry N. Abrams, 1998), 12.

72   Elizabeth Wilson writes about the 'childishness' of computers, and their subjective and affective treatment by Turing; see Elisabeth Wilson, 'Imaginable Computers: Affects and Intelligence in Alan Turing', in *Prefiguring Cyberculture: An Intellectual History*, ed. Darren Tofts, Annemarie Jonson and Alessio Cavallaro (Cambridge, MA and Sydney: MIT Press and Power Publications, 2002), 38–51.

73   Cf. 'Certain kinds of machines and some living organisms – particularly the higher living organisms – can, as we have seen, modify their patterns of behavior on the basis of past experience so as to achieve specific antientropic ends.' Norbert Wiener, *The Human Use of Human Beings: Cybernetics and Society/Norbert Wiener, with a New Introduction by Steve J. Heims* (London: Free Association, 1989), 48.

74   For example, by suggesting that humans and material items have agency, see Bruno Latour, 'Third Source of Uncertainty: Objects Too Have Agency', in *Reassembling the Social: An Introduction to Actor-network-theory*, Clarendon Lectures in Management Studies (Oxford: Oxford University Press, 2007).

75   Cf. e.g. 'What distinguishes man from animal is language, but this is not a natural given already inherent in the psychophysical structure of man; it is, rather, a historical production which, as such, can be properly assigned neither to man nor to animal. If this element is taken away, the difference between man and animal vanishes, unless we imagine a nonspeaking *man—Homo alalus*, precisely—who would function as a bridge that passes from the animal to the human', in Giorgio Agamben, *The Open*, trans. Kevin Attell (Stanford University Press, 2004), 36.

76   Donna Jeanne Haraway, *When Species Meet*, vol. 3, Posthumanities (Minneapolis: University of Minnesota Press, 2008), 69–70.

77   Lacan, Miller and Forrester, *Freud's Papers on Technique, 1953-1954*, 80.

78   Alexander R. Galloway, *Protocol: How Control Exists after Decentralization*, Leonardo (Cambridge, MA: MIT Press, 2004), 7.

79   Gitelman, *Always Already New*.

80   Harvey, *Animism*, 16.

81 Harvey, *Animism*, XI.

82 Giorgio Agamben, *'What Is an Apparatus?" and Other Essays*, Meridian, crossing aesthetics (Stanford, CA: Stanford University Press, 2009), 3. Interestingly, Harvey regards these matters in a similar way, writing that 'most often particular groups within every species are considered to hold and/or disseminate power or wisdom'; see Harvey, *Animism*, XVIII.

83 Agamben, *'What Is an Apparatus?' and Other Essays*, 15.

84 Vilém Flusser, *Towards a Philosophy of Photography* (London: Reaktion Books, 2012), 31.

85 Flusser, *Towards a Philosophy*, 32.

86 Agamben, *'What Is an Apparatus?' and Other Essays*, 19.

87 Kittler, *Gramophone, Film, Typewriter*, 89–90.

88 Agamben, *'What Is an Apparatus?' and Other Essays*, 21.

89 Andreas Hepp, *Deep Mediatization*, Key Ideas in Media and Cultural Studies (London and New York: Routledge, 2020), 109–10.

90 Andreas Hepp's works appeared five years after the publication of the first (Polish) edition of this book (author's note).

Chapter 1

1 The French name of peep shows, that is, optical toys in the form of a box fitted with a double eyepiece generating the impression of depth in the miniature of a selected architectural or landscape scenery created inside (author's note).

2 L. Mulvey, 'Visual Pleasure and Narrative Cinema', *Screen* 16, no. 3 (1 September 1975): 6–18.

3 See also Gaylyn Studlar, *In the Realm of Pleasure: Von Sternberg, Dietrich, and the Masochistic Aesthetic*, Columbia University Press Morningside ed. (New York: Columbia University Press, 1992); Bracha Ettinger, *The Matrixial Gaze* (Woodhouse: University of Leeds, 1995). Cynthia A. Freeland, 'Feminist Frameworks for Horror Films', in *Post-theory: Reconstructing Film Studies*, ed. David Bordwell Noel Carroll (Madison, WI: University of Wisconsin Press, 1996), 195–218. I would also add a selection of works by Patricia MacCormack, cited elsewhere in this work, as well as the extensive studies focused around the *Feminist Media Studies* journal.

4 Mulvey, 'Visual Pleasure and Narrative Cinema', 837.

5 Lusty Lady and Fantasy Unlimited (author's note).

6 Vicky Funari and Julia Query, *Live Nude Girls Unite!* (First Run Features, 2000).

7   Robert P. McNamara, 'Dramaturgy and the Social Organization of the Peep Shows', in *Sex, Scams, and Street Life: The Sociology of New York City's Times Square*, ed. Robert P. McNamara (Westport, CT: Praeger, 1995).

8   Jamie Berger, 'Wet Confessions: Autoethnography of a Peepshow Customer', in *Flesh for Fantasy: Producing and Consuming Exotic Dance*, ed. R. Danielle Egan, Katherine Frank and Merri Lisa Johnson (New York: Thunder's Mouth Press and Distributed by Publishers Group West, 2006).

9   It will, of course, be necessary to keep in mind that Moss's and Eaves's autobiographic stories take the form of literary text (author's note).

10   Funari and Query, *Live Nude Girls Unite!*

11   Erkki Huhtamo, 'The Pleasures of the Peephole: An Archaeological Exploration of Peep Media', in *The Book of Imaginary Media: Excavating the Dream of the Ultimate Communication Medium*, ed. Eric Kluitenberg (Rotterdam: De Balie; NAi Publishers, 2006).

12   See e.g. William Dieterle, *Salome* (Columbia Pictures, 1953), casting Rita Hayworth as the titular protagonist or, better still, scandalizing Ken Russel, *Salome's Last Dance* (Vestron Pictures, 1988).

13   Joris-Karl Huysmans, *Against the Grain [À Rebours]*, trans. Harrison Ainsworth (Project Gutenberg, 2004), http://www.gutenberg.org/files/12341/12341.txt.

14   Stavros Stavrou Karayanni, *Dancing Fear & Desire: Race, Sexuality, and Imperial Politics in Middle Eastern Dance*, Cultural Studies Series (Waterloo: Wilfrid Laurier University Press, 2004), 100.

15   Huysmans, *Against the Grain [À Rebours]*.

16   Georges Bataille, *Historia erotyzmu {History of Erotism]* (Kraków: Oficyna Literacka, 1992), 117–19. Originally published in French in 1951, see Georges Bataille, *L'histoire de l'érotisme. Le Surréalisme Au Jour Le Jour. Conférences 1951–1953. La Souveraineté*, ØEuvres Complètes (Paris: Gallimard, 1970).

17   Karayanni, *Dancing Fear & Desire*, 108.

18   Françoise Meltzer, *Salome and the Dance of Writing Portraits of Mimesis in Literature* (Chicago: University of Chicago Press, 1987), 25.

19   See Monika M. Elbert, 'Striking a Historical Pose: Antebellum Tableaux Vivants, Godey's Illustrations, and Margaret Fuller's Heroines', *New England Quarterly* 75, no. 2 (2002): 235; Mary Chapman, '"Living Pictures": Women and Tableaux Vivants in Nineteenth-century American Fiction and Culture', *Wide Angle* 18, no. 3 (1996): 22–52.

20   Harriet Beecher Stowe, *My Wife and I: Or, Harry Henderson's History* (New-York: J. B. Ford and company, 1871), http://archive.org/details/mywifeandiorhar00stowgoog., cited after: Grace Ann Hovet and Theodore R. Hovet, 'Tableaux Vivants: Masculine Vision and Feminine Reflections in Novels by Warner, Alcott, Stowe', *ATQ* 7, no. 4 (1993): 335.

21 Toni Bentley, *Sisters of Salome* (Lincoln: University of Nebraska Press, 2005).

22 Petra Dierkes-Thrun, *Salome's Modernity: Oscar Wilde and the Aesthetics of Transgression* (Ann Arbor: University of Michigan Press, 2011), 95.

23 Dierkes-Thrun, *Salome's Modernity*.

24 Bentley, *Sisters of Salome*, 64.

25 Funari and Query, *Live Nude Girls Unite!*

26 Interestingly, this is a two-way road in the peep show. The customer, too, can be regarded as an object to be watched; see the section titled 'The panopticon and the binarity of looking'.

27 David Nasaw, *Going Out: The Rise and Fall of Public Amusements* (Cambridge, MA: Harvard University Press, 1999), 121–2.

28 Kerry Segrave, *Vending Machines: An American Social History* (Jefferson, NC: McFarland, 2002), 10.

29 Segrave, *Vending Machines*, 11.

30 Amy Herzog, 'In the Flesh: Space and Embodiment in the Pornographic Peep Show Arcade', *Velvet Light Trap: A Critical Journal of Film & Television*, no. 62 (2008): 33.

31 Norman M. Klein, *The Vatican to Vegas: A History of Special Effects* (New York: New Press, distributed by Norton, 2004), 339–40.

32 Deleuze et al., *Anti-Oedipus*.

33 Jan Jagodzinski, *Postmodern Dilemmas: Outrageous Essays in Art & Art Education*, Studies in Curriculum Theory (Mahwah, NJ: Lawrence Erlbaum Associates, 1997), 19.

34 Klein, *The Vatican to Vegas*, 340.

35 The mixed private and public character of the shows is attested by the drawings included in Balzer's book, cited in the beginning, recording the repeat custom of pickpocketing the spectators gazing into the peep show's lens. See Balzer, *Peepshows*.

36 Exhibition item from Kodak Museum's collections in Rochester NY, USA. Source: author's own materials.

37 *Carnival Attraction at the Imperial County Fair, California. El Centro, California* by Russel Lee, public domain in the United States. Source: Farm Security Administration – Office of War Information Photograph Collection, Library of Congress, Reproduction number: LC-USF34-072233-D, available at http://commons.wikimedia.org/wiki/File:Carnival_attraction_of_the_Imperial_county_fair_ppmsc00119u.jpg.

38 Martin Quigley Jr, *Magic Shadows: The Story of the Origin of Motion Pictures* (Literary Licensing, LLC, 2012), 138.

39 Nasaw, *Going Out*.

40 Joseph W. Slade, *Pornography and Sexual Representation: A Reference Guide* (Greenwood Publishing Group, 2001), 1115.

41 Herzog, 'In the Flesh', 33.

42 Wes Goodman, 'Pornography, Peep Shows, and the Decline of Morality', *USA Today Magazine* 122, no. 2586 (1994): 32.

43 Pegan Moss, 'The Booth', *Peepshow Stories* (blog), 16 July 2003, www.peepshowstories. com. Moss's blog has been accessible until 2015; currently, it can be entered via Internet Archive only. A fragment from Eaves illustrates this process of reduction to numbers, bringing about mental associations with a concentration camp: 'A dancer who formerly went by Chelsea had changed her name to Agent 99, but everyone called her 99 for short. It made me imagine for a moment what it would be like if we all had numbers. I wondered if it would make a difference to the customers.' Elisabeth Eaves, *Bare: On Women, Dancing, Sex, and Power* (Random House LLC, 2011), 166.

44 Eaves, *Bare*, 63.

45 Eaves, *Bare*, 288.

46 Eaves, *Bare,* 60.

47 Moss, 'The Booth'.

48 Eaves, *Bare*, 64.

49 Eaves, *Bare,* 173.

50 Eaves, *Bare,* 68. Emphasis added by me.

51 Pegan Moss, 'Video Booths', *Peepshow Stories* (blog), 21 July 2003, http:// peepshowstories.com/2003/06/wall-of-porn-video-booths-there-is.html.

52 Moss, 'The Booth'.

53 McNamara, *Sex, Scams, and Street Life*, 63.

54 Carolyn J. Marr, 'Taken Pictures: On Interpreting Native American Photographs of the Southern Northwest Coast', *Pacific Northwest Quarterly* 80, no. 2 (1989): 52–61.

55 Eaves, *Bare*, 260.

56 Eaves, *Bare,* 89. Emphasis added by me.

57 Moss, 'The Booth'.

58 M. H Dunlop, *Sixty Miles from Contentment: Traveling the Nineteenth-century American Interior* (Boulder, CO: Westview Press, 1998), 161.

59 Dave Holmes, Patrick O'Byrne and Stuart J. Murray, 'Faceless Sex: Glory Holes and Sexual Assemblages: Faceless Sex', *Nursing Philosophy* 11, no. 4 (1 September 2010): 250–9.

60 Goodman, 'Pornography, Peep Shows, and the Decline of Morality'.

61 Jesse Katz, 'Under New Law, the Booths for Peep Shows Will Have No Doors', *Los Angeles Times*, 15 October 1988, https://www.latimes.com/archives/la-xpm-1988-09-15-ve-2626-story.html.

62 Eaves, *Bare*, 88.

63 Goodman, 'Pornography, Peep Shows, and the Decline of Morality'.

64 Eaves, *Bare*, 153.

65 Eaves, *Bare*, 97–8.

66 Arthur Kroker and Marilouise Kroker, *Body Invaders: Sexuality and the Postmodern Condition*, Culturetexts (Basingstoke: Macmillan Education, 1988), 22.

67 Kroker and Kroker, *Body Invaders*, 15.

Chapter 2

1 Donald Crafton, *Before Mickey: An Animated Anthology* (Cambridge, MA: MIT Press, 1982), 4.

2 Alan Cholodenko, *The Illusion of Life: Essays on Animation* (Sydney: Power Publications, 1991), 215.

3 Klein, *The Vatican to Vegas*, 251.

4 Klein, *The Vatican to Vegas*, 251.

5 Jerry Beck calls them combined films; see Jerry Beck, 'Combination Films: A Brief History', *Animation Magazine* 2, no. 1 (Summer 1988): 31–9.

6 It would be difficult to track who had been the first to use this term in reference to the animation genre discussed herein, but in the scholarly literature devoted to animation this is the term that prevails (author's note).

7 This homogeneity is a little misleading if one considers the popularity Fleischer's rotoscope gained in animation as an apparatus blurring the difference between actor's and animated cinemas (author's note).

8 This agreement sometimes need not include 'personal' relationships but can be a sphere of negotiation between the actor and the presented world created by the different film technologies. These aspects, along with the repositioning of the human subject as an element or layer in a cinematographic work, are what I discuss in the next chapter.

9 Michael Barrier, *Hollywood Cartoons: American Animation in Its Golden Age* (New York: Oxford University Press, Incorporated, 2003), 45.

10 Frank Thomas and Ollie Johnston, *Disney Animation: The Illusion of Life*, 1st ed. (New York: Abbeville Press, 1981), 74.

11 Thomas and Johnston, *Disney Animations*, 35.

12 The relevant fragment of the chapter will demonstrate that what we are dealing with is caricature rather than typical realism (author's note).

13 Of course, this was predated by a number of inventions acting as forerunners of animation – the taumatrope, phenakistoscope, zootrope, fantascope and more (author's note).

14 David L. Nathan and Donald Crafton, 'The Making and Re-Making of Winsor McCay's Gertie (1914)', *Animation* 8, no. 1 (1 March 2013): 23–46.

15 Crafton, *Before Mickey*, 173–4.

16 J. P. Telotte, 'Disney's Alice Comedies: A Life of Illusion and the Illusion of Life', *Animation* 5, no. 3 (11 January 2010): 331–40.

17 Crafton, *Before Mickey*, 284.

18 Erwin Feyersinger, 'Diegetic Short Circuits: Metalepsis In', *Animation* 5, no. 3 (11 January 2010): 279–94.

19 Feyersinger refers to the production stage while discussing the last on his list of types of metalepsis.

20 Crafton, *Before Mickey*, 11.

21 Crafton, *Before Mickey*, 177.

22 See also Pointer's book: Ray Pointer, *The Art and Inventions of Max Fleischer: American Animation Pioneer*, Illustrated ed. (Jefferson, NC: McFarland & Company, 2017).

23 Cholodenko, *The Illusion of Life*, 213.

24 Lev Manovich, *The Language of New Media* (Cambridge, MA: MIT Press, 2002).

25 I will be revisiting this issue in the chapter on digital effects. There, I will demonstrate the anthropological consequences arising for the subject from being a layer in a digital image.

26 Nathan Gilder, 'Theological Compatibilism & Animation: Vessel of Wrath', *ImageTexT: Interdisciplinary Comics Studies* 2, no. 2 (2006). http://imagetext. english.ufl.edu/archives/v2_2/gilder/.

27 Don Peri, *Working with Disney: Interviews with Animators, Producers, and Artists* (Jackson: University Press of Mississippi, 2011), 7.

28 Michael Barrier, *The Animated Man: A Life of Walt Disney* (Berkeley: University of California Press, 2007), 178.

29 Thomas and Johnston, *The Illusion of Life*, 332.

30 By nature, animation is a hybrid activity due to the often collective way in which it is created. On the one hand, the typical Disney animation is a very faithful depiction of the postures, gestures and mimical movements of live actors, and on the other hand the collectiveness manifests itself in the use of Fleischer's rotoscope, with technological support for the process of drawing the actor's silhouette.

31 Thomas and Johnston, *Disney Animation*, 332.

32 Thomas and Johnston, *Disney Animation,* 19.

33 Thomas and Johnston, *Disney Animation,* 19.

34 Thomas and Johnston, *Disney Animation,* 21.

35 Turkle, *Alone Together: Why We Expect More from Technology and Less from Each Other*. New York: Basic Books, 2011.

36 Thomas and Johnston, *Disney Animation*, 147.

37 Barrier, *The Animated Man*, 119.

38 Barrier, 128.

39 Thomas and Johnston, *Disney Animation,* 113–14.

40 Thomas and Johnston, *Disney Animation,* 323.

41 Thomas and Johnston, *Disney Animation,* 323.

42 Thomas and Johnston, *Disney Animation,* 114.

43 'How Disney Combines Living Actors with His Cartoon Characters', *Popular Science,* September 1944, 106.

44 Thomas and Johnston, *Disney Animation,* 527.

45 Thomas and Johnston, *Disney Animation,* 527.

46 *Behind the Ears: The True Story of Roger Rabbit,* documentary featured on the two-disc Vista Series DVD edition of 'Who Framed Roger Rabbit' film. (Disney Home Video, 2003). See also Ross Anderson, *Pulling a Rabbit Out of a Hat: The Making of Roger Rabbit* (Jackson: University Press of Mississippi Jackson, 2019).

47 *Behind the Ears: The True Story of Roger Rabbit.*

48 J. P. Telotte, *Animating Space: From Mickey to Wall-E* (Lexington, KY: University Press of Kentucky, 2010), 182.

49 Susan Ohmer, 'Who Framed Roger Rabbit?: The Presence of the Past', in *Storytelling in Animation: The Art of the Animated Image,* Vol. 2, ed. John Canemaker, Art of the Animated Image (Los Angeles, CA: The American Film Institute, 1988).

50 Cholodenko, *The Illusion of Life,* 220.

51 William Kozlenko, 'The Animated Cartoon and Walt Disney', in *The Emergence of Film Art. The Evolution and Development of the Motion Picture as an Art, from 1900 to the Present,* ed. Lewis Jacobs (New York: Hopikinson and Blake, 1969). Quoted after Telotte, *Animating Space,* 12.

52 http://humanityplus.org/philosophy/transhumanist-declaration/, URL of 20 November 2013.

53 Analyses of this type also begin to appear in film studies; see e.g. Johnson Cheu, *Diversity in Disney Films: Critical Essays on Race, Ethnicity, Gender, Sexuality and Disability* (Jefferson, NC: McFarland & Company, Inc., Publishers, 2013). There we can find a whole set of texts analysing Disney films from the perspective of studies into disability or monstrosity, or even analysis of Pixar's *Wall-E* referencing this area but enriched with other posthuman contexts. See also Jane Goodall, 'Hybridity and Innocence', in *The Illusion of Life 2: More Essays on Animation,* ed. Alan Cholodenko (Sydney: Power Publications, 2007) and Alan Cholodenko, 'Speculation on the Animatic Automaton', in *The Illusion of Life 2: More Essays on Animation,* ed. Alan Cholodenko (Sydney: Power Publications, 2007).

54 Barrier, *Hollywood Cartoons,* 47.

55 This motif, in way, is the harbinger of a real litigation taking place in 1930, which is described later on these pages.

56 Klein, *The Vatican to Vegas,* 253.

57 Klein, *The Vatican to Vegas,* 251–2.

58 Crafton, *Before Mickey*, 271.

59 Richard Fleischer, *Out of the Inkwell: Max Fleischer and the Animation Revolution* (Lexington: University Press of Kentucky and London, 2005), unnumbered pages between 82 and 83.

60 Fleischer, *Out of the Inkwell*, 103–4.

61 Haraway, *Simians, Cyborgs, and Women*.

62 Jim Korkis, 'The History of the Partners Statue: Part One', *Mouse Planet*, 26 October 2011, https://www.mouseplanet.com/9766/The_History_of_the_Partners_Statue_Part_One.

Chapter 3

1 See e.g. Richard Rickitt, *Special Effects: The History and Technique* (New York: Watson-Guptill Publications, 2007), Ron Fry and Pamela Fourzon, *The Saga of Special Effects: The Complete History of Cinematic Illusion, From Edison's Kinetoscope to Dynamation, Sensurround…and Beyond*, 1st ed. (Englewood Cliffs, NJ: Prentice-Hall, 1977), Raymond Fielding, *The Technique of Special-effects Cinematography*, 2nd ed., Library of Communication Techniques (London: Focal Press, 1969). Christopher Finch, *Special Effects: Creating Movie Magic*, 1st ed. (New York: Abbeville Press, 1984). See also: Andrzej. Gwóźdź, ed., *Kino po kinie: film w kulturze uczestnictwa [Cinema after Cinema. Film in Participatory Culture]* (Warsaw: Oficyna Naukowa, 2010).

2 Cf. e.g. Christopher Finch, *The CG Story: Computer-generated Animation and Special Effects* (New York: The Monacelli Press, 2013), Manovich, *The Language of New Media*.

3 After the first, Polish edition of this book in 2015, an interesting new analysis by Drew Ayers appeared, coinciding with the posthuman approach to special effects presented here; see Drew Ayers, *Spectacular Posthumanism: The Digital Vernacular of Visual Effects* (New York: Bloomsbury Academic, 2019). It will also be worth mentioning one more book published by Bloomsbury Academic and focused on a posthuman and materialist approach to cinema's apparatus: Elizabeth Ezra, *The Cinema of Things: Globalization and the Posthuman Object* (New York: Bloomsbury Academic, 2017).

4 Thomas G. Smith, *Industrial Light & Magic: The Art of Special Effects*, 1st ed. (New York: Ballantine Books, 1986), 137.

5 P. Vlahos, *Composite Photography Utilizing Sodium Vapor Illumination* (Google Patents, 1963), http://www.google.com/patents/US3095304.

6 Jean Kudar, Improvements in and relating to motion picture composite photography, GB633420 (A), issued 19 December 1949. http://worldwide.

espacenet.com/publicationDetails/biblio?FT=D&date=19491219&DB=&&CC=GB
&NR=633420A&KC=A&ND=1&locale=en_EP. In the abstract of Kudar's invention
he refers to his earlier patent: Composite kinematography, 25 November 1946, No.
34943.

7   P. Vlahos, *Comprehansive Electronic Compositing System* (Google Patents, 1987),
     https://www.google.com/patents/CA1228155A1?cl=en.

8   There exists a whole group of such pop-culture imaginations of nothingness. In
     Rosiński and Van Hamme's *Chninkel* (1988) comic, for example, a space appears
     that is referred to as the non-world, having no physical properties or content.
     Only story characters sent to that non-world exist in it; in Michael Ende's *The
     Neverending Story* (1984), the world of fantasy is absorbed by nothingness, which in
     the screen version takes the form of an ominous hurricane destroying all matter.

9   Jean-Paul Sartre, *Being and Nothingness: A Phenomenologica/Essay on Ontology*,
     trans. Hazel Barnes (New York: Pocket Books, 1978), 17–18.

10   What can also turn out to be interesting in this perspective is Deleuze's concept of
     indeterminate space, especially where he shows that such a space of uncertainty in
     (analog) cinema can be created by separation and shadow; this corresponds with
     the evolution of compositing techniques in film, as discussed above, along with the
     concept of the green screen; see Gilles Deleuze, *Cinema 1: The Movement-image*,
     trans. Hugh Hugh Tomlinson and Barbara Habberjam (London: Athlone, 1986).
     Here chapter VII. 'The Affection-image Qualities, Powers, Any-space-whatevers'.
     It is also worth noting that the specificity of such a space would not be the result
     of digital evolution alone, as Hansen demonstrates; see Mark B. N. Hansen, *New
     Philosophy for New Media* (Cambridge, MA: MIT Press, 2004), 204–7.

11   'State of the Art: A Cinefex 25th Anniversary Forum, Edited by Jody Duncan/
     Interviews by Don Shay and Joe Fordham', *Cinefex*, no. 100 (2005): 62–3.

12   Sartre, *Being and Nothingness*, 25. In his translation Hazel Barnes instead of
     'neantization' uses the word 'nihilation'.

13   Sartre, *Being and Nothingness,* 24.

14   Bill Desowitz, 'Sky Captain and the Virtual World of Today', *VFX World*, 5 February
     2004, https://www.awn.com/vfxworld/sky-captain-and-virtual-world-today.

15   Joe Fordham, 'Down the Rabbit Hole', *Cinefex*, no. 122 (2010): 69.

16   Rickitt and Harryhausen, *Special Effects*, 58.

17   Mark Cotta Vaz, *Industrial Light & Magic: Into the Digital Realm*, 1st ed. (New York:
     Ballantine Books, 1996), 170–3.

18   Barbara Robertson, 'Winds of War', *Cinefex*, no. 95 (2003): 70.

19   Ron Burnett, *How Images Think* (Cambridge, MA: MIT Press, 2005).

20   Erik Barnouw, *The Magician and the Cinema* (New York: Oxford University Press,
     1981), 77.

21   Joe Fordham, 'A Hero's Return', *Cinefex*, no. 106 (2006): 85.

22 Jody Duncan, 'Braving the Elements', *Cinefex*, no. 123 (2010): 112.

23 Joe Fordham, 'Reality Deconstructed', *Cinefex*, no. 126 (2011): 60–1.

24 Joe Fordham, 'Journey's End', *Cinefex*, no. 96 (2004): 106.

25 See Hugh Hart, 'Through Tim Burton's Looking Glass: Making Alice in Wonderland', *Wired*, 3 May 2010, www.wired.com/underwire/2010/03/wonderland-tech-tricks/.

26 Jody Duncan, 'Ghosts in the Machine', *Cinefex*, no. 99 (2004): 101.

27 Cf. e.g. Chapter 7 'Wire Flying and Levitation', in Robert E. McCarthy, *Secrets of Hollywood Special Effects* (Newton: Focal Press, 1992), 54–100.

28 Source: Andrew R. Boone, 'Snow White and the Seven Dwarfs', *Popular Science*, 52, January 1938, http://blog.modernmechanix.com/the-making-of-snow-white-and-the-seven-dwarfs/2/#mmGal.

29 Source: 'Big Chemist's Retort Built for Movie', *Popular Science*, February 1940, accessed 15 April 2021, http://blog.modernmechanix.com/big-chemists-retort-built-for-movie/.

30 'Sits in a Cabinet for Soundproof Tests', *Popular Science*, August 1930, accessed 15 April 2021, http://blog.modernmechanix.com/sits-in-a-cabinet-for-soundproof-tests/.

31 Jody Duncan, 'The Seduction of Reality', *Cinefex*, no. 120 (2010): 120.

32 Peter Lunenfeld, *Snap to Grid: A User's Guide to Digital Arts, Media, and Cultures* (Cambridge, MA: MIT, 2000).

33 N. Katherine Hayles, 'The Condition of Virtuality', in *Language Machines: Technologies of Literary and Cultural Production*, ed. Jeffrey Masten, Peter Stallybrass and Nancy J. Vickers, Essays from the English Institute (New York: Routledge, 1997). For the concept of virtuality itself, see also Michael Heim, *Virtual Realism* (New York: Oxford University Press, 1998).

34 Joe Fordham, 'Green Destiny', *Cinefex*, no. 94 (2003): 85.

35 Deleuze, *Cinema 1*. Here: Chapter VI 'The Affection-image. Face and Close Up'.

36 'State of the Art: A Cinefex 25th Anniversary Forum, Edited by Jody Duncan/Interviews by Don Shay and Joe Fordham', 76.

37 Jody Duncan, 'The Unusual Birth of Benjamin Button', *Cinefex*, no. 116 (2009): 88.

38 Deleuze, *Cinema 1*, 88.

39 Corresponding with this, in a way, is the transhuman definition of the expressionist face; according to Deleuze: 'In this way the face participates in the non-organic life of things as the primary pole of Expressionism. A striated, striped face, caught in a more or less fine net, catching the effects of a Venetian blind, of a fire, of foliage, of sun through trees'. Deleuze, 92.

40 Joe Fordham, 'Middle-Earth Strikes Back', *Cinefex*, no. 92 (2003): 85.

41 Duncan, 'The Unusual Birth of Benjamin Button', 88.

42 Fordham, 'Middle-Earth Strikes Back', 80.

43 Duncan, 'The Unusual Birth of Benjamin Button', 79.

44 Duncan, 'The Unusual Birth of Benjamin Button', 80.

45 Joe Fordham, 'Soldier Blue', *Cinefex*, no. 127 (2011): 66–74.

46 Rickitt, *Special Effects*, 164.

47 Jody Duncan, 'All the Way', *Cinefex*, no. 112 (2008): 45–6.

48 Duncan, 'All the Way', 46–7.

49 Duncan, 'The Seduction of Reality', 128–9.

50 Duncan, 'The Seduction of Reality', 137.

51 The use of prosthetics in *King Kong* is not limited to limb extensions or elaborate make-up. Peter Jackson installed a special device for Serkis, dubbed the 'Kongalizer', allowing the actor's voice to be transformed in the real time into the great gorilla's roaring audible in the film; see Joe Fordham, 'Return of the King', *Cinefex*, no. 96 (January 2004): 49–50.

52 Barbara Rauch's interesting artistic project and academic research in emotionality and consciousness studies also fall within this area. She compared animal 'facial' expressions to human ones with the use of 3D scans morphed together; see Barbara Rauch, 'Virtual Emotions, No Feelings', in *New Realities: Being Syncretic: IXth Consciousness Reframed Conference Vienna 2008*, ed. Ruth Schnell et al., 1st ed. (New York: Springer Vienna Architecture, 2008), 232–5.

53 See the document titled *Supercalifragilisticexpialidocious: Behind the Scenes of Disney's 1964 Film Mary Poppins* attached with *Mary Poppins. 50th Anniversary Edition*, Blu-Ray/DVD Disc, Walt Disney Studios Home Entertainment December 2013.

54 Joe Fordham, 'Lost World', *Cinefex*, no. 114 (2008): 111.

55 Joe Fordham, 'Under the Moons of Mars', *Cinefex*, no. 129 (2012): 50.

56 Jody Duncan, 'Deep Magic', *Cinefex*, no. 104 (2006).

57 Jody Duncan, 'Ring Masters', *Cinefex*, no. 89 (2002): 70.

58 Duncan, 'Ring Masters', 113.

59 Duncan, 'Ring Masters', 107–8.

60 'State of the Art: A Cinefex 25th Anniversary Forum, Edited by Jody Duncan/ Interviews by Don Shay and Joe Fordham', 57.

61 Jody Duncan, 'Passion Play', *Cinefex*, no. 97 (2004): 36.

62 Jody Duncan, 'Legacy System', *Cinefex*, no. 124 (2011): 42.

63 Duncan, 'State of the Art.

64 It will be expedient here to recall Tadeusz Miczka's observation that the paradigm of thanatology in film is widening; see Tadeusz Miczka, *O śmierci na ekranie [Death on the Screen]* (Katowice: Śląsk, 2013).

65 Duncan, 'State of the Art.

66 Duncan, 'State of the Art, 76.

67 Duncan, 'State of the Art.

68   Duncan, 'The Unusual Birth of Benjamin Button', 83.

69   Hayles, *How We Became Posthuman*.

70   A large body of other opinions correspond with this approach to intelligence and thinking; for example Ricardo Nemirovsky's and that of Francesca Ferrara; see Ricardo Nemirovsky and Francesca Ferrara, 'Mathematical Imagination and Embodied Cognition', *Educational Studies in Mathematics* 70, no. 2 (March 2009): 159–74.

Chapter 4

1   Lacan, *The Four Fundamental Concepts of Psycho-analysis*, 95.

2   The gaze (or reverie) will be understood as the stage of potential seduction in the ritual of gazing.

3   The 20th Century Fox Vice-President, Irving Berlin Kahn, is also mentioned alongside them (author's note).

4   Fred Barton and H. J. Schlafly, 'TelePrompter – New Production Tool', *Journal of Society of Motion Picture and Television Engineers* 58 (June 1952): 515.

5   'New Business Tool: The TelePrompTer', *Business Screen Magazine. Production Review* 14, no. 1 (1953): 112.

6   'TV's Cost Cutting Gadgets', *Sponsor*, 22 October 1952, 37.

7   Source: 'New Business Tool', 112.

8   'New Business Tool', 112.

9   'TV's Cost Cutting Gadgets', 37.

10   Barton and Schlafly, 'TelePrompter – New Production Tool', 515, 521.

11   'New Business Tool', 112.

12   'TV's Cost Cutting Gadget', 60.

13   'Have You Heard? TelePrompter Has a Big, New Station Deal (Press Ad)', *Sponsor*, (17 May 1954): 126.

14   'A Custom-Made Prompting System', *Business Screen. The Visual Communications Magazine* 33, no. 3 (June 1972): 28–32.

15   See 'Speech Q, Portable Prompter, Runs as Speaker's Own Speed', *Business Screen Magazine* 15, no. 8 (1954): 56.

16   Source: 'Speech Q, Portable Prompter, Runs as Speaker's Own Speed'.

17   Joseph Stromberg, 'A Brief History of the Teleprompter. How a Makeshift Show Business Memory Aid Became the Centerpiece of Modern Political Campaigning', *Smithsonian Magazine*, 22 October 2012, https://www.smithsonianmag.com/history/a-brief-history-of-the-teleprompter-88039053/#ixzz2hR6hjj1Y.

18   'New Business Tool', 113.

19   'New Business Tool', 112.

20   Frances Kish, 'The Advantages of Being Shy', *TV Radio Mirror*, January 1962: 71.

21   Louis Harris, 'Three-Headed Editor Required', *The Cine Technician* 22, no. 133 (January 1956): 25.

22   'New Business Tool', 113.

23   Jacques Derrida and Bernard Stiegler, *Echographies of Television: Filmed Interviews* (Cambridge and Malden, MA: Polity Press and Blackwell Publishers, 2002), 43.

24   Derrida refers to a French device for audience measuring, introduced in 1989 (author's note).

25   Derrida and Stiegler, *Echographies of Television*, 43.

26   Derrida and Stiegler, *Echographies of Television*, 4.

27   Paddy Scannell, 'Television and History: Questioning the Archive', *The Communication Review* 13, no. 1 (26 February 2010): 45–6.

28   Scannell, 'Television and History', 48.

29   Such as used in police interrogations or experimental psychology.

30   Cf. 'The gaze is not necessarily the face of our fellow being; it could just as easily be the window behind which we assume he is lying in wait for us. It is an x, the object when faced with which the subject becomes object.' in *Freud's Papers on Technique, 1953–1954*, ed. Jacques-Alain Miller, trans. John Forrester, vol. 1, Seminar of Jacques Lacan (New York: W. W. Norton & Company 1993), 220.

31   Speakers giving advice on how to work with a prompter actually emphasize the need to see the audience behind the text (author's note).

32   Sartre, *Being and Nothingness*, 257.

33   Sartre, *Being and Nothingness*, 257.

34   Sartre, *Being and Nothingness*, 281.

35   Sartre, *Being and Nothingness*, 257.

36   Steve Hardie appears to have developed a similar device prior to Morris; see http://nofilmschool.com/2012/09/interrotron-errol-morris-documentary/, URL of 18 October 2013.

37   Analysis of prompter locations in pseudo-documentaries would require separate analytical effort, for in each of them the apparatus is placed somewhat differently – sometimes closer to the camera, sometimes farther apart, but usually away from the lens (author's note).

38   Sartre, *Being and Nothingness*, 333.

39   Sartre, *Being and Nothingness*, 346.

40   I analyse this case in Chapter 6 (author's note).

41   Malfunctions of the equipment used in Barak Obama's public speeches, which destroy the mystification of directness and naturalness of this contact, have already

become a legend. Obama is ridiculed, among other things, for using the prompter even when meeting children; see e.g. Comedy Central television material from The Daily Show with Jon Steward, http://thedailyshow.cc.com/videos/1b43o1/obama-speaks-to-a-sixth-grade-classroom, URL of 12 November 2013.

Chapter 5

1 *Interview with Edwin Wycoff Attached to Winky Dink and You DVD* (Vanguard Cinema and Rembrandt Films, 2002).

2 *Interview with Edwin Wycoff Attached to Winky Dink and You DVD.*

3 James W. Roman, *From Daytime to Primetime: The History of American Television Programs* (Westport, CT: Greenwood Press, 2005). Ray E. Barfield, *A Word from Our Viewers: Reflections from Early Television Audiences*, [Praeger Television Collection Series] (Westport, CT: Praeger, 2008).

4 Mary E. Beadle, 'Winky Dink and You: The Beginnings of Interactive TV', *Paper Presented at the Annual Meeting of the BEA, Las Vegas Hotel (LVH), Las Vegas, NV*, 22 April 2014, http://citation.allacademic.com/meta/p_mla_apa_research_citation/6/2/6/7/7/p626774_index.html. John Carey and M. C. J. Elton, *When Media Are New: Understanding the Dynamics of New Media Adoption and Use*, The New Media World (Ann Arbor: Digital Culture Books and University of Michigan Press and University of Michigan Library, 2010). Here, the chapter titled 'The Long Road to Interactive Television'.

5 *Interview with Edwin Wycoff Attached to Winky Dink and You DVD.*

6 Mark Gawlinski, *Interactive Television Production* (Oxford: Focal, 2003).

7 Lynn Spigel, 'Seducing the Innocent', in *Ruthless Criticism: New Perspectives in U.S. Communication History*, ed. William Samuel Solomon and Robert Waterman McChesney (Minneapolis: University of Minnesota Press, 1993).

8 *Interview with Edwin Wycoff Attached to Winky Dink and You DVD.*

9 Fiona StewartPhil Turner Ian Smith, 'Winky Dink and You: Determining Patterns of Narrative for Interactive Television Design', in *Proceedings of the Second European Interactive Television Conference: Enhancing the Experience, Brighton, April 2004*, ed. Lyb Pemberton, Judith Masthoff and Richard Griffiths (Brighton: University of Brighton, 2004), 1–10.

10 The Paley Center in New York gave this episode the working title *Edgar the Auto.*

11 *Interview with Edwin Wycoff Attached to Winky Dink and You DVD.*

12 The Paley Center in New York gave this episode the working title *Gorilla Pranks.*

13 *Interview with Edwin Wycoff Attached to Winky Dink and You DVD.*

14   Jeffrey Sconce, *Haunted Media: Electronic Presence from Telegraphy to Television*,
     Console-Ing Passions (Durham, NC: Duke University Press, 2000), 191.

Chapter 6

1   See discussion on this: John Carey, 'Winky Dink to Stargazer: Five Decades Of
     Interactive Television' (paper presented on UnivEd Conference on Interactive
     Television, Edinburgh, Scotland, 1996). Wiesław Godzic discusses several different
     levels of television interactivity and the multitude of aspects of this concept; see
     Wiesław Godzic, 'Various Faces of Interactivity: Remarks on Television', *ICONO* 14,
     no. 15 (2010): 22–36.

2   '"Will Rich, Interactive Media Transform Television?" at TVOT NYC Intensive
     2012 MARCH 05, 2013', https://itvt.com/story/9593/will-rich-interactive-media-
     transform-television-tvot-nyc-intensive-2012, URL of 16 June 2013.

3   See James Blake, *Television and the Second Screen: Interactive TV in the Age of Social
     Participation* (Abingdon, Oxon; New York, N.Y: Routledge, 2016), 11.

4   In this chapter I focus on 'discontinuity' from the perspective of the presenter's
     activity, but this discontinuity also surfaces on the side of the active audience making
     the phone calls – there a characteristic binary opposition here between those who
     have managed to get on air and those who have failed to get hold of a free line – for
     example in *Salon Gry [Game Room]*(Polish TV Channel TVN 2009) they are greeted
     by the following message: 'TVN here. No luck this time, but you still have a chance.'

5   The record highs for such shows may have reached even 5,000–6,000 attempted
     calls per minute; see the answers of Jeff Henry of ITV before the culture, media and
     sport committee. Great Britain et al., *Call TV Quiz Shows: Report, Together with
     Formal Minutes, Oral and Written Evidence* (London: The Stationery Office Ltd.,
     2007), 39.

6   'Quiz Shows Are Gambling, Say MPs', *BBC News*, 25 January 2007, http://news.bbc.
     co.uk/2/hi/uk_news/6297205.stm.

7   Peter Lunenfeld, who in 2000 edited a collection of texts about new media under
     the collective title of *Digital Dialectic*, could be chosen as the patron for this way
     of thinking; (see Peter Lunenfeld, *The Digital Dialectic: New Essays on New Media*
     (Cambridge, MA: The MIT Press, 2000). His idea of marrying digital technology
     to the dialectic approach, however, is employed in an attempt to explain the
     relationship between the theory and the practice of new media. In my text, binarity
     will be described as a characteristic feature of communication activity.

8   The definition of a subject I rely on in this chapter can be construed on the basis
     of Žižek's concept when in one place in the *Plague of Fantasies* he regards a subject

as an instance delegating its goals to symbols intended to act on its behalf. The reconstructed picture of the interactive quiz and the evidence gathered from other areas suggests that the expansion of the infosphere has contributed to the emancipation of meanings from their previous subservient role to the subject, with which they begin to compete – 'a signifier is precisely an object-thing which substitutes for me, acts in my place'. Žižek, *The Plague of Fantasies*, 109.

9   The controversies appeared to be channelled into two principal currents. The first one, gathering together the supporters of artificial intelligence, involves a whole range of research studies, inventions and theoretical concepts of which the goal is to develop better and better AI systems; the second one, pessimistic as it is and increasingly sporadic nowadays, though previously rather frequent, forces a search for proof of the complete lack of any uniformity between human and 'computer' intelligence.

10   Jaron Lanier, 'Digital Maoism. The Hazards of New Online Collectivism', *Edge*, 29 May 2006, https://www.edge.org/conversation/jaron_lanier-digital-maoism-the-hazards-of-the-new-online-collectivism.

11   Bernard Stiegler, *Neganthropocene*, trans. Daniel Ross, Critical Climate Chaos (Open Humanities Press, 2018), http://www.openhumanitiespress.org/books/titles/the-neganthropocene.

12   Stiegler, *Neganthropocene,* 172–9.

13   Ian Hutchby in his study about the radio demonstrates how relationships of power are built in the discourse taking place between radio hosts and their callers; see Ian Hutchby, *Confrontation Talk: Arguments, Asymmetries, and Power on Talk Radio* (Mahwah, NJ: Routledge, 1996).

14   Niklas Luhmann, *Social Systems*, Writing Science (Stanford, CA: Stanford University Press, 1995).

15   James Silver, 'How to Win at Those Late-Night Quiz Shows', *The Guardian*, 17 January 2007, https://www.theguardian.com/media/2007/jan/17/broadcasting.ITV.

16   See *Quizmania (No Legs Caller)*, accessed 15 April 2021, https://www.youtube.com/watch?v=KzJotjN2imQ.

17   See, *Quizmania Australia Phones Down 1*, accessed 15 April 2021, http://www.youtube.com/watch?v=ePE0ljifhoY.

18   Désirée Ketabchi, 'Belgian Television Investigative Programme Exposes Social Injustice with Humour', *European Journalism Centre Magazine*, 3 November 2011, http://ejc.net/magazine/article/belgian-television-investigative-programme-exposes-social-injustice-with-hu#.WLfXXHqvzh4.

19   http://en.wikipedia.org/wiki/Basta_(TV_show), URL of 25 July 2013.

20   http://www.een.be/programmas/basta/de-mol-in-het-belspel, URL of 25 July 2014. De Weert published a list of solutions to mathematical puzzles in the show; see http://www.een.be/files/extra/programmas/basta/basta_110117_telsleutel.pdf

21 'Blue Peter Sorry over Fake Winner', *BBC News*, 14 March 2007, http://news.bbc. co.uk/2/hi/entertainment/6449919.stm.

22 Silver, 'How to Win at Those Late-night Quiz Shows'.

23 Iman Hamam, 'Satellite Arcades: Three-dimensional Puppets and the Coin-operated Interface', *Journal for Cultural Research* 16, no. 2–3 (2012): 239–59.

24 Seamus Simpson, 'Effective Communications Regulation in an Era of Convergence? The Case of Premium Rate Telephony and Television in the UK', *Convergence: The International Journal of Research into New Media Technologies* 16, no. 2 (5 January 2010): 221–2.

25 Mimi Curran, 'Participation Television: A Breakdown of Trust', *Journal of Direct, Data and Digital Marketing Practice* 9, no. 4 (4 January 2008): 385–9.

Chapter 7

1 Jacques Derrida, *Archive Fever: A Freudian Impression*, trans. Eric Prenowitz, 1 ed. (Chicago, IL: University of Chicago Press, 1998), 11.

2 Mark Derry, 'Naked Lunch: Talking Realcore with Sergio Messina', in *C'lickme: A Netporn Studies Reader*, ed. Katrien Jacobs, Marije Janssen and Matteo Pasquinelli (Amsterdam: Institute of Network Cultures, 2007), 17.

3 See the review published in *Sex News Daily*: '*Beautiful Agony* is not a porn site. It can become one of the most erotic websites on the internet. 'Support Agony – Buy a Subscription Today!', *Beautiful Agony*, accessed 15 April 2021, http://www. beautifulagony.com/public/main.php?page=joi. One project participant seems slightly hesitant, though, when she says: 'Even though, there is no nudity on BA, this website is in some sense pornography. There is nothing more obscene that the image of somebody's face during orgasm', 'Support Agony – Buy a Subscription Today!.'

4 Em & Lo, 'Beautiful Agony, the O-Face Video Website, Turns 5!', *Em & Lo. Sex, Love and Everything in Between*, 11 March 2009, https://www.emandlo.com/o-face-video-site-beautiful-agony-turns-five/.

5 Derrida, *Archive Fever*, 91.

6 Derrida, *Archive Fever*, 91.

7 Derrida, *Archive Fever*, 8–9.

8 Derrida, *Archive Fever*, 3.

9 Derrida, *Archive Fever*, 10.

10 Derrida, *Archive Fever*, 10–12.

11 Derrida, *Archive Fever*, 12.

12 Patricia Ward and George A. Dafoulas, *The Database Management Systems*, 1 ed. (Boston, MA: Thomson Learning, 2006), 2.

13 G. G. Chowdhury, *Text Retrieval Systems in Information Management* (New Dehli: New Age International, 1996), 19–21.

14 Martin Campbell-Kelly and William Aspray, *Computer: A History of the Information Machine* (Basic Books, 1996), 131–5.

15 Catherine Johnson-Roehr, 'In Search of Secret Museums', *Journal of Sex Research* 48, no. 1 (2010): 94–5.

16 'Gabinetto Segreto [Secret Cabinet]', accessed 6 October 2012, http://museoarcheologic onazionale.campaniabeniculturali.it/glossario/ploneglossarydefinition.2008-06-09. 8351409625/.

17 Lynn Hunt, *The Invention of Pornography, 1500–1800: Obscenity and the Origins of Modernity* (New York and Cambridge, MA: Zone Books, 1996), 9–10.

18 Steven Marcus, *The Other Victorians: A Study of Sexuality and Pornography in Mid-nineteenth-century England* (New Brunswick, NJ: Transaction Publishers, 2009), 67.

19 Marcus, *The Other Victorians*, 67.

20 Derrida, *Archive Fever*, 19.

21 Bruno Latour, 'Ces Réseaux Que La Raison Ignore – Laboratoires, Bibliothèques, Collections', in *Le Pouvoir Des Bibliothèques. La Mémoire Des Livres Dans La Culture Occidentale*, ed. Christian Jacob and Marc Baratin (Albin Michel, 1996), 23–46. Quoted after Ronald E. Day, *The Modern Invention of Information: Discourse, History, and Power* (Carbondale: Southern Illinois University Press, 2001), 25–6.

22 Derrida, *Archive Fever*, 18.

23 This aspect is not to be confused with Derrida's fundamental conception – 'archive fever'. Archiving is a compulsive passion of creating archives but the archive itself needs to be an isolated space, the exterior separated from the interior (author's comment).

24 Manovich, *The Language of New Media*, 225–8.

25 Derrida, *Archive Fever*, 17.

26 Derrida, *Archive Fever*, 2.

27 'Share Your Ecstasy with the Agony Community!', *Beautiful Agony*, accessed 15 April 2021, http://www.beautifulagony.com/public/main.php?page=submit.

28 Em & Lo, 'Beautiful Agony, the O-Face Video Website, Turns 5!'

29 Ishotmyself.com is a sister website presenting erotic selfies, author's comment.

30 Website's authors describe the participants of this project as 'artists', the word which is frequently used by participants themselves, author's comment.

31 William Gibson, *Idoru* (London: Penguin, 1997). I elaborate more on *Idoru* in Chapter 8.

32 Fifty such clips have been thoroughly analysed. All quotes directly come from recorded self-interviews, author's comment.

33 Anna E. Ward, 'Pantomimes of Ecstasy: BeautifulAgony.Com and the
    Representation of Pleasure', *Camera Obscura* 25, no. 1 73 (1 January 2010): 186.

34 Ward, 'Pantomimes of Ecstasy', 177.

35 In their book *Hacking the Future*, the Krokers mention a similar case of recursion
    (37–8). Here, a hacker and his friend meet in Berlin and organize a cybersexual
    happening using interactive costumes which stimulate the whole body remotely.
    Lots of people planned to take part in the experiment in which an advanced
    costume gave a person caressing conveyed by another experiment participant based
    in a different city. As it turned out, the day the project was supposed to be started,
    the information system of the device failed and it became recursive. The costume
    was cut off from the outside stimuli and it reacted only to the stimuli whose source
    was a user. In spite of the error, users could enjoy an incredible pleasure. See Arthur
    Kroker and Marilouise Kroker, *Hacking the Future: Stories for the Flesh-Eating
    1990s*, Culturetexts (New York: St. Martin's Press, 1996).

36 Ward, 'Pantomimes of Ecstasy', 171.

37 Ward, 'Pantomimes of Ecstasy', 166.

38 Lauren, *Beautiful Agony Forum*, accessed 15 April 2021, https://beautifulagony.
    com/forum/index.php.

39 Haraway, *Simians, Cyborgs, and Women.*

40 Georges Bataille, *Erotism: Death & Sensuality*, 1st City lights ed. (San Francisco:
    City Lights Books, 1986), 31 (my emphasis).

41 Bataille, *Erotism.*

42 Bataille, *Erotism*, 40.

43 Bataille, *Erotism*, 268.

44 Bataille, *Erotism*, 267.

45 Bataille, *Erotism*, 268.

46 Bataille, *Erotism*, 106.

47 Ward, 'Pantomimes of Ecstasy', 184.

Chapter 8

1   Gibson, *Idoru.*

2   'The World's Strangest Marriages', *Total Divorce* (blog), accessed 15 May 2015,
    http://www.totaldivorce.com/blog/2013/03/04/the-worlds-strangest-marriages-
    jzbdg/. See also Dolly Idlisan, 'Strangest Marriages in Japan', *Pop Japan*, 23 August
    2016, https://pop-japan.com/culture/strangest-marriages-in-japan/.

3   The discussion about intimate bonds with objects has very much in common with
    rapidly growing research on sexuality, erotism of machines and robots as well as on

technological love. See Dery, 'RoboCopulation'; Pettman, *Human Error*; Dominic Pettman, *Love and Other Technologies: Retrofitting Eros for the Information Age*, 1st ed. (New York: Fordham University Press, 2006), *Love and Sex with Robots* (New York: Springer Berlin Heidelberg, 2017); Ania Malinowska and Valentina Peri, eds., *Data Dating: Love, Technology, Desire* (Bristol: Intellect Ltd, 2021).

4   Aside from Harvey (Harvey, *Animism*), new animists include such researchers as Nurit Bird-David (Nurit Bird-David, '"Animism" Revisited: Personhood, Environment, and Relational Epistemology', *Current Anthropology* 40, no. S1 (February 1999): S67–91), Eduardo Viveiros de Castro (Eduardo Viveiros de Castro, 'Cosmological Deixis and Amerindian Perspectivism', *The Journal of the Royal Anthropological Institute* 4, no. 3 (1998): 469–88) and Signe Howell (Signe Howell Lise, 'Metamorphosis and Identity: Chewong Animistic Ontology', in *The Handbook of Contemporary Animism*, ed. Graham Harvey (Durham, UK: Acumen, 2013)).

5   I would like to offer special thanks to Imola Bulgozdi for the heads up about the wedding between a human being and a virtual character in Gibson's novel; Imola analyses the gender issues surfacing in that novel in her work: Imola Bulgozdi, *Artificial Intelligence and Gender Performativity in William Gibson's Idoru* (Brill, 2013).

6   Gibson, *Idoru*, 236.

7   Gibson, *Idoru*, 267.

8   Stanisław Lem, *Solaris* (Berkley Books, 1971).

9   Gibson, *Idoru*, 233.

10 Gibson, *Idoru*, 311.

11 Gibson, *Idoru*, 304–6.

12 For example, in animal studies bonding with 'furry children' is such a trap, see Monika Bakke, '"Between Us, Animals". Emotional Ties between Humans and Other Animals', trans. Jan Szelągiewicz, *Teksty Drugie* 1 (7), no. Special Issue English Edition (2015): 290–302.

13 Gibson, *Idoru*, 303.

14 Bataille, *Historia erotyzmu {History of Erotism]*, 128.

15 YouTuber YourChonny parodies on his channel, *inter alia*, kisses and having sex with the game character. See Yourchonny, 'Japanese Man Responds to Marrying a Nintendo Ds Character', 27 November 2009, https://www.youtube.com/watch?v=2D30hmYjIm4.

16 Gibson, *Idoru*, 247.

17 Kyung Lah, 'Tokyo Man Marries Video Game Character', *CNN*, 17 December 2009, http://edition.cnn.com/2009/WORLD/asiapcf/12/16/japan.virtual.wedding/index.html.

18 Noah et al., 'Agency Reconsidered', http://www.digra.org/wp-content/uploads/digital-library/09287.41281.pdf.

19 In all the testimonials of the OS community members the original spelling was retained.

20 Rudi from Germany, 'The Thing with the Soul: Expressed by Rudi in Germany', *Objectum Sexuality Internationale*, accessed 21 April 2021, http://objectum-sexuality.org/expressions-rudi.pdf.

21 K. Eva from The Netherlands, 'The Love Letter about Letters ... Expressed by Eva K. from The Netherlands', Objectum Sexuality Internationale, accessed 21 April 2021, http://www.objectum-sexuality.org/expressions-evak-2.pdf.

22 D. from Berlin, 'A Few More Thoughts ... Expressed by D. from Berlin, Germany', *Objectum Sexuality Internationale*, accessed 21 April 2021, http://objectum-sexuality.org/expressions-ds-2.pdf.

23 Grey Carter, 'Couple Celebrates Wedding by Murdering Virtual Girlfriend', *The Escapist*, 26 November 2012, https://v1.escapistmagazine.com/forums/read/7.394705-Couple-Celebrates-Wedding-by-Murdering-Virtual-Girlfriend.

24 Bataille invokes a figure of prostitute as an example of pure erotic object. In his point of view prostitutes 'put themselves forward as objects for the aggressive desire of men'; see the Chapter XII 'Erotic Object of Desire: Prostitution' in *Death and Sensuality. A Study of Eroticism and the Taboo*, Georges Bataille (New York: Walker, 1962), 131.

25 BC Hall, 'The Only Love for Me ... A Letter to the Outside World Expressed by BC Hall – Objectum-Sexual Sound Engineer', Objectum Sexuality Internationale, accessed 21 April 2021, http://www.objectum-sexuality.org/expressions-bc.pdf.

26 BC Hall.

27 Amy Marsh, 'Love among the Objectum Sexuals', *Electronic Journal of Human Sexuality* 13 (1 March 2010), http://www.ejhs.org/volume13/ObjSexuals.htm.

28 Marsh, 'Love among the Objectum Sexuals'.

29 Justin Clemens and Dominic Pettman, *Avoiding the Subject: Media, Culture and the Object* (Amsterdam: Amsterdam University Press, 2005), 40–1.

30 Turkle, *Alone Together*, 18.

31 Bataille, *Death and Sensuality. A Study of Eroticism and the Taboo*, 109–10.

32 Compare: 'Everything begins with the possibility of naming, which is both destructive of the thing and allows the passage of the thing onto the symbolic plane, thanks to which the truly human register comes into its own' in Lacan, *Freud's Papers on Technique, 1953–1954*, 1:219.

33 M. Adam, 'An Introspective View of Objectum Sexuality. Expressed by Adam M. from the USA, Mar 2011', Objectum Sexuality Internationale, accessed 21 April 2021, http://objectum-sexuality.org/expressions-am.pdf.

34 In the context of active and passive male and female roles, the Pygmalion's myth sounds masculine as well. However, the relationships between 'human' women and their creations within OS community prove that the roles of creator and the object of creation might not necessarily be gender biased.

35 Jacques Lacan, *Ecrits: The First Complete Edition in English*, ed. Bruce Fink (New York: W. W. Norton & Company 2006), 224–9.

36 Jacques Lacan, *The Ego in Freud's Theory and in the Technique of Psychoanalysis, 1954–1955*, vol. 2, The Seminar of Jacques Lacan (New York: W. W. Norton & Company 1988).

37 Lacan, *The Ego in Freud's Theory*, 259.

38 Lacan, *The Ego in Freud's Theory*, 260.

39 John Austin Langshaw, *How to Do Things with Words: The William James Lectures Delivered in Harvard University in 1955* (Oxford: Oxford University Press, 1962), 24.

40 Giorgio Agamben, *The Open: Man and Animal*, trans. Kevin Attell, Meridian, Crossing Aesthetics (Stanford, CA: Stanford University Press and London: Eurospan, 2004).

41 MacCormack, *Cinesexuality*.

42 Haraway, *Simians, Cyborgs, and Women*.

Chapter 9

1 Giorgio Agamben, *Homo Sacer: Sovereign Power and Bare Life*, trans. Daniel Heller-Roazen, 1st ed. (Stanford, CA: Stanford University Press, 1998).

2 See: Agamben, *The Open*.

3 M. Kamyszek, *Seria gier The Sims – porównanie edycji, struktura rozgrywki, profil graczy, strategie promocyjne ['The Sims Game Series – Comparative Analysis of Editions, Structure of the Game, Players' Profile, Promotional Strategies']*. Unpublished BA thesis, 2010.

4 The list includes various means of killing Sims present in different editions of the game.

5 The materials for the analysis come from the forums: http://forum.simy.bizserwer. pl; http://forum.thesims.pl/ http://forum.thesims3.com http://www.carls-sims-3-guide.com/, researched In 2011–2015. The translations retain small letters and punctuation of the original posts.

6 The names of the user are original nicknames from English and Polish forums (author's note).

7 Doda is a popular Polish pop singer (author's note).

8 http://forum.thesims.pl/showthread.php?t=9097&page=16, 15 December 2020.

9   http://forum.thesims.pl/archive/index.php/t-9097.html, 15 December 2020.

10 This type of cruelty may be generalized as death and cruelty being part of a work of art. By that I mean the forms of oppression towards non-human subjects, whose aim is the creation of an aesthetic object. For humans as non-humans used to be put on display in *tableau vivant*, where Pygmies or representatives of other tribes were shown during exhibitions organized in Europe or the United States. In case of animals a similar situation takes places in Wladyslaw Starewicz's early animations, which feature dissected insects. In literature this motif appears in Kafka's 'In the Penal Colony' (1919). See Franz Kafka, 'In the Penal Colony', in *Franz Kafka: The Complete Stories*, ed. Nahum N. Glatzer, Reprint ed. (New York: Schocken, 1995).

11 http://www.carls-sims-3-guide.com/forum/index.php?topic=10855.0, 15 December 2020.

12 http://forum.simy.bizserwer.pl/index.php?showtopic=7729, 15 December 2020.

13 http://forum.thesims.pl/showthread.php?t=9097&page=10, 15 December 2020.

14 http://forum.simy.bizserwer.pl/index.php?showtopic=7729, 15 December 2020.

15 http://forum.simy.bizserwer.pl/index.php?showtopic=7729, 15 December 2020.

16 http://alfadragons.my3gb.com/czy,zabijacie,swoich,simow,p.php, 15 December 2020.

17 http://forum.thesims3.com/jforum/posts/list/15/536481.page, 15 December 2020.

18 http://forum.thesims.pl/archive/index.php/t-9097.html, 15 December 2020.

19 http://forum.thesims.pl/archive/index.php/t-9097.html, 15 December 2020.

20 Boredom is simultaneously a motive for killing and desisting from executions.

21 http://forum.simy.bizserwer.pl/index.php?showtopic=7729, 15 December 2020.

22 http://www.carls-sims-3-guide.com/info/death.php, 15 December 2020.

23 http://forum.thesims.pl/showthread.php?t=9097&page=10, 15 December 2020.

24 http://forum.thesims3.com/jforum/posts/list/15/536481.page, 15 December 2020.

25 http://forum.thesims3.com/jforum/posts/list/15/536481.page, 15 December 2020.

26 http://www.carls-sims-3-guide.com/forum/index.php?topic=10855.25, 15 December 2020.

27 http://forum.thesims.pl/showthread.php?t=9097&page=10, 15 December 2020.

28 I refer here to the idea of the camp presented in both *Homo Sacer* and *Remnants of Auschwitz*. See Agamben, *Homo Sacer*. Giorgio Agamben, *Remnants of Auschwitz: The Witness and the Archive*, trans. Daniel Heller-Roazen (New York: Zone Books, 1999).

29 Agamben, *Remnants of Auschwitz*, 38–9.

30 In the Polish literature describing the life In concentration camps, the *Muselmann* (Muslim) appears, for example, in the works of Borowski and Grzesiuk, see Tadeusz Borowski, *Wybór opowiadań [Selected Stories]* (Warsaw: Państwowy Instytut Wydawniczy, 1983). Stanisław Grzesiuk, *Pięć lat kacetu [Five Years in Concentration Camp]* (Warsaw: Książka i Wiedza, 2008).

31 Turkle, *Alone Together*, 27–34.

32 See Jan Stasieńko, *Alien vs. predator?: gry komputerowe a badania literackie* [*Alien vs. Predator? Computer Games and Literary Studies*](Wrocław: Wydawnictwo Naukowe Dolnośląskiej Szkoły Wyższej Edukacji TWP, 2005). Here, the chapter: 'Mimesis i interaktywność jako kategorie badania świata przedstawionego' [Mimesis and Interactivity as categories of a story-world analysis]; I use here the term particular mimesis, which is connected with the idea of subversive playing and Espen Aarseth, 'I Fought the Law. Transgressive Play and The Implied Player', in *Situated Play, Proceedings of DiGRA 2007 Conference*, accessed 15 April 2021, http://www.digra.org/wp-content/uploads/digital-library/07313.03489.pdf.

33 Aarseth, 'I Fought the Law. Transgressive Play and the Implied Player'.

34 Kafka, 'In the Penal Colony'.

35 http://forum.simy.bizserwer.pl/index.php?showtopic=7729, 15 December 2020.

36 http://alfadragons.my3gb.com/czy,zabijacie,swoich,simow,p.php, 15 December 2020.

37 Agamben, *Homo Sacer*, 82 and 99.

Final word

1 Duncan, 'The Seduction of Reality', 124.

2 Agamben, *'What Is an Apparatus?'*, 18–19.

3 Auto-affect, in his opinion, is a characteristic enabling the subject to self-confirm itself in speech. See Jacques Derrida, 'The Voice That Keeps Silent', in *Voice and Phenomenon: Introduction to the Problem of the Sign in Husserl's Phenomenology*, trans. Leonard Lawlor, Northwestern University Studies in Phenomenology and Existential Philosophy (Evanston, IL: Northwestern University Press, 2011).

4 While many examples of such self-intimacy are described in the chapter about hybrid animation, this also occurs in the modern CGI cinema. For example, on *Avatar*'s set Weta Digital employees shot extreme zooms of themselves for reference (author's note).

5 See Pierre Teilhard de Chardin, 'Book Three: Thought, The Chapter II: The Deployment of the Noosphere', in *The Phenomenon of Man*, trans. Bernard Wall (Princeton, NJ: Harper Perennial, 1976), 191–212.

6 Duncan, 'The Seduction of Reality', 130.

7 Duncan, 'The Seduction of Reality', 133–4.

8 David Barboza, 'The Media Business: Advertising; Motorola Hopes a Computer-generated Character Will Link the Real World with the Virtual One', *The New York Times*, 25 April 2000, sec. Business, http://www.nytimes.com/2000/04/25/business/

media-business-advertising-motorola-hopes-computer-generated-character-will-link.html and '"Virtual Sensation," Mya Makes Her Debut At the Oscars; Motorola Announces Its First Cyber-assistant', *M2 PressWIRE*, 26 March 2000, http://www.m2.com/m2/web/story.php/20005B22C9F6EA4561EF802568AF005DCB6E. The author of the text in M2 PressWIRE writes about the symptomatic comparison between Mya and Hollywood stars: 'The questions running through Hollywood are: "How do I get to Mya? Who represents her? How can I sign her?"' Mary Flanagan, in turn, introduced Mya's peers, such as the first subjectivized newscaster Ananova, or the unrealized vision of a 'personified' internet search engine called Syndi; see Flanagan, 'The Bride Stripped Bare to Her Data'.

9   See e.g. Will Grice, 'Wahey Siri. Lonely People Are Having PHONE SEX with Apple's Siri and Other Voice Activated Assistants', *The Sun*, 27 October 2016, https://www.thesun.co.uk/news/2060119/lonely-pervs-are-having-phone-sex-with-siri/ and Mindshare and J. Walter Thomson, 'Speak Easy. The Future Answers To You', 20 January 2017, http://www.mindshareworld.com/sites/default/files/speakeasy.pdf.

10 Patrick St. Michel, 'A Brief History of Virtual Pop Stars', *The Pitch*, 15 July 2016, https://pitchfork.com/thepitch/1229-a-brief-history-of-virtual-pop-stars/.

11 Nick Remsen, 'Riccardo Tisci Gives Japan's Biggest Virtual Virtuoso an Haute Couture Makeover', *Vogue*, 2 May 2016, https://www.vogue.com/article/riccardo-tisci-hatsune-miku-haute-couture-makeover-avatar.

Bibliography

'A Custom-Made Prompting System'. *Business Screen. The Visual Communications Magazine* 33, no. 3 (June 1972): 28–32.

Aarseth, Espen. 'I Fought the Law. Transgressive Play and The Implied Player'. In *Situated Play, Proceedings of DiGRA 2007 Conference*. Accessed 15 April 2021. http://www.digra.org/wp-content/uploads/digital-library/07313.03489.pdf.

Adam, M. 'An Introspective View of Objectum Sexuality. Expressed by Adam M. from the USA, Mar 2011'. Objectum Sexuality Internationale. Accessed 21 April 2021. http://objectum-sexuality.org/expressions-am.pdf.

Agamben, Giorgio. *Homo Sacer: Sovereign Power and Bare Life*. Translated by Daniel Heller-Roazen. 1st ed. Stanford, CA: Stanford University Press, 1998.

Agamben, Giorgio. *The Open: Man and Animal*. Translated by Kevin Attell. Meridian, Crossing Aesthetics. Stanford, CA: Stanford University Press and London: Eurospan, 2004.

Agamben, Giorgio. *Remnants of Auschwitz: The Witness and the Archive*. Translated by Daniel Heller-Roazen. New York: Zone Books, 1999.

Agamben, Giorgio. *'What Is an Apparatus?' And Other Essays*. Meridian, Crossing Aesthetics. Stanford, CA: Stanford University Press, 2009.

Anderson, Ross. *Pulling a Rabbit out of a Hat: The Making of Roger Rabbit*. Jackson: University Press of Mississippi Jackson, 2019.

Austin, John Langshaw. *How to Do Things with Words: The William James Lectures Delivered in Harvard University in 1955*. Oxford: Oxford University Press, 1962.

Ayers, Drew. *Spectacular Posthumanism: The Digital Vernacular of Visual Effects*. New York: Bloomsbury Academic, 2019.

Bakke, Monika. '"Between Us, Animals". Emotional Ties Between Humans and Other Animals'. Translated by Jan Szelągiewicz. *Teksty Drugie* 1, no. 7, Special Issue English Edition (2015): 290–302.

Bakke, Monika. *Bio-transfiguracje: sztuka i estetyka posthumanizmu [Bio-transfigurations. Art and Esthetics of Posthumanism]*. Poznań: Wydawnictwo Naukowe Uniwersytetu im. Adama Mickiewicza, 2012.

Balzer, Richard. *Peepshows: A Visual History*. New York: Harry N. Abrams, 1998.

Barboza, David. 'The Media Business: Advertising; Motorola Hopes a Computer-generated Character Will Link the Real World with the Virtual One'. *The New York Times*, 25 April 2000, sec. Business. http://www.nytimes.com/2000/04/25/business/media-business-advertising-motorola-hopes-computer-generated-character-will-link.html.

Barfield, Ray E. *A Word from Our Viewers: Reflections from Early Television Audiences.* [Praeger Television Collection Series]. Westport and Conn: Praeger, 2008.

Barnouw, Erik. *The Magician and the Cinema.* New York: Oxford University Press, 1981.

Barrier, Michael. *The Animated Man: A Life of Walt Disney.* Berkeley: University of California Press, 2007.

Barrier, Michael. *Hollywood Cartoons: American Animation in Its Golden Age.* New York: Oxford University Press, Incorporated, 2003.

Barthes, Roland and Susan Sontag. *A Barthes Reader.* London: Cape, 1982.

Barton, Fred and H. J. Schlafly. 'TelePrompter – New Production Tool'. *Journal of Society of Motion Picture and Television Engineers* 58 (June 1952): 515–21.

Basu Thakur, Gautam and Jonathan Michael Dickstein, eds. *Lacan and the Nonhuman.* Cham: Palgrave Macmillan, 2018.

Bataille, Georges. *Death and Sensuality. A Study of Eroticism and the Taboo.* New York: Walker, 1962.

Bataille, Georges. *Erotism: Death & Sensuality.* 1st City lights ed. San Francisco: City Lights Books, 1986.

Bataille, Georges. *Historia erotyzmu [History of Erotism].* Kraków: Oficyna Literacka, 1992.

Bataille, Georges. *L'histoire de l'érotisme. Le Surréalisme Au Jour Le Jour. Conférences 1951-1953. La Souveraineté.* ØEuvres Complètes. Paris: Gallimard, 1970.

Beadle, Mary E. 'Winky Dink and You: The Beginnings of Interactive TV'. *Paper Presented at the Annual Meeting of the BEA, Las Vegas Hotel (LVH), Las Vegas, NV,* 22 April 2014. http://citation.allacademic.com/meta/p_mla_apa_research_citation/6/2/6/7/7/p626774_index.html.

Beck, Jerry. 'Combination Films: A Brief History'. *Animation Magazine* 2, no. 1 (Summer 1988).

Behind the Ears: The True Story of Roger Rabbit. Documentary featured on the 2-disc Vista Series DVD edition of 'Who Framed Roger Rabbit' film. Disney Home Video, 2003.

Bentley, Toni. *Sisters of Salome.* Lincoln: University of Nebraska Press, 2005.

Berger, Jamie. 'Wet Confessions: Autoethnography of a Peepshow Customer'. In *Flesh for Fantasy: Producing and Consuming Exotic Dance,* edited by R. Danielle Egan, Katherine Frank and Merri Lisa Johnson. New York: Thunder's Mouth Press and Distributed by Publishers Group West, 2006.

'Big Chemist's Retort Built for Movie'. *Popular Science,* February 1940. http://blog.modernmechanix.com/big-chemists-retort-built-for-movie/.

Bird-David, Nurit. '"Animism" Revisited: Personhood, Environment, and Relational Epistemology'. *Current Anthropology* 40, no. S1 (February 1999): S67–91.

Biro, Matthew. *The Dada Cyborg: Visions of the New Human in Weimar Berlin.* Minneapolis, MN and London: University of Minnesota Press, 2009.

Bishop, Philip E. 'Brecht, Hegel, Lacan: Brecht's Theory of Gest and the Problem of the Subject Studies'. *Twentieth and Twenty-first Century Literature* 10 (1986): 267–88.

Blake, James. *Television and the Second Screen: Interactive TV in the Age of Social Participation*. Abingdon, Oxon; New York, N.Y.: Routledge, 2016.

'Blue Peter Sorry over Fake Winner'. *BBC News*, 14 March 2007. http://news.bbc.co.uk/2/hi/entertainment/6449919.stm.

Boone, Andrew R. 'Snow White and the Seven Dwarfs'. *Popular Science*, January 1938. http://blog.modernmechanix.com/the-making-of-snow-white-and-the-seven-dwarfs/2/#mmGal.

Borowski, Tadeusz. *Wybór opowiadań [Selected Stories]*. Warsaw: Państwowy Instytut Wydawniczy, 1983.

Braidotti, Rosi. *The Posthuman*. Cambridge: Polity Press, 2013.

Bulgozdi, Imola. Artificial Intelligence and Gender Performativity in William Gibson's Idoru. In *collected volume: Navigating Cybercultures*, edited by Nicholas van Orden. Leiden, Boston: Brill, 2013.

Burnett, Ron. *How Images Think*. Cambridge, MA: MIT Press, 2005.

Campbell-Kelly, Martin and William Aspray. *Computer: A History of the Information Machine*. New York: Basic Books, 1996.

Carey, John. *Winky Dink to Stargazer: Five Decades of Interactive Television*. Edinburgh, Scotland: Conference of Interactive Television, 1996. http://www.columbia.edu/cu/business/courses/download/B9201-XX/carey/history_of_interactive_tv.pdf

Carey, John and M. C. J. Elton. *When Media Are New: Understanding the Dynamics of New Media Adoption and Use*. The New Media World. Ann Arbor: Digital Culture Books and University of Michigan Press and University of Michigan Library, 2010.

Carney, Sean. *Brecht and Critical Theory: Dialectics and Contemporary Aesthetics*. Vol. 2. Routledge Advances in Theatre and Performance Studies. London and New York: Routledge, 2005.

Carter, Grey. 'Couple Celebrates Wedding by Murdering Virtual Girlfriend'. *The Escapist*, 26 November 2012. https://v1.escapistmagazine.com/forums/read/7.394705-Couple-Celebrates-Wedding-by-Murdering-Virtual-Girlfriend.

Castricano, Carla Jodey. *Animal Subjects: An Ethical Reader in a Posthuman World*. Cultural Studies Series. Waterloo, ON: Wilfrid Laurier University Press, 2008.

Castro, Eduardo Viveiros de. 'Cosmological Deixis and Amerindian Perspectivism'. *The Journal of the Royal Anthropological Institute* 4, no. 3 (1998): 469–88.

Chapman, Mary. '"Living Pictures": Women and Tableaux Vivants in Nineteenth-century American Fiction and Culture'. *Wide Angle* 18, no. 3 (1996): 22–52.

Cheok, Adrian David and David Levy, eds. *Love and Sex with Robots*. Third International Conference, LSR 2017, London, UK, December 19–20, 2017, Revised Selected Papers, New York: Springer, 2018.

Cheu, Johnson. *Diversity in Disney Films: Critical Essays on Race, Ethnicity, Gender, Sexuality and Disability*. Jefferson, NC: McFarland & Company, Inc., Publishers, 2013.

Cholodenko, Alan. *The Illusion of Life: Essays on Animation*. Sydney: Power Publications, 1991.

Cholodenko, Alan. 'Speculation on the Animatic Automaton'. In *The Illusion of Life 2: More Essays on Animation*, edited by Alan Cholodenko. Sydney: Power Publications, 2007.

Chowdhury, G. G. *Text Retrieval Systems in Information Management*. New Delhi: New Age International, 1996.

Clemens, Justin and Dominic Pettman. *Avoiding the Subject: Media, Culture and the Object*. Amsterdam: Amsterdam University Press, 2005.

Colebrook, Claire, and Ian Buchanan. *Deleuze and Feminist Theory*. Edinburgh: Edinburgh University Press, 2000.

Crafton, Donald. *Before Mickey: An Animated Anthology*. Cambridge, MA: MIT Press, 1982.

Curran, Mimi. 'Participation Television: A Breakdown of Trust'. *Journal of Direct, Data and Digital Marketing Practice* 9, no. 4 (4 January 2008): 385–9.

D. from Berlin. 'A Few More Thoughts... Expressed by D. from Berlin, Germany'. *Objectum Sexuality Internationale*. Accessed 21 April 2021. http://objectum-sexuality.org/expressions-ds-2.pdf.

Day, Ronald E. *The Modern Invention of Information: Discourse, History, and Power*. Carbondale: Southern Illinois University Press, 2001.

Deleuze, Gilles. *Cinema 1: The Movement-image*. Translated by Hugh Hugh Tomlinson and Barbara Habberjam. London: Athlone, 1986.

Deleuze, Gilles and Félix Guattari. *Anti-Oedipus: Capitalism and Schizophrenia*. Minneapolis: University of Minnesota Press, 1983.

Deleuze, Gilles, Félix Guattari, Robert Hurley, Mark Seem, and Helen R. Lane. *Anti-Oedipus: Capitalism and Schizophrenia*. Continuum Impacts. London: Continuum, 2004.

Derrida, Jacques. *Archive Fever: A Freudian Impression*. Translated by Eric Prenowitz. 1 ed. Chicago, IL: University of Chicago Press, 1998.

Derrida, Jacques. 'Maddening the Subjectile'. In *Yale French Studies*, translated by Mary Ann Caws. 84, Boundaries: Writing&Drawing (1994): 154–71.

Derrida, Jacques. *Speech and Phenomena: And Other Essays on Husserl's Theory of Signs*. Evanston: Northwestern University Press, 1973.

Derrida, Jacques. 'The Voice That Keeps Silent'. In *Voice and Phenomenon: Introduction to the Problem of the Sign in Husserl's Phenomenology*, translated by Leonard Lawlor. Northwestern University Studies in Phenomenology and Existential Philosophy. Evanston, IL: Northwestern University Press. 2011.

Derrida, Jacques and Bernard Stiegler. *Echographies of Television: Filmed Interviews*. Cambridge and Malden, MA: Polity Press and Blackwell Publishers, 2002.

Derry, Mark. 'Naked Lunch: Talking Realcore with Sergio Messina'. In *C'lickme: A Netporn Studies Reader*, edited by Katrien Jacobs, Marije Janssen and Matteo Pasquinelli. Amsterdam: Institute of Network Cultures, 2007.

Dery, Mark. 'Robo Copulation: Sex Times Technology Equals the Future'. In *Escape Velocity: Cyberculture at the Cnd of the Century*, 2nd ed. New York: Grove Press, 1999.

Desowitz, Bill. 'Sky Captain and the Virtual World of Today'. *VFX World*, 5 February 2004. https://www.awn.com/vfxworld/sky-captain-and-virtual-world-today.

Detsi-Diamanti, Zoe, Katerina Kitsē-Mytakou and Effie Yiannopoulou. *The Future of Flesh: A Cultural Survey of the Body*. 1st ed. New York: Palgrave Macmillan, 2009.

Dierkes-Thrun, Petra. *Salome's Modernity: Oscar Wilde and the Aesthetics of Transgression*. Ann Arbor: University of Michigan Press, 2011.

Dieterle, William. *Salome*. Columbia Pictures, 1953.

Dolphijn, Rick and Iris der van Tuin. *New Materialism: Interviews et Cartographies*. 1st ed. New Metaphysics. Ann Arbor, MI: Open Humanities Press, 2012.

Dow, Suzanne and Colin Wright. *Psychoanalysis and the Posthuman*. Vol. 33, no. 3. Paragraph. Edinburgh: Edinburgh University Press, 2010.

Duncan, Jody. 'All the Way'. *Cinefex*, no. 112 (2008).

Duncan, Jody. 'Braving the Elements'. *Cinefex*, no. 123 (2010).

Duncan, Jody. 'Deep Magic'. *Cinefex*, no. 104 (2006).

Duncan, Jody. 'Ghosts in the Machine'. *Cinefex*, no. 99 (2004).

Duncan, Jody. 'Legacy System'. *Cinefex*, no. 124 (2011).

Duncan, Jody. 'Passion Play'. *Cinefex*, no. 97 (2004).

Duncan, Jody. 'Ring Masters'. *Cinefex*, no. 89 (2002).

Duncan, Jody. 'The Seduction of Reality'. *Cinefex*, no. 120 (2010).

Duncan, Jody. 'The Unusual Birth of Benjamin Button'. *Cinefex*, no. 116 (2009).

Dunlop, M. H. *Sixty Miles from Contentment: Traveling the Nineteenth-century American Interior*. Boulder, CO: Westview Press, 1998.

Eaves, Elisabeth. *Bare: On Women, Dancing, Sex, and Power*. New York: Random House LLC, 2011.

Elbert, Monika M. 'Striking a Historical Pose: Antebellum Tableaux Vivants, Godey's Illustrations, and Margaret Fuller's Heroines'. *New England Quarterly* 75, no. 2 (2002): 235.

Em & Lo. 'Beautiful Agony, the O-Face Video Website, Turns 5!' *Em & Lo. Sex, Love and Everything in Between*, 11 March 2009. https://www.emandlo.com/o-face-video-site-beautiful-agony-turns-five/.

Ettinger, Bracha. *The Matrixial Gaze*. Feminist Arts and Histories Network. Woodhouse: University of Leeds, 1995.

Eva K. from The Netherlands. 'The Love Letter about Letters… Expressed by Eva K. from The Netherlands'. Objectum Sexuality Internationale. Accessed 21 April 2021. http://www.objectum-sexuality.org/expressions-evak-2.pdf.

Ezra, Elizabeth. *The Cinema of Things: Globalization and the Posthuman Object*. New York: Bloomsbury Academic, 2017.

Feyersinger, Erwin. 'Diegetic Short Circuits: Metalepsis in'. *Animation* 5, no. 3 (11 January 2010): 279–94.

Fielding, Raymond. *The Technique of Special-effects Cinematography*. 2nd ed. Library of Communication Techniques. London: Focal Press, 1969.

Finch, Christopher. *The CG Story: Computer-generated Animation and Special Effects*. New York: The Monacelli Press, 2013.

Finch, Christopher. *Special Effects: Creating Movie Magic*. 1st ed. New York: Abbeville Press, 1984.

Flanagan, Mary. 'The Bride Stripped Bare to Her Data'. In *Data Made Flesh: Embodying Information*, edited by Robert Mitchell and Phillip Thurtle. New York and London: Routledge, 2003.

Fleischer, Richard. *Out of the Inkwell: Max Fleischer and the Animation Revolution*. Lexington: University Press of Kentucky and London, 2005.

Flusser, Vilém. *Towards a Philosophy of Photography*. London: Reaktion Books, 2012.

Fordham, Joe. 'A Hero's Return'. *Cinefex*, no. 106 (2006).

Fordham, Joe. 'Down the Rabbit Hole'. *Cinefex*, no. 122 (2010).

Fordham, Joe. 'Green Destiny'. *Cinefex*, no. 94 (2003).

Fordham, Joe. 'Journey's End'. *Cinefex*, no. 96 (2004).

Fordham, Joe. 'Lost World'. *Cinefex*, no. 114 (2008).

Fordham, Joe. 'Middle-Earth Strikes Back'. *Cinefex*, no. 92 (2003).

Fordham, Joe. 'Reality Deconstructed'. *Cinefex*, no. 126 (2011).

Fordham, Joe. 'Return of the King'. *Cinefex*, no. 96 (2004).

Fordham, Joe. 'Soldier Blue'. *Cinefex*, no. 127 (2011).

Fordham, Joe. 'Under the Moons of Mars'. *Cinefex*, no. 129 (2012).

Freeland, Cynthia A. 'Feminist Frameworks for Horror Films'. In *Post-theory: Reconstructing Film Studies*, edited by David Bordwell Noel Carroll. Madison, Wisconsin: University of Wisconsin Press, 1996, 195–218.

Freud, Sigmund. 'A Note upon the "Mystic Writing Pad"'. In *The Ego and the ID and Other Works*, translated by James Strachey and Anna Freud, Vol. XIX (1923–5). The Standard Edition of the Complete Psychological Works of Sigmund Freud. London: The Hogarth Press and the Institute of Psycho-Analysis, 1961.

Fry, Ron and Pamela Fourzon. *The Saga of Special Effects: The Complete History of Cinematic Illusion, From Edison's Kinetoscope to Dynamation, Sensurround…and Beyond*. 1st ed. Englewood Cliffs, NJ: Prentice-Hall, 1977.

Funari, Vicky and Julia Query. *Live Nude Girls Unite!* First Run Features, 2000.

Gabb, Jacqui. *Researching Intimacy in Families*. Pbk. ed. Palgrave Macmillan Studies in Family and Intimate Life. Basingstoke and New York: Palgrave Macmillan, 2010.

'Gabinetto Segreto [Secret Cabinet]'. Accessed 6 October 2012. http://museoarcheologiconazionale.campaniabeniculturali.it/glossario/ploneglossarydefinition.2008-06-09.8351409625/.

Galloway, Alexander R. *Protocol: How Control Exists after Decentralization*. Cambridge, MA: MIT Press, 2004.

Garoian, Charles R. *The Prosthetic Pedagogy of Art: Embodied Research and Practice.* Albany, NY: State University of New York Press, 2013.

Gawlinski, Mark. *Interactive Television Production.* Oxford: Focal, 2003.

Gibson, William. *Idoru.* London: Penguin, 1997.

Gilder, Nathan. 'Theological Compatibilism & Animation: Vessel of Wrath'. *ImageTexT: Interdisciplinary Comics Studies* 2, no. 2 (2006).

Gitelman, Lisa. *Always Already New: Media, History and the Data of Culture.* Cambridge, MA: MIT Press, 2006.

Gitelman, Lisa, ed. *'Raw Data' Is an Oxymoron.* Infrastructures Series. Cambridge, MA and London: The MIT Press, 2013.

Godzic, Wiesław. 'Various Faces of Interactivity: Remarks on Television'. *ICONO 14*, no. 15 (2010): 22–36.

Goodall, Jane. 'Hybridity and Innocence'. In *The Illusion of Life 2: More Essays on Animation*, edited by Alan Cholodenko. Sydney: Power Publications, 2007.

Goodman, Wes. 'Pornography, Peep Shows, and the Decline of Morality'. *USA Today Magazine* 122, no. 2586 (1994): 32.

Grice, Will. 'Wahey Siri. Lonely People Are Having PHONE SEX with Apple's Siri and Other Voice Activated Assistants'. *The Sun*, 27 October 2016. https://www.thesun.co.uk/news/2060119/lonely-pervs-are-having-phone-sex-with-siri/.

Grzesiuk, Stanisław. *Pięć lat kacetu [Five Years in Concentration Camp].* Warsaw: Książka i Wiedza, 2008.

Gwóźdź, Andrzej, ed. *Kino po kinie: film w kulturze uczestnictwa [Cinema after Cinema. Film in Participatory Culture].* Warsaw: Oficyna Naukowa, 2010.

Halberstam, Judith and Ira Livingston. *Posthuman Bodies. Unnatural Acts.* Bloomington: Indiana University Press, 1995.

Hall, B. C. 'The Only Love for Me… A Letter to the Outside World Expressed by BC Hall –Objectum-Sexual Sound Engineer'. Objectum Sexuality Internationale. Accessed 21 April 2021. http://www.objectum-sexuality.org/expressions-bc.pdf.

Hamam, Iman. 'Satellite Arcades: Three-dimensional Puppets and the Coin-Operated Interface'. *Journal for Cultural Research* 16, no. 2–3 (2012): 239–59.

Hansen, Mark B. N. *New Philosophy for New Media.* Cambridge, MA: MIT Press, 2004.

Haraway, Donna. *The Companion Species Manifesto: Dogs, People and Significant Otherness.* Chicago, IL: Prickly Paradigm Press, 2009.

Haraway, Donna Jeanne. *Simians, Cyborgs, and Women: The Reinvention of Nature.* New York: Routledge, 1991.

Haraway, Donna Jeanne. *When Species Meet.* Vol. 3. Posthumanities. Minneapolis: University of Minnesota Press, 2008.

Harris, Louis. 'Three-Headed Editor Required'. *The Cine Technician* 22, no. 134 (January 1956): 24–26.

Hart, Hugh. 'Through Tim Burton's Looking Glass: Making Alice in Wonderland'. *Wired*, 3 May 2010. www.wired.com/underwire/2010/03/wonderland-tech-tricks/.

Harvey, Graham. *Animism: Respecting the Living World.* New York: Columbia University Press, 2006.

'Have You Heard? TelePrompter Has a Big, New Station Deal (Press Ad)'. *Sponsor*, 17 May 1954.

Hayles, N. Katherine. 'The Condition of Virtuality'. In *Language Machines: Technologies of Literary and Cultural Production*, edited by Jeffrey Masten, Peter Stallybrass and Nancy J. Vickers. Essays from the English Institute. New York: Routledge, 1997.

Hayles, N. Katherine. *How We Became Posthuman: Virtual Bodies in Cybernetics, Literature, and Informatics.* Chicago, IL: University of Chicago Press, 1999.

Heim, Michael. *Virtual Realism.* New York: Oxford University Press, 1998.

Herzog, Amy. 'In the Flesh: Space and Embodiment in the Pornographic Peep Show Arcade'. *Velvet Light Trap: A Critical Journal of Film & Television*, 62 (Fall 2008): 29–43.

Holmes, Dave, Patrick O'Byrne and Stuart J. Murray. 'Faceless Sex: Glory Holes and Sexual Assemblages: Faceless Sex'. *Nursing Philosophy* 11, no. 4 (1 September 2010): 250–9.

Hovet, Grace Ann and Theodore R. Hovet. 'Tableaux Vivants: Masculine Vision and Feminine Reflections in Novels by Warner, Alcott, Stowe'. *ATQ* 7, no. 4 (1993): 335.

'How Disney Combines Living Actors with His Cartoon Characters'. *Popular Science*, September 1944.

Howell, Signe, Lise. 'Metamorphosis and Identity: Chewong Animistic Ontology'. In *The Handbook of Contemporary Animism*, edited by Graham Harvey. Durham, UK: Acumen, 2013.

Huhtamo, Erkki. 'The Pleasures of the Peephole: An Archaeological Exploration of Peep Media'. In *The Book of Imaginary Media: Excavating the Dream of the Ultimate Communication Medium*, edited by Eric Kluitenberg. Rotterdam: De Balie; NAi Publishers, 2006.

Huhtamo, Erkki and Jussi Parikka, eds. *Media Archaeology: Approaches, Applications, and Implications.* Berkeley, CA: University of California Press, 2011.

Hunt, Lynn. *The Invention of Pornography, 1500–1800: Obscenity and the Origins of Modernity.* New York and Cambridge, MA: Zone Books, 1996.

Hutchby, Ian. *Confrontation Talk: Arguments, Asymmetries, and Power on Talk Radio.* Mahwah, NJ: Routledge, 1996.

Huysmans, Joris-Karl. *Against The Grain [À Rebours]*, translated by Harrison Ainsworth. Project Gutenberg, 2004. http://www.gutenberg.org/files/12341/12341.txt.

Ian Smith, Fiona StewartPhil Turner. 'Winky Dink and You: Determining Patterns of Narrative for Interactive Television Design'. In *Proceedings of the Second European Interactive Television Conference: Enhancing the Experience, Brighton, April 2004*, edited by Lyb Pemberton, Judith Masthoff and Richard Griffiths, 1–10, 2004.

Idlisan, Dolly. 'Strangest Marriages in Japan'. *Pop Japan*, 23 August 2016. https://pop-japan.com/culture/strangest-marriages-in-japan/.

Ihde, Don. *Ironic Technics*. Copenhagen: Automatic Press/VIP, 2008.

Interview with Edwin Wycoff Attached to Winky Dink and You DVD. Vanguard Cinema and Rembrandt Films, 2002.

Jagodzinski, Jan. *Postmodern Dilemmas: Outrageous Essays in Art & Art Education*. Studies in Curriculum Theory. Mahwah, NJ: Lawrence Erlbaum Associates, 1997.

Johnson-Roehr, Catherine. 'In Search of Secret Museums'. *Journal of Sex Research* 48, no. 1 (2010): 94–5.

Kac, Eduardo. *Telepresence & Bio Art: Networking Humans, Rabbits & Robots*. Studies in Literature and Science. Ann Arbor: University of Michigan Press, 2005.

Kafka, Franz. 'In the Penal Colony'. In *Franz Kafka: The Complete Stories*, edited by Nahum N. Glatzer, Reprint edition. New York: Schocken, 1995.

Karayanni, Stavros Stavrou. *Dancing Fear & Desire: Race, Sexuality, and Imperial Politics in Middle Eastern Dance*. Cultural Studies Series. Waterloo: Wilfrid Laurier University Press, 2004.

Katz, Jesse. 'Under New Law, the Booths for Peep Shows Will Have No Doors'. *Los Angeles Times*, 15 October 1988. https://www.latimes.com/archives/la-xpm-1988-09-15-ve-2626-story.html.

Ketabchi, Désirée. 'Belgian Television Investigative Programme Exposes Social Injustice with Humour'. *European Journalism Centre Magazine*, 3 November 2011. http://ejc.net/magazine/article/belgian-television-investigative-programme-exposes-social-injustice-with-hu#.WLfXXHqvzh4.

Kish, Frances. 'The Advantages of Being Shy'. *TV Radio Mirror*, January 1962.

Kittler, Friedrich A. *Gramophone, Film, Typewriter*. Writing Science. Stanford, CA: Stanford University Press, 1999.

Klein, Norman M. *The Vatican to Vegas: A History of Special Effects*. New York: New Press: distributed by Norton, 2004.

Kluszczyński, Ryszard W. 'From Film to Interactive Art: Transformations In Media Arts'. In *MediaArtHistories, Red. Oliver Grau*, s. 207–28. Cambridge, MA and London: MIT Press, 2007.

Korkis, Jim. 'The History of the Partners Statue: Part One'. *Mouse Planet*, 26 October 2011. https://www.mouseplanet.com/9766/The_History_of_the_Partners_Statue_Part_One.

Kozlenko, William. 'The Animated Cartoon and Walt Disney'. In *The Emergence of Film Art. The Evolution and Development of the Motion Picture as an Art, from 1900 to the Present*, edited by Lewis Jacobs. New York: Hopikinson and Blake, 1969.

Kroker, Arthur and Marilouise Kroker, eds. *Body Invaders: Panic Sex in America*. Culturetexts. New York: St. Martin's Press, 1987.

Kroker, Arthur and Marilouise Kroker. *Body Invaders: Sexuality and the Postmodern Condition*. Culturetexts. Basingstoke: Macmillan Education, 1988.

Kroker, Arthur and Marilouise Kroker. *Hacking the Future: Stories for the Flesh-Eating 1990s*. Culturetexts. New York: St. Martin's Press, 1996.

Kroker, Arthur and Marilouise Kroker. *The Last Sex: Feminism and Outlaw Bodies.* Culturetexts. New York: St. Martin's Press, 1993.

Kudar, Jean. Improvements in and Relating to Motion Picture Composite Photography. *GB633420 (A)*, issued 19 December 1949.

Lacan, Jacques. *Ecrits: The First Complete Edition in English*, edited by Bruce Fink. New York: W. W. Norton & Company, 2006.

Lacan, Jacques. *The Ego in Freud's Theory and in the Technique of Psychoanalysis, 1954–1955*. Vol. 2. The Seminar of Jacques Lacan. New York: W. W. Norton & Company, 1988.

Lacan, Jacques. *The Ethics of Psychoanalysis, 1959–1960*. Vol. 7. The Seminar of Jacques Lacan. New York: W. W. Norton & Company, 1997.

Lacan, Jacques. *The Four Fundamental Concepts of Psycho-analysis*. New York and London: W. W. Norton & Company, 1998.

Lacan, Jacques. *Freud's Papers on Technique, 1953–1954*, edited by Jacques-Alain Miller. Translated by John Forrester. Vol. 1. Seminar of Jacques Lacan. New York: W. W. Norton, 1993.

Lah, Kyung. 'Tokyo Man Marries Video Game Character'. *CNN*, 17 December 2009. http://edition.cnn.com/2009/WORLD/asiapcf/12/16/japan.virtual.wedding/index.html.

Langan, Debra and Deborah Davidson. 'Rethinking Intimate Questions: Intimacy as Discourse'. In *Canadian Families: Diversity, Conflict and Change*, edited by Ann Duffy and Nancy Mandell, 33–60. Toronto: Nelson Education, 2011.

Lanier, Jaron. 'Digital Maoizm. The Hazards of New Online Collectivism'. *Edge*, 29 May 2006. https://www.edge.org/conversation/jaron_lanier-digital-maoism-the-hazards-of-the-new-online-collectivism.

Latour, Bruno. 'Ces Réseaux Que La Raison Ignore – Laboratoires, Bibliothèques, Collections'. In *Le Pouvoir Des Bibliothèques. La Mémoire Des Livres Dans La Culture Occidentale*, edited by Christian Jacob and Marc Baratin, 23–46. Paris: Albin Michel, 1996.

Latour, Bruno. 'Third Source of Uncertainty: Objects Too Have Agency'. In *Reassembling the Social: An Introduction to Actor-network-theory*, Clarendon Lectures in Management Studies. Oxford: Oxford University Press, 2007.

Lauren. *Beautiful Agony Forum*. Accessed 15 April 2021. https://beautifulagony.com/forum/index.php.

Lem, Stanisław. *Solaris*. New York: Berkley Books, 1971.

Levi, Primo. *If This Is a Man*. Reprint. London: Abacus, 1987.

Luhmann, Niklas. *Social Systems*. Writing Science. Stanford, CA: Stanford University Press, 1995.

Lunenfeld, Peter. *The Digital Dialectic: New Essays on New Media*. Cambridge, MA: MIT Press, 2000.

Lunenfeld, Peter. *Snap to Grid: A User's Guide to Digital Arts, Media, and Cultures.* Cambridge, MA: MIT, 2000.

MacCormack, Patricia. *Cinesexuality.* Queer Interventions. Aldershot: Ashgate, 2008.

Malinowska, Ania and Valentina Peri, eds. *Data Dating: Love, Technology, Desire.* Bristol: Intellect Ltd, 2021.

Manovich, Lev. *The Language of New Media.* Cambridge, MA: MIT Press, 2002.

Marcus, Steven. *The Other Victorians: A Study of Sexuality and Pornography in Mid-Nineteenth-century England.* New Brunswick, NJ: Transaction Publishers, 2009.

Marr, Carolyn J. 'Taken Pictures: On Interpreting Native American Photographs of the Southern Northwest Coast'. *Pacific Northwest Quarterly* 80, no. 2 (1989): 52–61.

Marsh, Amy. 'Love among the Objectum Sexuals'. *Electronic Journal of Human Sexuality* 13 (1 March 2010). http://www.ejhs.org/volume13/ObjSexuals.htm.

McCarthy, Robert E. *Secrets of Hollywood Special Effects.* Newton: Focal Press, 1992.

McGlotten, Shaka. *Virtual Intimacies: Media, Affect, and Queer Sociality.* Albany: State University of New York Press, 2013.

McNamara, Robert P. *Sex, Scams, and Street Life: The Sociology of New York City's Times Square.* Westport, CT: Praeger, 1995.

Meltzer, Françoise. *Salome and the Dance of Writing Portraits of Mimesis in Literature.* Chicago: University of Chicago Press, 1987.

Miczka, Tadeusz. *O śmierci na ekranie [Death on the Screen].* Katowice: Śląsk, 2013.

Mindell, David A. *Between Human and Machine: Feedback, Control, and Computing before Cybernetics.* Johns Hopkins Studies in the History of Technology. Baltimore: Johns Hopkins University Press, 2002.

Mindshare and J. Walter Thomson. 'Speak Easy. The Future Answers To You'. 20 January 2017. http://www.mindshareworld.com/sites/default/files/speakeasy.pdf.

Mitchell, Robert. *Bioart and the Vitality of Media.* In Vivo: The Cultural Mediations of Biomedical Science. Seattle: University of Washington Press, 2010.

Moss, Pegan. 'The Booth'. *Peepshow Stories* (blog), 16 July 2003. www.peepshowstories.com.

Moss, Pegan. 'Video Booths'. *Peepshow Stories* (blog), 21 July 2003. http://peepshowstories.com/2003/06/wall-of-porn-video-booths-there-is.html.

Mulvey, L. 'Visual Pleasure and Narrative Cinema'. *Screen* 16, no. 3 (1 September 1975): 6–18.

Nasaw, David. *Going Out: The Rise and Fall of Public Amusements.* Cambridge, MA: London: Harvard University Press, 1999.

Nathan, David L. and Donald Crafton. 'The Making and Re-making of Winsor McCay's Gertie (1914)'. *Animation* 8, no. 1 (1 March 2013): 23–46.

Nayar, Pramod K. *Posthumanism.* Themes in Twentieth- and Twenty-first-century Literature and Culture. Cambridge: Polity, 2014.

Nemirovsky, Ricardo and Francesca Ferrara. 'Mathematical Imagination and Embodied Cognition'. *Educational Studies in Mathematics* 70, no. 2 (March 2009): 159–74.

'New Business Tool: The TelePrompTer'. *Business Screen Magazine. Production Review* 14, no. 1 (1953).

Noah, Wardrip-Fruin, Mateas Michael, Dow Steven and Sali Serdar. 'Agency Reconsidered'. *Breaking New Ground: Innovation in Games*, Play, *Practice and Theory. Proceedings of DiGRA 2009*, 2009. http://www.digra.org/wp-content/uploads/digital-library/09287.41281.pdf.

Noah, Wardrip-Fruin, Mateas Michael, Dow Steven and Sali Serdar. 'Agency Reconsidered'. *Breaking New Ground: Innovation in Games*, Play, *Practice and Theory. Proceedings of DiGRA 2009*, 2009. http://www.digra.org/wp-content/uploads/digital-library/09287.41281.pdf.

Nusselder, André. *Interface Fantasy: A Lacanian Cyborg Ontology*. Short Circuits. Cambridge, MA: MIT Press, 2009.

Ohmer, Susan. 'Who Framed Roger Rabbit?: The Presence of the Past'. In *Storytelling in Animation: The Art of the Animated Image*, Vol. 2, edited by John Canemaker, Los Angeles, CA: The American Film Institute, 1988.

Onishi, Bradley. 'Information, Bodies, and Heidegger: Tracing Visions of the Posthuman'. *Sophia* 50, no. 1 (2011): 101–12.

Parisi, Luciana. *Abstract Sex: Philosophy, Bio-technology and the Mutations of Desire*. Transversals. London and New York: Continuum, 2004.

Peri, Don. *Working with Disney: Interviews with Animators, Producers, and Artists*. Jackson: University Press of Mississippi, 2011.

Pertierra, Raul. 'Mobile Phones, Identity and Discursive Intimacy'. *Human Technology* 1, no. 1 (2005): 23–44.

Pettman, Dominic. *Human Error: Species–Being and Media Machines*. Vol. 14. Posthumanities. Minneapolis: University of Minnesota Press, 2011.

Pettman, Dominic. *Love and Other Technologies: Retrofitting Eros for the Information Age*. 1st ed. New York: Fordham University Press, 2006.

Pointer, Ray. *The Art and Inventions of Max Fleischer: American Animation Pioneer*. Illustrated ed. Jefferson, NC: McFarland & Company, 2017.

Quigley Jr, Martin. *Magic Shadows: The Story of the Origin of Motion Pictures*. New York: Biblo and Tannen, 1969.

'Quiz Shows Are Gambling, Say MPs'. *BBC News*, 25 January 2007. http://news.bbc.co.uk/2/hi/uk_news/6297205.stm.

Quizmania Australia Phones Down 1. Accessed 15 April 2021. http://www.youtube.com/watch?v=ePE0ljifhoY.

Quizmania (No Legs Caller). Accessed 15 April 2021. https://www.youtube.com/watch?v=KzJotjN2imQ.

Raiti, Gerard C. 'Mobile Intimacy: Theories on the Economics of Emotion with Examples from Asia'. *M/C Journal* 10, no. 1 (2007). http://journal.media-culture.org.au/0703/02-raiti.php.

Rauch, Barbara. 'Virtual Emotions, No Feelings'. In *New Realities: Being Syncretic: IXth Consciousness Reframed Conference Vienna 2008*, edited by Ruth Schnell, Roy Ascott, Gerald Bast, Wolfgang Fiel and Margarete Jahrmann. 1st ed. New York: Springer Vienna Architecture, 2008.

Remsen, Nick. 'Riccardo Tisci Gives Japan's Biggest Virtual Virtuoso an Haute Couture Makeover'. *Vogue*, 2 May 2016. https://www.vogue.com/article/riccardo-tisci-hatsune-miku-haute-couture-makeover-avatar.

Rickitt, Richard. *Special Effects: The History and Technique.* New York: Billboard, 2000.

Rickitt, Richard. *Special Effects: The History and Technique.* New York: Watson-Guptill Publications, 2007.

Rickitt, Richard and Ray Harryhausen. *Special Effects: The History and Technique.* London: Aurum, 2006.

Robertson, Barbara. 'Winds of War'. *Cinefex*, no. 95 (2003).

Roman, James W. *From Daytime to Primetime: The History of American Television Programs.* Westport, CT: Greenwood Press, 2005.

Rudi from Germany. 'The Thing with the Soul: Expressed by Rudi in Germany'. *Objectum Sexuality Internationale*. Accessed 21 April, 2021. http://objectum-sexuality.org/expressions-rudi.pdf.

Russel, Ken. *Salome's Last Dance.* Vestron Pictures, 1988.

Sartre, Jean-Paul. *Being and Nothingness: A Phenomenologica Essay on Ontology.* Translated by Hazel Barnes. New York: Pocket Books, 1978.

Scannell, Paddy. 'Television and History: Questioning the Archive'. *The Communication Review* 13, no. 1 (26 February 2010): 37–51.

Sconce, Jeffrey. *Haunted Media: Electronic Presence from Telegraphy to Television.* Console-Ing Passions. Durham, NC: Duke University Press, 2000.

Scott, Kristi. 'Transhumanism vs. /and Posthumanism'. *Ethical Technology*, 14 July 2011. http://ieet.org/index.php/IEET/more/scott20110714.

Segrave, Kerry. *Vending Machines: An American Social History.* Jefferson, NC: McFarland, 2002.

'Share Your Ecstasy with the Agony Community!' *Beautiful Agony*. Accessed 15 April 2021. http://www.beautifulagony.com/public/main.php?page=submit.

Silver, James. 'How to Win at Those Late-night Quiz Shows'. *The Guardian*, 17 January 2007. https://www.theguardian.com/media/2007/jan/17/broadcasting.ITV.

Simpson, Seamus. 'Effective Communications Regulation in an Era of Convergence? The Case of Premium Rate Telephony and Television in the UK'. *Convergence: The International Journal of Research into New Media Technologies* 16, no. 2 (5 January 2010): 217–33.

'Sits in a Cabinet for Soundproof Tests'. *Popular Science*, August 1930. http://blog.modernmechanix.com/sits-in-a-cabinet-for-soundproof-tests/.

Slade, Joseph W. *Pornography and Sexual Representation: A Reference Guide*. Westport, Conn.: Greenwood Press, 2001. Greenwood Publishing Group, 2001.

Smith, Thomas G. *Industrial Light & Magic: The Art of Special Effects*. 1st ed. New York: Ballantine Books, 1986.

Sorgner, Stefan. 'Nietzsche, the Overhuman, and Transhumanism'. *Journal of Evolution and Technology* 20, no. 1 (2009): 29–42.

'Speech Q, Portable Prompter, Runs as Speaker's Own Speed'. *Business Screen Magazine* 15, no. 8 (1954): 56.

Spigel, Lynn. 'Seducing the Innocent'. In *Ruthless Criticism: New Perspectives in U.S. Communication History*, edited by William Samuel Solomon and Robert Waterman McChesney. Minneapolis: University of Minnesota Press, 1993.

St. Michel, Patrick. 'A Brief History of Virtual Pop Stars'. *The Pitch*, 15 July 2016. https://pitchfork.com/thepitch/1229-a-brief-history-of-virtual-pop-stars/.

Stasieńko, Jan. *Alien vs. predator?: gry komputerowe a badania literackie*. Wrocław: Wydawnictwo Naukowe Dolnośląskiej Szkoły Wyższej Edukacji TWP, 2005.

'State of the Art: A Cinefex 25th Anniversary Forum, edited by Jody Duncan/Interviews by Don Shay and Joe Fordham'. *Cinefex*, no. 100 (2005).

Stiegler, Bernard. *Neganthropocene*. Translated by Daniel Ross. Critical Climate Chaos. London: Open Humanities Press, 2018.

Stone, Allucquere Rosanne. 'Will the Real Body Please Stand Up?: Boundary Stories about Virtual Cultures'. In *Cyberspace: First Steps*, edited by Michael Benedikt. Cambridge, MA: MIT Press, 1991.

Stowe, Harriet Beecher. *My Wife and I: Or, Harry Henderson's History*. New York: J. B. Ford and Company, 1871. http://archive.org/details/mywifeandiorhar00stowgoog.

Stromberg, Joseph. 'A Brief History of the Teleprompter. How a Makeshift Show Business Memory Aid Became the Centerpiece of Modern Political Campaigning'. *Smithsonian Magazine*, 22 October 2012. https://www.smithsonianmag.com/history/a-brief-history-of-the-teleprompter-88039053/#ixzz2hR6hjj1Y.

Studlar, Gaylyn. *In the Realm of Pleasure: Von Sternberg, Dietrich, and the Masochistic Aesthetic*. Columbia University Press Morningside ed. New York: Columbia University Press, 1992.

'Support Agony – Buy a Subscription Today!' *Beautiful Agony*. Accessed 15 April 2021. http://www.beautifulagony.com/public/main.php?page=joi.

Teilhard De Chardin, Pierre. 'Book Three: Thought, The Chapter II: The Deployment of the Noosphere'. In *The Phenomenon of Man*, translated by Bernard Wall. Princeton, NJ: Harper Perennial, 1976.

Telotte, J. P. *Animating Space: From Mickey to Wall-E*. Lexington, KY: University Press of Kentucky, 2010.

Telotte, J. P. 'Disney's Alice Comedies: A Life of Illusion and the Illusion of Life'. *Animation* 5, no. 3 (11 January 2010): 331–40.

Thacker, Eugene. *Biomedia*. Vol. 11. Electronic Mediations. Minneapolis: University of Minnesota Press, 2004.

Total Divorce. 'The World's Strangest Marriages'. Accessed 15 May, 2015. http://www.totaldivorce.com/blog/2013/03/04/the-worlds-strangest-marriages-jzbdg/.

Thomas, Frank and Ollie Johnston. *Disney Animation: The Illusion of Life*. 1st ed. New York: Abbeville Press, 1981.

Thomas, Frank and Ollie Johnston. *The Illusion of Life: Disney Animation*. 1st ed. New York: Hyperion, 1995.

Turkle, Sherry. *Alone Together: Why We Expect More from Technology and Less from Each Other*. New York: Basic Books, 2011.

Turkle, Sherry. *Evocative Objects: Things We Think with*. Cambridge, MA: MIT Press, 2007.

Turkle, Sherry. *Life on the Screen: Identity in the Age of the Internet*. New York: Simon & Schuster, 1995.

Turkle, Sherry. *The Second Self: Computers and the Human Spirit*. 20th anniversary ed., 1st MIT Press ed. Cambridge, MA and London: MIT, 2005.

'TV's Cost Cutting Gadgets'. *Sponsor*, 22 October 1952.

Vaz, Mark Cotta. *Industrial Light & Magic: Into the Digital Realm*. 1st ed. New York: Ballantine Books, 1996.

'"Virtual Sensation" Mya Makes Her Debut at the Oscars; Motorola Announces Its First Cyber-Assistant'. *M2 PressWIRE*. 26 March 2000. http://www.m2.com/m2/web/story.php/20005B22C9F6EA4561EF802568AF005DCB6E.

Vlahos, P. *Comprehansive Electronic Compositing System*. Google Patents, 1987. https://www.google.com/patents/CA1228155A1?cl=en.

Vlahos, P. *Composite Photography Utilizing Sodium Vapor Illumination*. Google Patents, 1963. http://www.google.com/patents/US3095304.

Waldby, Cathy. *The Visible Human Project: Informatic Bodies and Posthuman Medicine*. Biofutures, Biocultures. London: Routledge, 2000.

Ward, Anna E. 'Pantomimes of Ecstasy: BeautifulAgony.Com and the Representation of Pleasure'. *Camera Obscura* 25, no. 1 (73) (1 January 2010): 161–95.

Ward, Patricia and George A. Dafoulas. *The Database Management Systems*. 1 ed. Australia: Thomson Learning, 2006.

Whitehead, Neil L. 'Post-Human Anthropology'. *Identities* 16, no. 1 (2009): 1–32.

Whitehead, Neil L. and Michael Wesch. *Human No More: Digital Subjectivities, Unhuman Subjects, and the End of Anthropology*. Boulder: University Press of Colorado, 2012.

Wiener, Norbert. *The Human Use of Human Beings: Cybernetics and Society/Norbert Wiener; with a New Introduction by Steve J. Heims*. London: Free Association, 1989.

Wilson, Elisabeth. 'Imaginable Computers: Affects and Intelligence in Alan Turing'. In *Prefiguring Cyberculture: An Intellectual History*, edited by Darren Tofts, Annemarie

Jonson and Alessio Cavallaro. Cambridge, MA and Sydney: MIT Press and Power Publications, 2002.

Wolfe, Cary. *What Is Posthumanism?* Vol. 8. Posthumanities Series. Minneapolis: University of Minnesota Press, 2010.

Yourchonny. 'Japanese Man Responds to Marrying a Nintendo Ds Character'. 27 November 2009. https://www.youtube.com/watch?v=2D30hmYjIm4.

Zielinski, Siegfried. *Deep Time of the Media: Toward an Archaeology of Hearing and Seeing by Technical Means*, Electronic Culture: History, Theory, Practice. Cambridge, MA: MIT Press, 2006.

Žižek, Slavoj. *The Plague of Fantasies*. Wo Es War. London; New York: Verso, 1997.

Zylinska, Joanna. *Bioethics in the Age of New Media*. Cambridge, MA: MIT Press, 2009.

Index